LAN Desktop Guide
to Security
NetWare® Edition

LAN Desktop Guide
to Security
NetWare® Edition

Ed Sawicki

SAMS

A Division of Prentice Hall Computer Publishing

11711 North College, Carmel, Indiana 46032 USA

To Merryl, Beth, and Mark

International Standard Book Number: 0-672-30085-0
Library of Congress Catalog Card Number: 92-60110

95   94   93   92   8   7   6   5   4   3   2   1

Interpretation of the printing code: the rightmost number of the first series of numbers is the year of the book's printing; the rightmost number of the second series of numbers is the number of the book's printing. For example, a printing code of 92-1 shows that the first printing of the book occurred in 1992.

Screen reproductions in this book were created by means of the program Collage Plus from Inner Media, Inc., Hollis, NH.

Printed in the United States of America

CREDITS

Publisher
Richard K. Swadley

Associate Publisher
Marie Butler-Knight

Managing Editor
Elizabeth Keaffaber

Product Development Manager
Lisa A. Bucki

Acquisitions Editor
Stephen R. Poland

Development Editors
Wayne Blankenbeckler
Gregg Bushyeager

Production Editor
Lisa C. Hoffman

Copy Editors
Howard Peirce
Diana Francoeur

Cover Illustrator
Polly McNeal

Designers
Scott Cook
Michele Laseau

Indexer
John Sleeva

Production Team
Claudia Bell
Scott Boucher
Keith Davenport
Kate Godfrey
Carrie Keesling
Julie Kichler
Julie Pavey
Linda Quigley
Louise Shinault
Kevin Spear
Phil Worthington

*Special thanks to James P. McCarter
for ensuring the technical accuracy of this book.*

CONTENTS

INTRODUCTION

I don't recall when I first became interested in computer security. Growing up in New York provided me with the basics. New Yorkers tend to be suspicious and careful. Visit a New York City apartment building and you'll see some of the best physical security in the world. When I was a teenager and first visited Alabama, I was surprised that many people didn't lock their doors at night. Most administrators of local area networks run their networks as if they live in Alabama, when they really should be acting more like New Yorkers.

I've been involved with local area networks since about 1982. I run a company called the Accelerated Learning Center, which has been offering courses on NetWare-based LANs since 1983. We had a 3COM LAN running in 1982 and a NetWare-based LAN running in early 1983. We've had every version of NetWare running on our LAN since then, except NetWare Lite. In the early years, our network was run rather loosely, with little emphasis on security. Today, security is a strong consideration when we add users or applications to the network.

I've been surprised to find how many of our students ignore security when they set up their networks. A few years ago, I conducted a course in New York City for a business school where they did not have a network administrator. They had three user accounts on their NetWare file server—SUPERVISOR, GUEST, and STUDENT. The STUDENT account was security-equivalent to the SUPERVISOR account, and the SUPERVISOR account had no password.

Many of our students have said that they set their user accounts equivalent to SUPERVISOR accounts because they don't want to deal with "that rights stuff." Most say this is allowable because their users don't know enough to be threats.

What they don't realize is that even though their users may not be a threat, there are other threats which may be far more sophisticated. These are *computer viruses* and *Trojan Horse programs.*

The Need for Security

Sometime in 1990, a colleague that works in a bank told me that I was paranoid about security when I said that file servers should be locked away. I also said that I had refused warranty repair on a new hard disk that had failed because my data was still on the broken drive. I didn't want that valuable data to leave my office.

However, think about this: If I'm a small business owner and I'm unwilling to have someone break into my file server and steal or destroy my data, or allow data to leave my office on a broken hard disk, why would a bank allow the same things to happen? Surely the data that a bank possesses represents far more money than my data. So, that a bank employee has such a cavalier attitude towards security demonstrates just how little regard some of us have for the value of the information we're entrusted with. Of course, I could be paranoid.

In early 1991, I was in London watching a BBC broadcast which showed a van parked outside the New Scotland Yard. The van had an antenna on the roof. Inside the van, there were men watching a television screen that was connected to a radio receiver. They were looking at images of CRT screens inside the building. The CRT screens inside the New Scotland Yard were radiating FAX-like emissions which were being intercepted and displayed inside the van. I did some research and learned how I too could easily implement this surveillance technique with low-cost equipment.

It's important I point out my interest in security is not to exploit these techniques for evil purposes. My concern is education. At the Accelerated Learning Center, our goal is to teach people how to better run their networks. Tightening up security on your network is part of the job of running your network.

My associates and I have known for a few years how to break into a NetWare file server. We *didn't* tell our students because we didn't want to be responsible for training an army of people to break into file servers. We discovered that Novell training courses taught service technicians how to break into NetWare file servers. So, in mid-1991, we set out to conduct courses on NetWare security, so network administrators knew the risk they were facing. We wanted them to know, for example, that they might not want to allow the service technicians to be alone with their file servers.

During the next few months, we learned a great deal about how NetWare handles security. We discovered that NetWare was strong in some areas and weak in others. We wondered how easy it would be to bypass the security mechanisms in NetWare—and we found out. One of our instructors demonstrated to Novell how to break into a NetWare file server. Novell later fixed this problem.

We were also concerned about the damage computer viruses could do to a network. At the time, we knew of no viruses that exploited unique features of NetWare. So, we wrote programs to simulate what future viruses and Trojan Horse programs could do. Our first demonstration "virus" was a program meant to do hostile things to the NetWare Bindery. Our second program was a LOGOUT Trojan Horse program meant to fool a user into believing he or she had logged out.

Months later, we developed programs to capture user passwords and store them in a file. We were thinking like the enemy. This was good because we could now focus on how to protect against these hostile programs and hostile actions.

In September 1991, we held our first NetWare Security course in Amsterdam, followed by one in London the next week. This was a wonderful experience. The people who had gathered there were genuinely interested in securing their networks. However, our market research showed that while the Europeans were concerned about security, most people in North America and Australia were not.

In 1992, we ran NetWare Security courses in Washington, D.C., and discovered that U.S. government agencies were very concerned about security and "corporate America" was not that interested. Bud Hovell from MTEK (a company that shares space in our office building) provided some insight into this.

He published a survey on the Internet which asked Network Administrators the question: *"Who sets computer policy in your organization?"* He discovered that in most cases, computer policy was set by Network Administration staff. Top management was generally not involved in setting or endorsing computer policy. This is a mistake, because a network administrator does not always have insight into the value of corporate data—and therefore does not know what's needed to protect it.

Then, on March 6, 1992, Michelangelo appeared on the scene. There had been computer viruses before, but the Michelangelo virus was different. Michelangelo was famous. Most people heard about Michelangelo from their television sets. I was in London at the time. On March 5, there was mention of Michelangelo nearly every hour on both CNN International and the BBC. People all over the world were becoming aware of the threat.

The Purpose of This Book

This book is meant to teach you the basics of securing your NetWare-based network. If you follow the procedures and recommendations in this book, you'll have a network which is far more secure than the average LAN. This does not mean that your network will be bulletproof. It will simply be break-in and virus resistant.

You should be reading this book if you're involved in managing the data stored within your network. For example, if you are a Network Administrator, you are responsible for data stored on your network. You should also read this book if you manage the people who manage the data stored on your network. Finally, you should read this book if you are responsible for security in your organization.

By the way, this book uses the term *Network Administrator* as a general purpose way of referring to a variety of job titles. Many organizations have people who are called System Supervisors, Network Managers, Network Supervisors, and so on. This book does not attempt to define these job titles or distinguish between them.

While this book is Novell NetWare-specific, many of the concepts described here also apply to other networking environments as well. So if you manage a network which includes Banyan VINES, Microsoft LAN Manager, or UNIX/TCP-IP/NFS, you will likely find this book useful.

Since this book is meant to ground you in the essentials of NetWare security, it does not get into the more advanced concepts. For example, I stop short of getting into C2 security concepts. This is part of a U.S. Department of Defense standard for evaluating trusted computer systems. Novell plans to have a C2-rated NetWare product sometime in the future. If you're interested in C2 networking now, you should call Centel Federal Systems, whose address and phone number is listed in Appendix B.

Surveillance

One of the problems in securing a NetWare LAN is the ability of any two machines on the network to establish a connection between themselves without first seeking permission or registering that connection. This makes it possible for any two programs or users on the network to communicate without the knowledge of Network Administrators.

You may be using a product which exploits this "feature" of NetWare. Products like Intel's NetSight Analyst, Fresh Technology's LAN Assist, and Triticom's Argus/N are examples of products that allow you to look at another workstation screen on the network. You would normally use these products for technical support purposes. If a user calls you for help with a problem, you can look at their screen and control their keyboard when you attempt to diagnose the problem.

However, these products can also be used for surveillance purposes. If you're the Network Administrator, you probably don't mind when it's you doing the looking. After all, you're the administrator—this is authorized surveillance. You probably would mind if the surveillance was being done by another user. How do you protect against unauthorized surveillance?

It's also possible for a virus or Trojan Horse program to run in a user's workstation and send user data to another machine on the network. A password-capturing virus, for example, would be able to send user passwords to a user covertly capturing these passwords. How do you protect against these hostile programs?

There's no easy answer to these problems. Novell's IPX makes this too easy to do. I have a way to solve this problem—an *authorized network traffic monitor.* A machine, connected to the network, would monitor packets flowing over the cable and look for activity between two network nodes which have no business communicating. If it finds such packets, it would send alerts to the network administrators or to the security officer. Unfortunately, nobody has a product yet that does this.

Speaking of surveillance, remember the problem of being able to receive signals from a workstation's CRT? How would you solve this problem? While this book does not tell you how, you may want to give STX Information Security Group a call. Their phone number is in Appendix B. They have solutions to help solve this surveillance problem. They'll send you literature you'll find enlightening. I especially like the "HERF generator." Read the literature to see what I mean.

One other thing—Novell is the name of a corporation and NetWare is the name of Novell's principal product line. Many people use the two terms as if they're synonyms. They're not. You can't install a corporation on your file server. This has little to do with security, but you'll have an easier time knowing this.

Tying It All Together

This book primarily tells you about the security features of NetWare and third-party products and how to best take advantage of these features. However, product features alone do not result in secure networks. The second component is people. You'll need to implement policies and procedures to help ensure that people do what they're supposed to.

For example, it would be very difficult and expensive to implement a foolproof technological solution to the problem of users leaving their workstations unattended and logged in. The best solution is gaining their cooperation by explaining to them the reasons why they should log out when they leave their work area. This means training. Part of a Network Administrator's job is ensuring that users receive training so they know how to comply with the policies and procedures for using the network.

Many organizations have not established a computer policy and have only sketchy procedures for how the network should be administered and run. You should spend time to develop a computer policy. Your computer users should know what the organization's attitude is regarding the use of computer equipment and the information stored there.

For example, you wouldn't want to find yourself in court defending your right to examine the electronic mail archives of users. If your organization has no stated computer policy, a court may find you guilty of invading the privacy of your computer users.

To start you on your way, I've included a sample computer policy statement in Appendix D. This is a very simple statement which you will most likely want to add to. If policy statements are a new area for you and you feel that you need help, there are consulting companies that specialize in this area. One such company is MTEK, whose address and phone number is in Appendix B.

How This Book Is Organized

In a few chapters in this book, I point out the need for physical security, but don't go into the specifics of how to achieve that. If you want to provide physical security for your file server, for example, I don't tell you how to hang the doors and what kind of door locks to use. There are consultants who specialize in this area.

One of my fondest memories was when a student in Singapore invited me to his office to see his "file server room." He was proud of the lock on the door and the large plate glass window which allowed the room to be viewed from most places in the office. He was a little disappointed when I pointed out that anyone could gain entry into the room by climbing over the wall. They had ceiling tiles in the file server room which lifted up, exposing the plenum space above.

Chapter 1 deals with setting up User, User Group, Workgroup Manager, and Account Manager accounts. It also deals with ways to secure these accounts by placing login restrictions on the accounts. If you're a seasoned Network Administrator, there are still things to be learned here. For example, it's rare that I meet a Network Administrator that knows the *real* reason why a GUEST account exists or what an Account Manager can do.

Chapter 2 deals primarily with securing user workstations and user accounts from a break-in. Novell's Intruder Detection feature is described in detail, as well as ways of dealing with that age-old problem—users leaving their logged-in workstations unattended.

Chapter 3 tells you about diskless workstations and how to make them work on a NetWare-based network. Diskless workstations are controversial. Some people hate them and some like them. Regardless of your feelings about them, you need to understand that they have security benefits that make them hard to ignore.

In a recent article in a computer-user magazine, the author modified his rule of "One User, one processor" to include " ... and one hard disk." You (and the author) need to understand that local disks (hard or floppy) are as much a liability as they are a benefit. From the security point of view, local disks represent risk. Don't ignore diskless workstations just because it doesn't fit in with "The Law."

Chapter 4 focuses on securing your file server from those who might wish to break into it and steal or destroy your data. I tell you how to break into a NetWare file server, but be sure to read and understand the reasons why. You'll read about how you can protect your server from break-ins, for which the ultimate solution is physical security.

Chapter 5 deals with computer viruses and Trojan Horse programs. It's important that you understand some of the basic philosophy of the book. I take an attitude towards computer viruses which may be different from what you might expect. Rather than focus on telling you how to scan for viruses on your network, this book will focus on virus prevention. It's my view that by the time you detect a virus, it's often too late to prevent damage. I'd prefer to take the extra time to attempt to prevent virus infection.

Chapter 6 tells you about file server-based programs that you can use to protect your data from hostile programs. Some of these programs, like MONITOR and NLM-Profile, simply tell you about conditions on your file server which might indicate the presence of a hostile program. Other programs, such as SiteLock and NET-Check, take an active role in preventing hostile programs from doing damage.

Chapter 7 describes the NetWare Bindery—probably in more detail than you ever wanted. Since the Bindery is central to NetWare security mechanisms, it's important to understand it. This chapter also tells you about Novell's SECURITY program. This examines the Bindery and reports on potential security problems that it finds.

You should pay particular attention to Chapters 8 and 9 and the recommendations which appear at the end of those chapters. Chapter 8 covers the concepts of file and directory attributes. If you take advantage of attributes, you can go a long way toward securing the data on your file server against deliberate attack from hostile users and programs. The same applies to the concept of rights in Chapter 9. There are compelling reasons to use NetWare 3.x rather than NetWare 2.x, as 3.x has useful attributes that 2.x does not.

Chapter 10 concerns itself with protecting your data files from scrutiny by those who should not be able see your data— even though NetWare gives them the rights to do so. The Network Administrators, for example, have access rights to all files stored on the file server. Yet, there is some data that they should not access. How do you protect your data files from the administrators? The answer is *encryption*. This chapter deals with encryption features found within popular application programs, as well as external encryption—when the application itself does not support encryption.

Chapter 11 covers menuing systems. Many Network Administrators do not feel secure if users have the ability to get to the DOS prompt. If this is your concern, this chapter deals with ways of locking users into their menus.

Chapter 12 focuses entirely on issues of time and date. Time is a security mechanism in NetWare. NetWare has a long way to go to provide more robust handling of time zones, server time synchronization, and 12-hour versus 24-hour time formats.

xxiii

Chapter 13 deals with audit trails. If you come from a mainframe environment, audit trails may be conspicuous by their absence in NetWare. However, there are third-party audit trail products. This chapter focuses on LT Auditor, from Blue Lance.

You'll also find a section on backups and archives in Appendix A; the list of third-party products in Appendix B; a useful command reference in Appendix C; the sample computer policy in Appendix D; and lastly, a glossary of security terms and features.

How to Use This Book

This book is designed to be a desktop guide, so we have established special features to make it easier to use. These include special icons to emphasize specific points in the text and typographical conventions.

Icons

The icons are designed to draw your attention to information considered to be interesting or especially important. The icons used are as follows:

 The Tip icon offers advice or teaches an easier way to do something.

 The Note icon presents interesting tidbits of information related to the surrounding discussion.

 The Caution icon warns you about potential problems and helps to steer you clear of disaster.

 The Step icon precedes a list of steps to guide you through procedures.

This icon indicates that the information in the connected paragraph concerns only NetWare 2.x.

 This icon indicates that the information in the connected paragraph concerns only NetWare 3.x.

Typographical Conventions

In the *text*, terms will be treated as follows:

User-typed entries will appear in **bold computer font.**

Information that is on-screen will appear in computer font.

DOS NetWare commands and switches will appear in regular UPPERCASE.

DOS/NetWare filenames and NetWare groups, directories, and group names will appear in regular UPPERCASE.

New terms introduced to the reader will appear in *regular italics.*

Command Line Syntax

There are a number of NetWare commands that are entered at the DOS prompt. The convention used for command line entries is as follows:

```
REVOKE rights [FOR path] FROM [USER|GROUP] name
[options]
```

Command lines will always appear in the computer font above.

Parameters that must be entered as they appear are shown in uppercase computer font. (Example: REVOKE)

Parameters that are to be supplied by the user appear in lowercase, italic computer font. (Example: *rights*)

Parameters enclosed in brackets "[ ]" indicate that the parameter is optional. (Example: [FOR *path*])

Parameters that are separated by a vertical bar "|" indicate that either of the parameters may be used. (Example: [USER|GROUP])

Switches are sometimes listed by their full names. Uppercase letters in a switch indicate the minimum information required to specify the switch. For example, to specify /No Tabs, you can type /NT.

Acknowledgments

Thanks to:

Howard and Kristin Marks of Networks Are My Life for making introductions and getting this book off the ground.

Dave Chamberlain of the Accelerated Learning Center. This book could not have been as complete and products could not have been as thoroughly tested without his help.

The people at Sams Applications Software for taking my raw words and refining them. These include Gregg Bushyeager, Wayne Blankenbeckler, Lisa Hoffman, and others that I know only by initials. Thanks, HP (Howard Peirce).

Zika Milenkovic of Professional Development Associates for helping to make the NetWare Security course successful—thereby making the book possible.

The many students in my NetWare Security courses who asked such interesting questions and offered useful suggestions for improvements to the course and, therefore, the book. Thanks to those students who thought of such evil things to do to a NetWare file server.

Cathryn and Melissa of the Accelerated Learning Center for tolerating me and taking care of business while this project was underway.

The people at Nu-Mega for reviewing the sections on server-based security.

The LAN Support Group for sharing a few of their secrets.

This book could not have contained as much information about non-Novell products as it does without the cooperation of those vendors (too numerous to mention), who sent evaluation copies of their products. I hope that you consider the objective treatment your product received here to be accurate and fair. Thanks for your help.

It seems perverse to thank the author of the Michelangelo virus for making the computer user community more aware of the threats to the security of our data—but thanks are in order—whoever you are. Call me. We'll do lunch.

Trademarks

All terms mentioned in this book that are known to be trademarks or service marks are listed below. Sams cannot attest to the accuracy of this information. Use of a term in this book should not be regarded as affecting the validity of any trademark or service mark.

Bindview Plus and BVDEBUG are registered trademarks of LAN Support Group Inc.

BootWare and Bootware MSD are registered trademarks of LANWORKS Technologies Inc.

Central Point Anti-Virus and PC Secure are registered trademarks of Central Point Software Inc.

Certus LAN is a registered trademark of Certus International.

Excel is a registered trademark of Microsoft Corp.

FANSI-Console is a registered trademark of Hersey Micro Consulting Inc.

LANSight Support, NetPort II, and LANProtect are registered trademarks of Intel Corp.

LANTrail is a registered trademark of NetWave, Inc.

Lotus 1-2-3 is a registered trademark of Lotus Development Corp.

LT Auditor is a registered trademark of Blue Lance.

MetzLock is a registered trademark of Metz Software.

NET-Check and NLM Profile are registered trademarks of Nu-Mega.

NetAssure is a registered trademark of Centel Federal Systems Inc.

NetMenu is a registered trademark of Network Enhancement Tools.

NETOFF is a registered trademark of Citadel Systems.

NetUtils and Dr. Solomon are registered trademarks of Ontrack Computer Systems Inc.

NetWare (all versions) is a registered trademark of Novell Inc.

Norton Anti-Virus is a registered trademark of Symantec.

Password Coach is a registered trademark of Baseline Software.

PKZIP is a registered trademark of PKWare Inc.

Quattro Pro is a registered trademark of Borland International.

Saber Menuing System is a registered trademark of Saber Software.

SECUREcard is a registered trademark of Datamedia Corp.

Serv+ is a registered trademark of Procomp USA, Inc.

SiteLock is a registered trademark of Brightwork Development.

STXPRESS Stealth is a registered trademark of STX Information Security Group.

Time Master is a registered trademark of Jovandi International.

V^2Scan, CryptDir, and SCANT are registered trademarks of Accelerated Learning Center.

VIRUSCAN and NETSCAN are registered trademarks of McAfee Associates.

NetWare Accounts

To use NetWare file and print services, you must first log in to a NetWare file server. This requires that you have an account on the server. NetWare enforces security by allowing access only to valid accounts. You're probably accustomed to thinking of accounts as belonging to people, but other entities can also have accounts. A print server is an example of an entity that must also log in to a NetWare file server to service print jobs in a print queue.

In this chapter we'll deal with the following account types and concepts.

- Introduction to Accounts
- User Accounts
- User Group Accounts
- Workgroup Management
- Account Management
- Security Equivalence
- User Account Passwords
- Account Restrictions
- Print Server Passwords

Introduction to Accounts

If you're a seasoned Network Administrator, most of this chapter will seem elementary, but there may still be some things here that are new to you. For example, you may not know why there is a *GUEST* account. Novell includes a GUEST account to make it easy to print to print queues on other file servers.

User Accounts

When you install NetWare on your file server, two user accounts are automatically created. They are called *SUPERVISOR* and *GUEST*. When you log in to the file server as a Supervisor, you can create other user and group accounts.

 Note: NetWare uses a database called the Bindery to hold information about accounts. The Bindery is described in detail in Chapter 7.

SUPERVISOR Account

The purpose of the *SUPERVISOR* account is to manage accounts on the file server. It is special in many ways. It is the only user account that:

- Can never be deleted—even by the Supervisor.
- Has rights to all directories and all files within directories.
- Can create and delete user accounts and user group accounts.
- Can create and delete Workgroup Managers.
- Can create and delete print queues.
- Can assign Console Operators.
- Can create and modify the system login script.

- Can set default user account restrictions.
- Can set intruder detection parameters.
- Can assign a password to a print server.
- Can assign a full name to a print server.
- Can define servers that can charge for their services.

GUEST Accounts

The purpose of the *GUEST* account is to allow users to access your server's print queues, using the NPRINT and CAPTURE programs, even when the users don't have accounts on your server. This feature of NetWare is not well documented (or not documented at all) in Novell's manuals. Novell's CAPTURE and NPRINT programs behave in the following ways:

1. A user who doesn't have a connection to your server (the user is connected to another server) may specify a print queue on your server when using the CAPTURE command.

2. CAPTURE will attempt to log in that user to your file server as *GUEST*.

3. If the GUEST account on your server has no password and GUEST is a queue user for the target print queue, the user will attach to your server and place a print job in the print queue.

> **Note:** CAPTURE maintains this connection to your server after the print job is sent. This activity is transparent to the user. If NPRINT is used instead of CAPTURE, the connection is terminated after the print job is submitted to the print queue on your server.

If the GUEST account has a password or if GUEST is not a queue user for the target print queue, CAPTURE will prompt the user for an account name and a password for your server. It will then try to attach to your server by using the account name and password that the user supplied.

4

The *GUEST* account has rights to its own mailbox directory, but is also security-equivalent to the group EVERYONE. Therefore, it also has the rights to the SYS:PUBLIC and SYS:MAIL directories.

Some Network Administrators view the GUEST account as a security threat. Since GUEST is equivalent to EVERYONE, any guest has access to programs in the SYS:PUBLIC directory and has Create rights in the SYS:MAIL directory structure. You may want to maintain a GUEST account, but you may not want it to have equivalence to EVERYONE.

 Tip: You can remove the GUEST account from membership in the group EVERYONE while still allowing the guest to deposit print jobs in print queues. To do this, make sure that you add user GUEST as a QUEUE USER to the print queue(s) with the PCONSOLE program.

If you don't want users without accounts on your server to deposit print jobs in your print queues, you can delete the GUEST account with the SYSCON program.

Creating User Accounts

You must be a Supervisor or a Workgroup Manager to create user accounts. You can create user accounts with the following Netware programs:

- SYSCON
- MAKEUSER
- USERDEF
- NWSETUP

SYSCON

The SYSCON program is a menu-oriented program which is used by the Supervisor to perform the following functions related to account restrictions.

- Create user accounts
- Delete user accounts
- Change user passwords
- Assign "long names" to a user's account
- Restricting logins by time-of-day
- Restricting logins by day-of-week
- Restricting logins by network address
- Restricting concurrent connections
- Require users to have passwords
- Require unique passwords
- Require that users change their passwords periodically

  SYSCON can be used by a user to:

- Change his or her password
- Change his or her login script
- Examine account restrictions

MAKEUSER

The MAKEUSER program is used by the Supervisor to create or delete user accounts in bulk. The Supervisor writes a script which controls how users are created.

   The MAKEUSER program and the script file(s) are located in the SYS:SYSTEM directory on the server. Only the Supervisor may run the MAKEUSER program. Table 1.1 lists script commands. MAKEUSER scripts can contain the following commands:

6

Table 1.1   MAKEUSER script commands.

Command	Description
Account_Expiration	Specifies when a user account expires.
Accounting	Specify the account balance and the low balance limit for the user account.
Connections	Specifies the maximum number of concurrent connections to the file server.
Create	Create a user account and specify password.
Delete	Specify user accounts to delete.
Groups	Specify that new user accounts are assigned to the group(s) specified.
Home_Directory	Specify the directory under which a newly-created user's home directory will be created.
Login_Script	Specify the filename that contains the newly-created user's login script.
Max_Disk_Space	Specify the number of disk blocks a newly-created user has available.
Password_Length	Specify the minimum number of characters for the user's password.
Password_Period	Specify the number of days between forced password changes.
Password_Required	Require that a user must have a password.
Purge_User_Directory	Specify that a user's home directory and subdirectories are deleted when the user account is deleted.
Rem	Used to place comments in the MAKEUSER script file.
Restricted_Time	Specify a range of times that a user cannot be logged in to the file server.
Stations	Specify the workstation addresses that a user is allowed to login from.
Unique_Password	Specify that a user cannot reuse old passwords.

USERDEF

The USERDEF program is used to create users in bulk—similar to MAKEUSER. However, USERDEF is more powerful than MAKEUSER and provides more functions. The additional capabilities provided by USERDEF are:

■ Assign disk space limitations to multiple users

■ Create print job configurations for all newly created users

These two additional functions make the Supervisor's job a lot easier. Before USERDEF, copying print job configurations to user mailbox directories was tedious. Now, USERDEF automates this process.

NWSETUP

The NWSETUP program was introduced with NetWare 2.2 as a way to more easily setup a Netware file server. Scasoned Network Administrators will likely ignore NWSETUP and choose to use SYSCON, MAKEUSER, or USERDEF instead.

Creating User Accounts with SYSCON

You can use SYSCON when you need to quickly create one or two user accounts. If you need to create two or more user accounts, consider using either MAKEUSER or USERDEF instead.

Follow the next procedure to create a new user account with the SYSCON program.

 Creating a New User Account

1. At the DOS prompt, type **SYSCON** and press **Enter**.	The SYSCON Available Topics menu appears.
2. Select User Information.	A list of existing user account names appears in the User Names list.
3. Press the **Ins** key.	The User Name box appears. Figure 1.1 shows what the screen looks like at this point. In this example, the account name JOHNP is being created.
4. Type the new user account name and press **Enter**.	The new user account name is added to the User Names list.

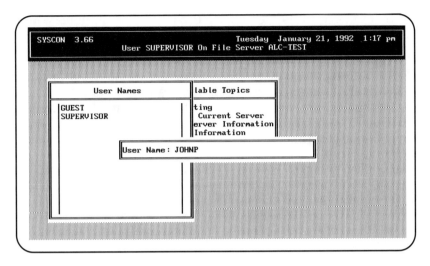

```
SYSCON  3.66                              Tuesday  January 21, 1992  1:17 pm
                        User SUPERVISOR On File Server ALC-TEST


           ┌──────────────────────┬──────────────────┐
           │      User Names       │lable Topics      │
           │ GUEST                 │ting              │
           │ SUPERVISOR            │  Current Server  │
           │                       │erver Information │
           │                       │Information       │
           │         ┌─────────────────────────────────────┐
           │         │User Name: JOHNP                      │
           │         └─────────────────────────────────────┘
           │                       │
           │                       │
           │                       │
           └──────────────────────┴──────────────────┘
```

Figure 1.1   Creating a new user account with SYSCON.

Length of Account Names

NetWare account names may contain up to 47 characters. However, there are compelling reasons to keep account names short.
One important reason for keeping account names short concerns
the use of home directory names. It is common practice to create
home directories for users. The name of the home directory is
usually the user's account name.

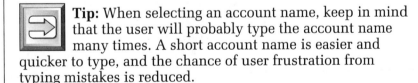

Tip: When selecting an account name, keep in mind
that the user will probably type the account name
many times. A short account name is easier and
quicker to type, and the chance of user frustration from
typing mistakes is reduced.

You can use a simple statement in a login script to map a
drive letter to the user's home directory if the user's account
name has eight or fewer characters. The following statement in a
login script does this:

MAP H:=SYS:HOME\%LOGIN_NAME

If your account name is JOHNP, this MAP command will assume that your home directory is SYS:HOME\JOHNP.

 Directory names in NetWare 3.x must comply with DOS naming conventions. The directory name should not be more than eight characters with an optional three-character extension. So if you're running NetWare 3.x, you must restrict user account names to the same conventions in order to take advantage of this simple home directory mapping.

 NetWare 2.x directory names are allowed to have up to fourteen characters, and a period can be used anywhere in the name except in the first character position. So, it's possible to have user account names containing up to fourteen characters as well. If your server is running NetWare 2.x, it's still best to restrict directory names to DOS naming conventions to be compatible with NetWare 3.x.

Remember that periods are allowed in account names. Thus, you can create longer account names that follow DOS directory naming conventions. Imagine creating user names like JOANNE.BRO or BROWN.JON. These names will work well with the preceding MAP command.

Valid Characters in Account Names

Some of the 128 ASCII characters cannot be used in NetWare account names. Space and tab characters cannot be used because they are used as command-line delimiters by DOS, nor can the 32 ASCII control characters be used. ASCII control characters are the first 32 characters in the ASCII code set. An example of an ASCII control character is the BEL character often expressed as "control G." Table 1.2 lists additional characters that cannot be used.

Table 1.2 Invalid characters in NetWare account names.

Character	Name
=	equal sign
>	greater than sign
|	vertical bar
+	plus sign
[	left bracket
]	right bracket
\	backslash
/	slash
*	asterisk
;	semicolon
:	colon
.	period
,	comma
?	question mark
"	double quote

Misleading Account Names

Older versions of Novell's SYSCON program allowed you to use the Alt key to enter unusual characters for account names. For example, consider the following account names:

■ 25¢

■ BIG CHEESE

In the first example, the cents sign was created by holding down the Alt key while pressing **155** on the numeric keypad. In the second example (BIG CHEESE), a space was simulated by holding down the Alt key while pressing **255**. If a user tried to log in to the BIG CHEESE account by typing a space character between the *G* and *C* characters, NetWare would think that the account name was BIG and that CHEESE was a parameter.

Recent versions of SYSCON do not allow characters above ASCII 127.

While you may be using a version of SYSCON that does allow this, recent versions of Novell's LOGIN program do not allow these characters in account names. Older versions of the LOGIN program do allow these characters, however.

It's not a good idea to use characters above ASCII 127 in account names because Novell programs no longer support this.

User Group Accounts

A *user group account* is one whose purpose is to provide a single identity for a collection of users who are members of the group. User groups are important because a Network Administrator can manage a potentially large group of users simply by managing one account. An example is a group called ACCOUNTING. If all users in the Accounting Department are members of the ACCOUNTING group, these users can be assigned directory rights very easily just by assigning those rights to the ACCOUNTING group.

The rules for group membership are:

- A user account can be a member of more than one user group account.
- Any number of user accounts may be members of the user group account.
- A user group account cannot be a member of another user group account.

When you install NetWare on your file server and run SYSCON the first time, a user group called EVERYONE is automatically created. As you create user accounts, they are automatically assigned as members to the EVERYONE group.

Creating User Group Accounts

You can create your own user group accounts if you are a Supervisor or Workgroup Manager. The next set of steps describes the procedure.

Creating a User Group Account

1. At the DOS prompt, type **SYSCON** and press **Enter**.

   The SYSCON `Available Topics` menu appears.

2. Select `Group Information`.

   A list of existing user group account names appears in the `Group Names` list.

3. Press the **Ins** key.

   The `New Group Name` box appears. Figure 1.2 shows what the screen looks like at this point. In this example, a group called ACCOUNTING is being created.

4. Type the new user group account name and press **Enter**.

   The new user group account name is added to the `User Names` list.

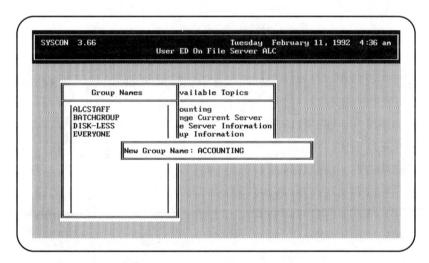

Figure 1.2   Creating a group account with SYSCON.

Workgroup Management

NetWare supports the concept of workgroup management involving a *Workgroup Manager* and an *Account Manager*. Rather than having the Supervisor manage all users or having several supervisor-equivalent accounts to manage a large network, the Supervisor can delegate the job of managing users to a Workgroup Manager. The Workgroup Manager can, in turn, delegate some of the work to an Account Manager. To see how Workgroup Manager and Account Manager accounts are useful, examine the following scenario.

A network must serve five departments in an organization:

- Sales
- Marketing
- Engineering
- Accounting
- Manufacturing

The Network Administrator can create a Workgroup Manager account for each of the departments. The names of these accounts may be the department names. That is, the user account called SALES is a Workgroup Manager account for the Sales department.

Each department can then manage its own users with its Workgroup Manager account. The Workgroup Manager can create new users which are then part of the workgroup. He or she can delete workgroup users as well.

When the Supervisor created the Workgroup Manager accounts, he or she probably created a volume or a directory tree that was unique to that department. The Workgroup Manager was given all rights to the volume or the tree. Workgroup users can be assigned rights to directories that the Workgroup Manager has Access Control rights to.

 Note: A Workgroup Manager cannot give rights to users that are not already possessed by the Workgroup Manager.

Creating a Workgroup Manager

If you're a Supervisor, you can create a Workgroup Manager account simply by creating a user account. The following steps describe how to do this.

 Creating a Workgroup Manager Account

1. At the DOS prompt, type **SYSCON** and press **Enter**.	The SYSCON Available Topics menu appears.
2. Select Supervisor Options.	The Supervisor Options menu appears.
3. Select Workgroup Managers.	The Workgroup Managers list appears. There may already be user account names in the list.
4. Press the **Ins** key to insert a new account in the list.	The Other Users and Groups list appears.
5. Select a user or user group account. You may select more than one account by using the **F5** key.	The account names are highlighted as you select them.
6. Press **Enter** when you've selected the Workgroup Manager account(s).	The new account is added to the Other Users and Groups list.

Account Management

The Workgroup Manager or Supervisor can create Account Managers and assign user accounts to the *Account Managers*. If you're an Account Manager, you can control the following for user accounts that you manage:

- Trustee rights
- Account balance

- Full Name
- Account, time, station, and volume restrictions
- Password
- Membership to groups managed by the Account Manager
- Login script
- Assign the user to another Account Manager (that you manage)
- Assign the user to another Workgroup Manager (that you manage)
- Assign the user to be a manager of another user in the workgroup
- Assign the user to be security-equivalent to another user or group that you manage

 Note: It's possible for an Account Manager to manage a Workgroup Manager, though the reason for doing this is questionable.

An Account Manager cannot create new users or delete existing users. The Account Manager is someone to handle the day-to-day problems that users may encounter running their application programs.

Creating an Account Manager

If you're a Workgroup Manager, you can create an Account Manager account simply by creating a user account. The following steps show you how.

 Creating an Account Manager Account

1. At the DOS prompt, type **SYSCON** and press **Enter**.

   The SYSCON Available Topics menu appears.

2. Select `User Information`.   The `User Names` list appears.

3. Select the account name you'd like to make an Account Manager.   The `User Information` menu appears.

4. Select the `Managed Users and Groups` item.   The `Managed Users and Groups` list appears.

5. Press the **Ins** key.   The `Other Users and Groups` list appears.

6. Select a user or user group account. These will be the accounts that this Account Manager will manage. You can select more than one account by using the **F5** key.   The account names are highlighted as you select them.

7. Press **Enter** when you've selected the account(s).   The new accounts are added to the `Managed Users and Groups` list.

Security Equivalence

When a user account becomes a member of a user group account, it is *security-equivalent* to the user group account. Any rights assigned to the user group account are available to the members of the user group.

Security-equivalence may occur between two user accounts as well. A user account may be made equivalent to another user account. This is accomplished with the SYSCON program. The next steps explain how.

 Creating a Security-Equivalent User Account

1. At the DOS prompt type **SYSCON** and press **Enter**.   The SYSCON `Available Topics` menu appears.

2. Select `User Information`.	A list of existing user account names appears in the `User Names` list.
3. Select the user account name that you want to be security-equivalent.	The `User Information` menu appears.
4. Select `Security Equivalence`.	Existing equivalent account names appears in the `Security Equivalences` list.
5. Press the **Ins** key.	The `Other Users and Groups` list appears.
6. Select the name of a user or group account and press **Enter**.	The new account is added to the `Security Equivalences` list.

Rules for Equivalence

When you set a user account equivalent to another account, you need to understand the impact to the users. These are the rules for equivalence that you should understand.

■ Security-equivalence has a "depth" of one. That is, if user B is equivalent to user A and user C is equivalent to user B, user C is *not* necessarily equivalent to user A. This prevents supervisor-equivalence from accidentally being assigned to a user or group.

■ If user B is equivalent to user A, user A is *not* necessarily equivalent to user B. Equivalence is unidirectional.

■ If user B is equivalent to user A, user A may be made equivalent to user B. This means that all rights assigned to one of the users are automatically available to the other.

Backdoor Accounts

Rather than having just one Supervisor account, you should have at least one other user account which is security-equivalent to the Supervisor account. This is called a *backdoor account*. Backdoor accounts can be used for the following reasons:

18

- To gain entry into the system if the Supervisor account should be locked out by the intruder detection feature of NetWare.

- Since the Supervisor account is well known, it may be the target for viruses or hostile users. A backdoor account can be used with lesser risk.

- You may want to covertly monitor the actions of a user. The user may not wish to attempt hostile actions while a Network Administrator (Supervisor) is logged in. The user may think that the backdoor account is a plain user account.

 Tip: Do not use a provocative name for the backdoor account. A name like SUPER1 will get attention. A name that is no more interesting than a normal user account is recommended.

Supervisor's Working Account

It's rare that Network Administrators spend all of their time performing administration functions that require supervisor equivalence. Much of their time is usually spent running applications that do not require supervisor equivalence.

Administrators should have working accounts for themselves that are not equivalent to the Supervisor account. This lessens the risk of a successful attack from a hostile user or program. As you'll see later in this book, a computer virus that can run with Supervisor privileges can do whatever damage it wants.

 Tip: Do not create a home directory, an application menu and an EMAIL mailbox for the SUPERVISOR account. This makes it less likely that you'll stay logged in as SUPERVISOR.

User Account Passwords

Each user account may be protected with a password. The Network Administrator has a great deal of control over user password requirements. The Administrator can require that:

■ The user be forced to have a password.

■ The password be a minimum length.

■ The user not be allowed to change the password.

■ The password be changed periodically and can specify the period.

■ A new password be different from the last eight passwords.

Creating/Changing Passwords

An Administrator can create or change a user's password. Here's how:

 Creating/Changing a Password

1. At the DOS prompt, type **SYSCON** and press **Enter**.	The SYSCON Available Topics menu appears.
2. Select User Information.	A list of existing user account names appears in the User Names list.
3. Select the name of the user account for which you want to change the password.	The User Information menu appears.
4. Select Change Password.	The Enter New Password prompt appears.
5. Type the user's new password and press **Enter**.	The Retype New Password prompt appears.
6. Retype the user's new password and press **Enter**.	The new password is set and you're back at the User Information menu.

Password Format

A NetWare *password* may consist of any ASCII characters except the 32 control characters. Passwords are *case-insensitive*—any lowercase alphabetic characters are converted to uppercase. So, the user may enter the password with Caps Lock on or off.

> **Tip:** A space character is valid in a password, but the password cannot begin or end with a space. Since spaces can be contained in a password, a user's password may look like a phrase or a sentence. This makes a long password easier to remember.

A NetWare password may have up to 127 characters. If a user is required to have a password, the Supervisor specifies a minimum length for the password. The Supervisor may specify any length between 1 and 20 characters as the minimum length. The default minimum length is 5 characters.

Thinking of a password can be difficult. A password must be something that you can remember but that others can't guess. Network Administrators and users often have very different ideas about what a "good" password is. The Network Administrator is more focused on passwords that are difficult to guess. The user is more focused on passwords that are easy to remember and type. Clearly, a solution that makes all people happy is best. This section of the book deals with the trade-offs between security and simplicity.

User-Generated Passwords

Without training, most users create passwords that are not very secure. Users tend to use a birthdate or the name of their spouse, child, dog, cat, and so forth. This kind of information is simply too easy to get or guess.

When you train your users about passwords, you can recommend the techniques used by computer service bureaus and time-share companies.

- CompuServe assigns users a password that consists of two ordinary words separated by a special character. A CompuServe password may be "green$rice."

- MCI Mail assigns user passwords that are pronounceable words such as "pasunabi." MCI's algorithm is to begin with a consonant and then alternate vowels and consonants.

Most users tend to avoid numeric passwords because of their complexity and the difficulty in committing them to memory. Some may use a password with numerals if it represents something that is easy to remember like a birthdate, social security number, and other "personal" numbers. Unfortunately, these are too easy for an intruder to discover if the intruder knows the identity of the user.

Dictionary Passwords

Like passwords that consist of a "personal number," dictionary passwords have the advantage of being easy to remember but the disadvantage of being discoverable by a sophisticated intruder. As Table 1.3 shows, for a five-character password, there are fewer than 5,000 possibilities if the five-character password must be a dictionary word. In contrast, there are 60 million possibilities with a random five-character password.

In the next section of this chapter, Table 1.3 estimates the number of dictionary words for given word lengths. This data was taken from a publication that did not assume uppercase-only words, so the numbers given are best case. As you can see from the table, the most effective password length for dictionary passwords is seven. Even with this best-case length, the effectiveness is many orders of magnitude less than a random character password. If users resort to dictionary passwords, requiring long passwords may not make sense since, as you can see from the chart, the number of dictionary words diminishes after a length of seven.

The message here is that passwords should not be "words" at all. A more appropriate term for passwords is "passcodes," but most of us are accustomed to calling them passwords even if they're not "words."

Pronounceable Passwords

A good compromise between random characters and a dictionary password is a *pronounceable password*. This is a string of characters that consists of alternating consonants and vowels. This combination of characters is pronounceable even though it's usually a nonsense word. Users don't typically resent having to change their passwords because the process of deciding the next password can be fun.

A pronounceable password is much more effective for a given length than a dictionary word. Table 1.3 shows the effectiveness of passwords of various lengths (with the password techniques previously described). The table assumes that the password starts with a consonant.

Table 1.3   Possible number of password combinations.

Password Length	Random Characters	Dictionary Words	Pronounceable Words
3	46,656	1,193	2,205
4	1,679,616	3,025	11,025
5	60,466,176	4,619	231,525
6	2,176,782,336	6,470	1,157,625
7	78,364,164,096	7,356	24,310,125
8	282,110,990,745	6,999	121,550,625
9	10,155,960,000,000	6,073	2,552,563,125

 Caution: If you do have an account on another machine, such as a mainframe, avoid using the same password for your NetWare password. If someone were to discover your password on one system, the person would also have access to the other system.

If you need to remember more than two or three passwords, consider storing the passwords in a secure place rather than on a piece of paper that you leave in your desk drawer. The problem with most secure places is that they are usually not convenient to access. Conversely, places which are convenient to access are usually not secure.

> **Tip:** One inexpensive solution to finding secure but accessible storage for your passwords is what some companies call a *digital diary,* such as the Casio SF-7500. There are several other brands and models that will work as well. You can store all of your passwords in the password-protected memory area of the digital diary. Now you need to remember only one password—the one for the digital diary.

Checking Security of Passwords

You should be concerned that users are choosing secure passwords. But how can you monitor their choices when you can't view user passwords? One answer is BindView Plus from the LAN Support Group. It can scan the Bindery and produce a report showing you the password status of user accounts. Figure 1.3 shows a sample report.

```
BindView+ v3.0b (Advanced Mode)          Saturday  March 28, 1992  2:55 pm
F/S: ALC                      User Password Analysis              Width:  76

┌───────────┬─────────┬─────────┬─────────┬─────────┬─────────┬──────────────┐
│ User Name │ Password│Password │Password │Password │Password │     Date     │
│           │Required?│Exists?  │Same As  │Same As  │in Full  │  Password    │
│           │         │         │Initials?│Login ID?│ Name    │   Expires    │
├───────────┼─────────┼─────────┼─────────┼─────────┼─────────┼──────────────┤
│ ADMIN     │      NO │    YES  │    NO   │    NO   │    NO   │<Never Expires>│
│ BACKUP    │     YES │    YES  │    NO   │    NO   │    NO   │<Never Expires>│
│ BATCH     │      NO │    YES  │    NO   │    NO   │    NO   │<Never Expires>│
│ CATHRYN   │     YES │    YES  │    NO   │    NO   │    NO   │<Never Expires>│
│ CONSOLE_OP│     YES │    YES  │    NO   │    NO   │    NO   │<Never Expires>│
│ GUEST     │      NO │    NO   │    NO   │    NO   │    NO   │<Never Expires>│
│ LAURA     │     YES │    YES  │   YES   │    NO   │    NO   │ MAY  7, 1992 │
│ LINDA     │     YES │    YES  │    NO   │    NO   │   YES   │ MAY  7, 1992 │
│ MELISSA   │     YES │    YES  │    NO   │    NO   │    NO   │<Never Expires>│
│ MERRYL    │     YES │    YES  │    NO   │    NO   │    NO   │<Never Expires>│
│ REMOTE    │      NO │    NO   │    NO   │    NO   │    NO   │<Never Expires>│
│ SUPERVISOR│      NO │    YES  │    NO   │    NO   │    NO   │<Never Expires>│
└───────────┴─────────┴─────────┴─────────┴─────────┴─────────┴──────────────┘

↑↓→←  <Esc>  <PgUp>  <PgDn>  <Home>  <End>  <Ctrl-Left>  <Ctrl-Right>
```

Figure 1.3   BindView Plus Security report.

24

Notice in the sample report that the account called *LINDA* has a password that is contained within the Full Name. When this user account was created, a Full Name was added, which was Linda White. When Linda changed her password, she chose "WHITE." BindView Plus discovered that Linda's password was contained within the full name.

The report also shows a user LAURA whose password is the same as her initials. When Laura's account was created, the Full Name was set to "Laura A. Petry." Laura later set her password to "LAP," which are her initials based on the Full Name.

The sample report also shows that the SUPERVISOR account is not required to have a password—a significant security problem.

Account Restrictions

NetWare allows the Network Administrator to place restrictions on user accounts. These restrictions control the user's access to the server. Restrictions can be placed on the following:

- Time-of-day and day-of-week access
- Network and node address
- Concurrent connections
- Password changes
- Disk space limits

You control account restrictions with the SYSCON program. Within SYSCON you can set both default account restrictions and user account restrictions.

Note: You cannot set restrictions for a group and have those restrictions apply to members of a group. Account restrictions only apply to individual user accounts.

Default Account Restrictions

SYSCON has default account restrictions that apply to each new user account that you create. If you want different default account restrictions, you can change them but you must be a Supervisor. The next procedure describes how to change the default account restrictions.

 Changing the Default Account Restrictions

1. At the DOS prompt, type **SYSCON** and press **Enter**.

   The Available Topics menu appears.

2. Select Supervisor Options.

   The Supervisor Options menu appears.

3. Select Default Account Balance/Restrictions.

   The Default Account Balance/Restrictions screen appears. Figure 1.4 shows how this screen appears.

4. Make the appropriate changes to the default account restrictions.

   The screen shows the new default account restrictions.

5. Press **Esc** to save your changes.

   You're back at the Supervisor Options menu.

```
┌─────────────────────────────────────────────────────┐
│         Default Account Balance/Restrictions         │
├─────────────────────────────────────────────────────┤
│ Account Has Expiration Date:            No           │
│    Date Account Expires:                             │
│ Limit Concurrent Connections:           Yes          │
│    Maximum Connections:                 2            │
│ Create Home Directory for User:         Yes          │
│ Require Password:                       Yes          │
│    Minimum Password Length:             5            │
│ Force Periodic Password Changes:        Yes          │
│    Days Between Forced Changes:         40           │
│    Limit Grace Logins:                  Yes          │
│       Grace Logins Allowed:             1            │
│ Require Unique Passwords:               Yes          │
│ Account Balance:                        50000        │
│ Allow Unlimited Credit:                 Yes          │
│    Low Balance Limit:                                │
└─────────────────────────────────────────────────────┘
```

Figure 1.4   Default Account Restrictions.

The restrictions on the Default Account Balance/Restrictions screen are described separately in the next sections.

Account Has Expiration Date

The Account Has Expiration Date restriction lets you set a date when the user account should expire. Normally this restriction is set to No. If you set it to Yes and enter a future date, all new user accounts you create will be disabled on this date. A *disabled account* means that the account still exists but that the user cannot log in to the server.

If you enter a date in the past, any new accounts will expire when you create them. When the user tries to log in to the server, the message `This account has expired or been disabled by the Supervisor` will appear. The Supervisor can then enable the user's account. The practical application for this is elusive, so expiration dates should be dates in the future.

Limit Concurrent Connections

By default, the Limit Concurrent Connections restriction is set to No. This means that a user can log in to the file server any number of times concurrently from any number of workstations. Allowing a user to do this represents a security problem because the user is likely to leave one or more of the workstations unattended. You would normally set this restriction to Yes and then set the maximum connections to one.

 Note: If a few users legitimately need two or more concurrent connections, set the restriction in their user account restrictions—not in the default account restrictions.

Create Home Directory for User

By default, the Create Home Directory for User restriction is set to Yes. This means that SYSCON will ask if you want to create a home directory for a user at the time you create the new user account. If you set this restriction to No, SYSCON will not ask if you want to create a home directory.

Some Network Administrators don't want users to have home directories. They feel that home directories are just repositories for junk since some users don't do a good job of housekeeping. Most Administrators don't feel that way, however, and allow users to have home directories.

Require Password

Not requiring passwords for users is a major security problem. The correct setting for the Require Password restriction should always be Yes. You then need to set the Minimum Password Length. This is the minimum length password that must be specified when the user changes his or her password. The default length is five characters but may range from one to twenty.

 Note: Although the Minimum Password Length may be as high as twenty characters, a user may choose to have a longer password since the maximum length for a password may be 127 characters.

Force Periodic Password Changes

The Force Periodic Password Changes restriction is significant only if users are required to have passwords. If this restriction is set to No, users may use the same password forever. It is a security problem to keep the same password forever because as a password "ages," it becomes less secure. If someone wanted to try to guess your password, the person would eventually succeed— given enough time. You make this less likely if you change your password occasionally.

The correct setting for this restriction is Yes. You now have to define how often users will be forced to change their passwords. The default is 40 days. There is no correct value, since this tends to be a controversial topic. Some people feel that if users must change their passwords too often, they will choose new passwords which are not secure or will write their passwords somewhere where others can discover it.

Most Network Administrators in a commercial organization choose values between 30 and 60 days. It would not be unusual in a military organization, for example, to have weekly or daily password changes.

An interesting difference exists between NetWare 2.x and NetWare 3.x when a new user account is required to have a password but doesn't. This assumes that the user is required to change passwords periodically.

 With NetWare 2.2 servers, the administrator can set a user account's password expiration date to a future date. This would allow the user to log in without a password until that future date.

 With NetWare 3.x servers, if the administrator sets the password expiration date to a future date, the server will automatically expire the password when the user tries to log in.

If you force periodic password changes, you'll also need to define *Grace Login* parameters. A Grace Login means that you're logging in to the server with an expired password.

If you choose No for Limit Grace Logins, users will be able to log in forever with expired passwords. Clearly, "No" is not the right setting. When you select Yes, you then need to define the number of Grace Logins that you will allow. The default is six. You must assign at least one Grace Login.

 Note: If a user runs out of Grace Logins, he or she will not be able to log in to change the password. The Supervisor will have to grant more Grace Logins or change the password expiration date in order for the user to log in again.

Require Unique Passwords

The Require Unique Passwords restriction determines if users are allowed to "reuse" passwords that they've used in the past. If you set this restriction to No, users may change their password and specify an old password for the new password. The only restriction will be that the user cannot specify the current password as a new password. Users can have the same two passwords forever even though they're required to change their passwords periodically.

 Caution: Setting the restriction Require Unique Passwords to No makes it pointless to require password changes at all. So, the correct setting is Yes.

The old passwords are stored in the NetWare Bindery. The Bindery stores only eight old passwords. When you change your password, your old password is moved to the Bindery. When there are eight old passwords in the Bindery, a new password change causes the oldest expired password in the Bindery to be discarded.

 Note: You may think that you can get around the unique password restriction by changing your password nine times. Then you'll be able to reuse an old password that is no longer in the Bindery. NetWare prevents this by only allowing you to move one old password to the Bindery each day. So, if you change your password more than once during a day, only the first old password for that day is moved to the Bindery.

Changing a User's Account Restrictions

You can change a user's account restrictions if they should be different from the default account restrictions. Here's how.

 Changing a User's Account Restrictions

1. At the DOS prompt, type **SYSCON** and press **Enter**.

The Available Topics menu appears.

2. Select User Information.	The list of User Names appears.
3. Select a user account by highlighting one of the user names in the list. Press **Enter**.	The User Information menu appears.
4. Select Account Restrictions.	The Account Restrictions For User xxxx screen appears, where xxxx is the user account name. Figure 1.5 shows how this screen appears.
5. Make changes to the user's account restrictions.	The screen shows the user's account restrictions.
6. Press **Esc** to save your changes.	You're back at the User Information menu.

```
┌────────────────────────────────────────────────────┐
│          Account Restrictions For User LAURA         │
├──────────────────────────────────────────────────────
│Account Disabled:                     No              │
│Account Has Expiration Date:          No              │
│   Date Account Expires:                              │
│Limit Concurrent Connections:         Yes             │
│   Maximum Connections:               2               │
│Allow User To Change Password:        Yes             │
│Require Password:                     Yes             │
│   Minimum Password Length:           6               │
│Force Periodic Password Changes:      Yes             │
│   Days Between Forced Changes:       40              │
│   Date Password Expires:             May 7, 1992     │
│   Limit Grace Logins:                Yes             │
│      Grace Logins Allowed:           6               │
│      Remaining Grace Logins:         6               │
│Require Unique Passwords:             Yes             │
└──────────────────────────────────────────────────────
```

Figure 1.5   User Account Restrictions.

Default Time Restrictions

You can restrict user access to a file server based on time-of-day and day-of-week. Just as there are default account restrictions, there are also default time and day restrictions. You define the defaults with SYSCON.

Changing the Default Time and Day Restrictions

1. At the DOS prompt, type **SYSCON** and press **Enter**.

   The `Available Topics` menu appears.

2. Select `Supervisor Options` and press **Enter**.

   The `Supervisor Options` menu appears.

3. Select `Default Time Restrictions`.

   The `Default Time Restrictions` screen appears. Figure 1.6 shows how this screen appears.

4. Each asterisk character represents a half-hour period of time. Remove asterisks with the space bar to disallow that time period. You can allow a time period by pressing the *****.

   The new default time restrictions appear.

5. Press **Esc** to save your changes.

   You're back at the `Supervisor Options` menu.

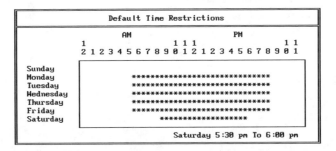

Figure 1.6   *Default Time Restrictions.*

The example in Figure 1.6 shows that users are allowed to log in to the server between 5:30 am and 8:00 pm on Monday through Friday. Additionally, users can log in on Saturday between 8:30 am and 5:30 pm.

If a user is already logged in, he or she will be told twice to log out when a disallowed time period occurs. The first message occurs about one minute into the disallowed time period. The second message occurs about six minutes later. If the user has not logged out by about eight minutes into the disallowed time period, NetWare will clear the user's connection.

Changing a User's Time Restrictions

Changing the default time restrictions for a particular user is easily accomplished. The next procedure explains how to do it.

 Changing the Default Time Restrictions

1. At the DOS prompt, type **SYSCON** and press **Enter**.

   The `Available Topics` menu appears.

2. Select `User Information` and press **Enter**.

   A list of user account names appears in the `User Names` list.

3. Select a user.

   The `User Information` menu appears.

4. Select `Time Restrictions`.

   The `Allowed Login Times For User xxxx` screen appears, where xxxx is the user account name you selected from the list. See Figure 1.7.

5. Each asterisk character represents a half-hour period of time. Remove asterisks with the space bar to disallow that time period. You can allow a time period by pressing *****.

   The new user time restrictions appear.

6. Press **Esc** to save your changes.

   You're back at the `User Information` menu.

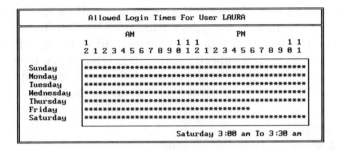

Figure 1.7   User Time Restrictions.

Print Server Passwords

Just as user accounts may have passwords, a print server account may have a password. A print server account is defined with the PCONSOLE program. Figure 1.8 shows how a password is assigned with PCONSOLE for the print server account called ALCPRT.

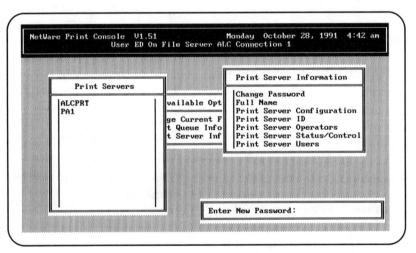

Figure 1.8   Assigning a Print Server a Password.

When you start the print server, it will prompt you for the password because it needs this password to establish a connection with the file server. Figure 1.9 shows how PSERVER prompts for the password.

```
┌─────────────────────────────────────────────────────────────────┐
│ ╔═══════════════════════════════════════════════════════════════╗ │
│ ║          Novell NetWare Print Server V1.21                    ║ │
│ ║                Server ALCPRT Initializing                     ║ │
│ ╚═══════════════════════════════════════════════════════════════╝ │
│ ┌──────────────────────────────┬────────────────────────────────┐ │
│ │ 0: Not installed             │ 4: Not installed               │ │
│ │                              │                                │ │
│ ├──────────────────────────────┼────────────────────────────────┤ │
│ │ 1: Not installed             │ 5: Not installed               │ │
│ │      ┌───────────────────────────────────────────┐            │ │
│ │      │ Password for file server ALC:             │            │ │
│ ├──────└───────────────────────────────────────────┘────────────┤ │
│ │ 2: Not installed             │ 6: Not installed               │ │
│ │                              │                                │ │
│ ├──────────────────────────────┼────────────────────────────────┤ │
│ │ 3: Not installed             │ 7: Not installed               │ │
│ │                              │                                │ │
│ └──────────────────────────────┴────────────────────────────────┘ │
└─────────────────────────────────────────────────────────────────┘
```

Figure 1.9   How PSERVER prompts for a password.

Passwords are assigned to print server accounts to prevent someone from starting up a print server that masquerades as the real print server. For example, the printer that prints checks is located on the fourth floor in a locked room. The print server is named CHEK_PRT and is a PC running the PSERVER program. The print server services the print queue called CHECKS. Is it possible for someone to obtain financial information by "stealing" it from the print queue?

Yes—by running PSERVER on any machine on the network and calling it CHEK_PRT. This bogus print server will now service print jobs in the CHECKS print queue.

In most organizations, sensitive or confidential information to which a user normally does not have access can be had by waiting for the information to be printed.

Only a Supervisor can add a print server account to the Bindery and assign that print server account a password. Security controls used for user account passwords, such as minimum password lengths, are not used for print server account passwords. It is assumed that Supervisors are aware of security matters and don't need to be forced into proper security practices.

If your organization has a computer security officer, you probably have no need for additional security controls for print server accounts. Unfortunately, many organizations do not have staff whose primary responsibility is computer or network security. A Network Administrator who has numerous responsibilities can easily lose track of print server account passwords. For the present, print server account security requires that procedures be implemented to ensure that passwords change periodically. In the future, NetWare should provide print server accounts with automatic security mechanisms such as those that exist for user account passwords.

2

Workstation Security

This chapter focuses on securing the workstation from hostile users using features built into NetWare, as well as features of third-party products, such as Watchdog. Intruder Detection is a security feature that you should take advantage of. To not use intruder detection is to ignore one of the more powerful features of NetWare. However, Intruder Detection is not foolproof, as you'll soon discover.

You'll also see that Novell's LOGIN program has "features" that hinder your ability to secure your network. You'll learn why you should upgrade an ancient version of NetWare to take advantage of encrypted passwords.

- ■ Intruder Detection
- ■ Encrypted Passwords
- ■ LOGIN Security Problems
- ■ Auto-Logout
- ■ Watchdog

Intruder Detection

An *intruder* is someone who attempts to access someone else's account. This is generally done by guessing at the password for the user's account.

If the intruder succeeds, he or she has all rights that the owner of the account has. As you might expect, the typical target is the Supervisor account or the accounts of supervisor-equivalents. Fortunately, there is no easy way for a non-Supervisor to discover which other accounts are supervisor-equivalent. If a non-Supervisor runs SYSCON to see if a user account is equivalent to Supervisor, he or she would see a screen similar to Figure 2.1.

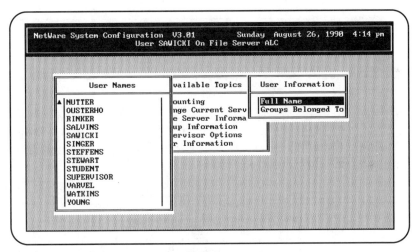

Figure 2.1   A User's view of SYSCON.

In this example, a non-Supervisor called SAWICKI tries to get information about a user called STEWART. The only information available is the user's full name and the groups that the user belongs to. This means that unless an intruder knows that a user account is equivalent to SUPERVISOR, the intruder will probably focus on breaking into the SUPERVISOR account.

At times, though, it's fairly obvious which users are likely to be equivalent to SUPERVISOR. If a user whose name is Jones is one of the Network Administrators, it's a good assumption that an account called JONES is equivalent to SUPERVISOR.

Tip: A technique for avoiding exposure of a SUPER-VISOR account is to give to a Supervisor-equivalent an account name that is unrelated to the person's name. Additionally, you may want to create an account called JONES that has no rights, just to give the intruder something harmless to go after.

An intruder does not typically know the password of the account in advance, so a break-in involves guessing at the password. This guessing may be done manually or it may be automated by a program. Fortunately, NetWare is very strong in this area. It can detect intruders and, optionally, lock the account that the intruder is trying to break into.

Note: The Network Administrator must enable intruder detection since it is disabled by default.

To enable intruder detection, select `Supervisor Options` on the SYSCON main menu. You'll see the screen shown in Figure 2.2. When you select `Intruder Detection/Lockout` from this menu, you see the screen in Figure 2.3.

```
                  Supervisor Options

       Default Account Balance/Restrictions
       Default Time Restrictions
       Edit System AUTOEXEC File
       File Server Console Operators
       Intruder Detection/Lockout
       System Login Script
       View File Server Error Log
       Workgroup Managers
```

Figure 2.2   Supervisor Options menu in SYSCON.

```
                 Intruder Detection/Lockout

 Detect Intruders:                Yes

 Intruder Detection Threshold
 Incorrect Login Attempts:        4
 Bad Login Count Retention Time:  0  Days    0  Hours    15 Minutes

 Lock Account After Detection:    Yes
   Length Of Account Lockout:     0  Days    0  Hours    5  Minutes
```

Figure 2.3   Intruder Detection/Lockout screen in SYSCON.

You can turn intruder detection on or off at any time. However, there is little reason to turn it off. As Figure 2.3 shows, you must enter parameters defining the events that must take place to detect an intruder.

 Note: As defined by NetWare, an intruder is someone who types the wrong password a certain number of times within a certain period of time.

In Figure 2.3, intruder detection is set for four wrong passwords within 15 minutes. The "correct" settings here are elusive. You should keep the `Bad Login Count Retention Time` fairly low to discourage break-ins but not so low that users who often mistype their passwords trip the intruder detection mechanism and possibly become locked out. Unfortunately, these parameters apply to all users. There is no way to give specific users or groups their own settings. Even though Novell allows you to set this time to 40 days, 23 hours and 59 minutes, this seems unusually long.

 Note: NetWare considers an incorrect login attempt to be one in which the user types one or more incorrect keystrokes (not including the Enter key), in response to the `Enter your password:` prompt. If you only press the Enter key in response to the password prompt, that is not considered a login attempt and is not included in the Incorrect Login Attempts count.

Account Lockout

NetWare gives you the choice of locking the account that the intruder is trying to break into. You can specify the amount of time that must pass before the account becomes unlocked. If you specify a long period, such as two or more days (to cover a weekend), this ensures that the user will notify the Supervisor of the intruder. The user will not be able to log in until the Supervisor unlocks the account. Short lockout periods ensure that a program which guesses at passwords will not function while still allowing the user to log in after a short lockout.

In Figure 2.3, account lockout is turned on and accounts are locked for five minutes.

When an account does become locked, the Supervisor can run SYSCON to get information about the locked account and the intruder. Figure 2.4 shows that the account is locked and will be reset in 4 minutes and 29 seconds. The `Last Intruder Address` is the node address of the workstation the intruder attempted the break-in from.

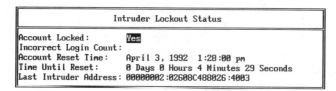

```
                        Intruder Lockout Status
Account Locked:           Yes
Incorrect Login Count:
Account Reset Time:       April 3, 1992  1:28:00 pm
Time Until Reset:         0 Days 0 Hours 4 Minutes 29 Seconds
Last Intruder Address: 00000002:02608C488026:4003
```

Figure 2.4   Intruder Lockout Status screen in SYSCON.

Address of Intruder

The `Intruder Lockout Status` screen, shown in Figure 2.4, gives the address of the intruder. In this case, the address is `00000002:02608C488026:4003`. This three-level address is formatted as follows:

`NETWORK ADDRESS:NODE ADDRESS:IPX SOCKET`

- The `NETWORK ADDRESS` (here, `00000002`), is the address of the cabling system. This is the address you assign the LAN card in your file server.

- The `NODE ADDRESS` (here, `02608C488026`), is the address of the LAN card in the workstation.

- The `IPX SOCKET` (here, `4003`), is the socket number that the program used to make the login request. An IPX socket is a concept that is beyond the scope of this book, but the IPX socket information is not required in determining the physical location of the workstation used by the intruder.

2 — Workstation Security

To catch the intruder in the act, you'll need the ability to quickly translate the internetwork address to a physical location. This is best done at the time the LAN cards are installed in the workstations. The installer(s) should keep detailed notes about the LAN card node addresses. These notes can then be compiled as a simple table and included in your network documentation.

 Tip: To quickly locate a workstation, create a table similar to sample Table 2.1. Sort the table first by network address, then by node address. You should have a table for every network address on your internetwork.

Table 2.1   Sample network address table.

| Network address: 00000001 | | | |
Node Address	Floor	Mailstop	Primary User
000000000008	3	32/192	John Savage
000000000011	3	32/187	Betty Littlefield
000000000015	3	33/001	Tom Bentley
000000000023	3	32/192	Dan Williams
000000000034	3	32/191	Bob Kane
000000000035	3	32/190	Chris Martin
00000000006B	3	33/050	Joe Jackson
000000000095	3	34/200	Jennifer Walsh
0000000000BA	3	33/412	Valerie Voss
0000000000C0	3	32/192	Peter Arnett
0000000000C8	3	33/050	James Baker
0000000000EA	3	33/001	print server

Node Address Problems

ARCNET, Token-Ring, and any network topology where the node address can be locally administered represent a problem for the intruder address. It's easy for someone to change the node address of an ARCNET card. This is especially true for those LAN cards in which the vendor "thoughtfully" put the node address switches on the back panel so that you don't have to remove the cover of the machine to access the switches.

An intruder can change the node address of the card in a PC before attempting the break-in. Some cards, such as Token-Ring can have a locally administered address downloaded into them by software that the user can run. Some diskless workstations have a keyboard setup screen that allows you to change the node address very quickly.

It is easy for a workstation to assume a different node address if you are using Novell's ODI drivers and a LAN card which allows its node address to change. Currently, ODI drivers can change the node address of the following EtherNet cards:

- 3C501

- 3C503

- 3C505

- 3C523

- NE1000

- NE2000

- NE/2

- NE2-32

Additionally, any Token-Ring card that uses Novell's TOKEN driver can be changed as well.

You can quickly change the node address by changing the contents of the NET.CFG file. Under the heading "Link Driver," include the statement NODE ADDRESS X where X is any hexidecimal address you want the card's node address to be.

When these problem situations exist, it may be difficult to do anything with the intruder address information, since a node address that is not on your list of installed workstations doesn't tell you where the machine is located.

However, there are specific actions that you can take to attempt to locate the intruder:

2 — Workstation Security

- If you have accounting enabled at your server, you can search the audit log to see which users have logged out or logged in close to the time that the intruder alert occurred.

- You can use diagnostic packages, such as NetWare Care, to see which node addresses existed on the network at the time of an intruder alert. Those persons whose node addresses contain no irregularities can be eliminated as suspects for the short term.

 Note: Intruder detection and account lockout apply to all accounts on the server equally. There is no way to provide different intruder detection parameters for different users or groups. If you think that intruder detection should take place whenever a user types a password wrong two times within one minute and that the account should be locked for 24 hours when that occurs, you'll have to live with the results (users and their managers may be unhappy).

Encrypted Passwords

NetWare versions below 2.15c allowed passwords to flow between the workstation and the file server in clear text. The term "clear text" often refers to textual data which is unencrypted. Anyone who could capture packets and display their contents could learn the passwords of any user, given enough time. Starting with NetWare 3.0 and NetWare 2.15c, Novell added encryption of passwords to the operating system and to programs that must log in to a server (such as LOGIN.EXE).

Assuming that the user logs in with the LOGIN.EXE program, the encryption works in the following way:

1. LOGIN.EXE sends a message to the server asking for an encryption key.

2. The server returns a 64-bit key to the workstation. The key is different each time the workstation requests a key.

3. LOGIN.EXE uses the key to encrypt the password.

4. Since the server knows the key that was used to encrypt the password, it is able to decrypt the password.

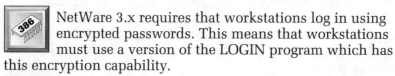 NetWare 3.x requires that workstations log in using encrypted passwords. This means that workstations must use a version of the LOGIN program which has this encryption capability.

 Version 2.10 of LOGIN.EXE was able to use encrypted passwords. If you have version 2.10 or a later version of LOGIN.EXE, you can log in with encrypted passwords. If you don't know the version of your LOGIN.EXE program, you can use Novell's VERSION program to find out.

If your version of LOGIN does not support encrypted passwords, get a later version of LOGIN that does support encryption.

Caution: When updating the version of LOGIN.EXE on your file server, remember that it normally resides in three directories: SYS:LOGIN, SYS:PUBLIC, and SYS:SYSTEM. Make sure you put the new copy of LOGIN.EXE in all three directories.

In addition to the LOGIN program using encrypted passwords, there are other programs that can log in to a file server and use encrypted passwords. Some of these programs are:

- ATTACH
- CAPTURE
- DSPACE
- FCONSOLE
- FILER

- MAP
- NPRINT

So, if you need to update your copy of LOGIN.EXE, it's likely that other NetWare programs need updating as well.

There may be reasons why you need to allow your NetWare 3.x file server to accept passwords which are unencrypted. The most common reason is that you're using a print server product such as the Intel NetPort. NetPort does not know how to encrypt passwords because, in the past, Novell did not release information about how to acomplish this.

 Note: Castelle began shipping a print server product which encrypts passwords before Novell made this information generally available.

The solution is to tell your server to allow logins where passwords are sent in unencrypted form. You do this with the following statement entered at the file server console or placed in the server's AUTOEXEC.NCF file:

```
SET ALLOW UNENCRYPTED PASSWORDS=ON
```

 Note: Now that Novell has given developers a way to encrypt passwords, vendors like Intel are releasing products that use encrypted passwords, such as Intel's NetPort II.

NetWare 2.15c and later versions of NetWare 2.x will accept either encrypted or unencrypted passwords. You do not need to take any action to tell the file server to allow unencrypted passwords.

NetWare 3.x differs from NetWare 2.x in that it lets the Network Administrator decide whether unencrypted passwords should be allowed. Netware 2.x does not give you a choice.

Caution: If you have NetWare 2.x and NetWare 3.x servers on the same network, make sure all users run a current version of the LOGIN program that supports encrypted passwords. Otherwise, users will only be able to log in to a NetWare 3.x server if you tell the server to `Allow Unencrypted Passwords`. Allowing unencrypted passwords diminishes the additional security of a NetWare 3.x server.

LOGIN Security Problems

The LOGIN program that Novell includes with NetWare has two fundamental security flaws that you should know about. The first involves the ability of a user to bypass the login scripts. The second allows a user to automate the entry of a password.

Bypassing Login Scripts

The LOGIN program supplied by Novell allows a DOS command-line argument to use an alternate file as a login script. This by-passes both the system login script and the user login script. This is a serious problem, because Network Administrators may assume that certain programs are loaded as a result of the system login script.

For example, you may set up your server so that when a user logs in to the system, the system login script causes an audit trail program to load in the user's workstation. By bypassing the system login script, a user gains control of the auditing process. Allowing a user to bypass the system login script is very poor security.

Automating Password Entry

The LOGIN program allows DOS redirection of the keyboard. This means that instead of getting keystrokes from the actual keyboard, the "keystrokes" can be gotten from a file. The user could create a file on a local drive that contains his or her password. Then, the AUTOEXEC.BAT program could read the password from the file.

As an example, a user named Diana could create a file called PASSWORD on drive C:. The PASSWORD file would contain Diana's password in ASCII text. Here is what Diana's AUTOEXEC.BAT might look like:

```
PROMPT $P$G
PATH C:\SYS;C:\DOS
IPX.COM
NETX.COM
F:
LOGIN DIANA < C:\PASSWORD
```

The last line in the AUTOEXEC.BAT file runs Novell's LOGIN program that gets the user's password from the PASSWORD file by using DOS redirection (the < character).

This represents a significant security problem, because anyone with physical access to the workstation can read the PASSWORD file and see the user's password.

Auto-Logout

One of the more common problems in any interactive computing environment is maintaining security when the user leaves the terminal or workstation unattended without first logging out of the system. A NetWare environment is as vulnerable as other systems in this regard. NetWare does not have any built-in mechanism to deal with this security problem.

There are a few ways to deal with this problem. The simplest and least costly solution is user training. However, you may want a mechanism in place that takes over if a user forgets. In this section of the book, we'll give examples of third-party products that can be used to help solve the problem.

Training

The best solution to the problem of an unattended workstation is training. You must convince users that security is essential even in a work environment that seems nonhostile. They must understand that if they leave their workstations unattended, there is opportunity for someone to have unauthorized access to their files.

A typical training session will include questions such as, "Do I need to logout if I leave my desk for only one minute to make a photocopy?" You need to be prepared to give decisive answers to such questions. Otherwise, your users will wonder just how important security is.

You can, for example, tell users that if they are out of sight of their workstation for more than one minute, they should log out.

NetOFF

NetOFF is a third-party program that automatically logs out a user if there is no activity at the user's workstation for a specified time. It is a Terminate-and-Stay-Resident (TSR) program that consumes less than 2 KB of workstation memory. NetOFF is available from Citadel Systems, whose address and phone number is included in Appendix B, "Third-Party Products."

When you load NetOFF, you specify a timeout period in minutes. If this amount of time passes without workstation activity, the user will be logged out from any file server he or she is connected to. A message appears on the bottom line of the workstation screen notifying the user that he or she has been logged out.

 Caution: NetOFF currently gives no warning that auto-logout is imminent. The user finds out after it happens.

NetOFF considers activity to be:

- Keystrokes
- Open files or printer
- Disk and network I/O

NetOFF does give you some control over what constitutes activity. You can declare, for example, that an open file is not a reason to keep the user logged on in the absence of other activity. A user could have gone home and left a word processing document still on the screen.

When you load NetOFF, you'll see a screen similar to the one shown in Figure 2.5. The time-out parameter is a numeric value between 1 and 60. By default, this number represents minutes, but the /H switch can be used to represent hours or /S for seconds.

```
H:\HOME\ED>netoff
NetOFF 2.00 is being installed......

NetOFF 2.00 Current Settings 30 - Minute(s) delay time
        Server (N)otification.......: DISABLED
        Open (F)ile check...........: ENABLED
        Misc (I)nteruppt check......: ENABLED
        (T)est mode.................: DISABLED

H:\HOME\ED>
```

Figure 2.5   Loading NetOFF.

The /Q switch installs NetOFF "quietly" (no banner displayed on the screen). Use this switch if you don't want users to know that NetOFF is being loaded. Of course, they will know something is up when they are logged out.

The /N+ switch causes NetOFF to post a message to the server's NET$LOG.MSG file whenever an auto-logout occurs. This will provide a record of users who are frequently being logged off by NetOFF.

The /F- switch causes NetOFF to ignore open files as activity.

The /U switch removes NetOFF from memory.

METZ Lock

METZ Lock is a Windows-based locking product sold by Metz Software whose address and phone number is in Appendix B, "Third-Party Products." METZ Lock is a better way of dealing with unattended workstations than NetOFF, but it only works while a user is running Windows.

I'll refer to it as *ML*. After you install ML and set parameters, it will take over the screen, keyboard, and mouse after a pre-defined time period of inactivity elapses. The screen will blank and will display an "icon" that moves around to prevent the image from being burned into your screen phosphor. When you press a key, you'll see the window shown in Figure 2.6. After you enter your password and select OK, you're returned to the window that you were at when ML locked your machine.

Figure 2.6   Providing your password to MetzLock.

Main Configuration

You can customize ML by running the program or selecting the ML icon. Figure 2.7 shows the main configuration dialog box. ML offers three modes from which you can select:

- **Manual Locking** requires you to lock your workstation manually by double-clicking on the ML icon or by using the hot key. There is no automatic locking.

- **Automatic Locking** means that ML automatically locks your workstation after a period of inactivity. The period of inactivity is determined by the Timeout value you enter.

- **Screen Saver Only** means that your workstation screen will blank and display a moving icon, but will not be locked. Pressing any key or moving the mouse will return the screen to the way it was before.

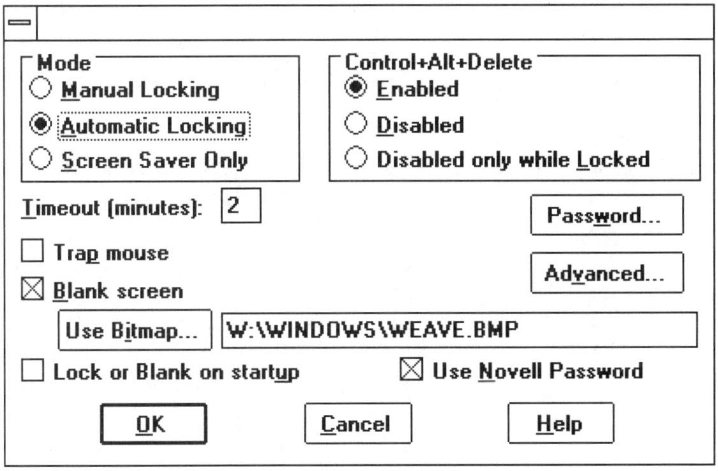

Figure 2.7 *METZ Lock main configuration screen.*

ML can disable "warm booting" by preventing your workstation from reacting to the Ctrl-Alt-Del key combination. Optionally, you can disable warm booting only when the workstation is locked.

You can choose between having ML use your NetWare password and defining a password that is significant only to ML. A NetWare password is stored in the NetWare Bindery. The password is not case-sensitive. The ML password is encrypted and stored in your WIN.INI file. The password is case-sensitive.

You'll probably want to use your NetWare (Novell) password for your ML password. Just check the box marked Use Novell Password. When you do, ML will refer to the NetWare Bindery for checking your password. If you change your password within ML, your NetWare password will change in the Bindery. ML knows how to encrypt NetWare passwords, so you don't need to Allow Unencrypted Passwords on your NetWare 3.x server.

> **Note:** If you use your NetWare password for ML, intruder detection will apply if it is enabled. Should someone try to break into your workstation while it is unattended (and ML is in control), and should they enter the wrong password several times, your account would be locked.

Advanced Configuration

Figure 2.8 shows the advanced parameters over which you have control.

- **Hotkey Sequence:** You can define the hotkey sequence that will activate ML as well as hide the ML icon so that it doesn't show on your screen. This makes ML "stealthy."

- **Password Expiration:** You can set ML so that it expires your password periodically. Since this feature already exists in NetWare, you may choose not to use it.

- **Daily Locking:** You can set ML so that it locks your workstation everyday at a certain time. If that time arrives and you are still using your workstation, ML will wait for a period of inactivity that you specify.

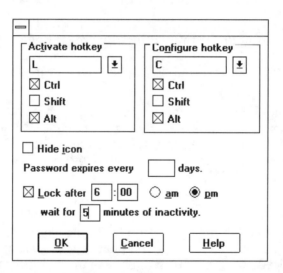

Figure 2.8   METZ Lock advanced configuration screen.

Watchdog

Watchdog is a security product from Fischer International designed to control access to a workstation. Your workstation must have a local hard disk to use Watchdog. It was not designed with networking in mind, but it can be used in a networking environment to provide additional security that NetWare does not provide.

Watchdog provides two primary functions:

- Access control to the workstation
- Access control to directories on the workstation's local hard disk

Access control to the workstation is achieved by requiring that the user specify an account name and password(s) to Watchdog before the workstation will boot DOS and run the AUTOEXEC.BAT file.

Watchdog provides you with security features for directories on the workstation's local hard disk similar to the features that NetWare provides for directories on the file server. Without Watchdog, you had the ability to secure files and directories on your file server, but not on local drives—in other words, a security "hole." With Watchdog, you can now secure the entire user environment.

Access Control

To use a Watchdog-equipped workstation, a user must have a Watchdog user ID and password assigned by the Watchdog System Administrator. This information is stored on the local hard disk drive. When the workstation is booted, the Watchdog login screen prompts the user for his or her Watchdog ID and passwords. Figure 2.9 shows what the Watchdog opening screen looks like.

The Watchdog user password can be up to 12 characters. The Administrator can enforce a minimum password length. The passwords are case-sensitive, but a user can choose to have an alternate password, which may be the same password but opposite case of the primary password. If the primary password is "dy12h4," for example, the alternate password may be "DY12H4."

Users can choose to create their own passwords or have Watchdog create a pronounceable password for them. This assumes that the Administrator has configured Watchdog to allow users to change their own passwords. The length of the generated password is the minimum password length. If no minimum password length is set, the generated password is 12 characters.

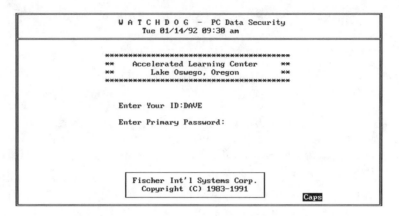

```
              W A T C H D O G  -  PC Data Security
                    Tue 01/14/92 09:30 am

          ********************************************
          **      Accelerated Learning Center      **
          **           Lake Oswego, Oregon         **
          ********************************************


              Enter Your ID:DAVE

              Enter Primary Password:




                ┌──────────────────────────────┐
                │  Fischer Int'l Systems Corp.  │
                │    Copyright (C) 1983-1991    │
                └──────────────────────────────┘ [Caps]
```

Figure 2.9   Watchdog Login Screen.

Periodic Password Changes

Like NetWare, Watchdog can require users to change their Watchdog passwords periodically. The Administrator can set this so that the password expires in 1 to 999 days.

One-Time Passwords

The Administrator can assign a user a one-time password which allows a user to log in with that password one time only. This is useful when you don't want the Administrator to know user passwords. During that one-time login, the user would typically choose a different password so that he or she could log in again in the future.

Dual Password Protection

A dual password feature helps prevent Trojan Horse programs from emulating the login sequence and obtaining user IDs and passwords. Trojan Horse programs will be described later in this book. The System Administrator can choose to enable this feature. If dual-passwords are enabled, Watchdog prints a *token* to the screen after the user enters the Watchdog user ID and password.

This token is a four-character string unique to the user and should be known only to the user. The token appears on the screen briefly (about one-half second). If the token is correct, the user then enters the secondary password.

If the token does not appear or the token is wrong, the user can assume that Watchdog security has been compromised. The user would then not enter the secondary password. If the user is distracted and doesn't see the token, pressing the Enter key will return the user to the primary password.

Intruder Detection

If the user enters the password(s) wrong three times, the user must wait 30 seconds before being able to enter the password(s) again. If the pasword(s) is entered wrong an additional three times, the user must wait 60 seconds before being able to try again. Each additional wrong attempt doubles the wait time.

Bootup Protection

Whenever the PC is booted, the Watchdog program loads immediately after DOS loads and *before* the AUTOEXEC.BAT file executes. This sequence protects against someone trying to circumvent Watchdog security by booting from a floppy disk. If the PC is booted from a floppy, the PC's hard disk is not recognized by DOS. Any attempts to access programs or data on the hard disk will fail.

Watchdog Armor

The Watchdog Armor card is an available option. This half-slot card contains a protected clock that can be set only by the System Administrator. It has DES encryption circuitry to make DES encryption of files (on local drives) faster. When this card is installed, the PC will not boot from the floppy drive at all. If an attempt is made to boot from the floppy, the Armor card redirects the boot to the hard disk.

 Note: The Watchdog Armor product can be defeated if you can remove the Armor card from the bus of the workstation.

3

Diskless Workstations

Few issues in the networking industry are more controversial than diskless workstations. Proponents and opponents are passionate in their views and clash often in forums like CompuServe and Letters to the Editor sections of trade journals. You probably consider diskless workstations to be oddities and ignore them. After all, your users need "real" workstations.

Yet, diskless workstations are hard to ignore when you realize the benefits—especially the security benefits. If you lost a bit of sleep in March of 1992 during the Michelangelo affair, perhaps you should consider going diskless.

- Pros and Cons
- How Diskless Workstations Boot
- A Simple Installation
- Common Problems

Pros and Cons

Diskless workstations are a popular way to achieve a more secure network environment. Basically, a diskless workstation is a PC that has no local diskette drives or hard disk drives. When it boots, it loads DOS from a boot file located on the server disk. To do this, a boot PROM must be installed in the diskless workstation.

While diskless workstations provide increased security, they are also controversial. It seems that people either like them or hate them, with little middle ground. Why do they inspire such strong reactions?

Advantages

Advocates point out that the advantages of diskless workstations far outweigh any disadvantages. While the most important advantage is enhanced security, there are others as well which have little to do with security.

Security: There are no floppy disk drives, so users cannot remove valuable and proprietary data from the system and carry it out of the office easily. The converse is also true. Users cannot easily bring in program and data files (which may be virus infected) and copy them to the server. It makes a network administrator's or a security officer's life a little easier.

Simplicity: For office workers who are intimidated by computers, diskless workstations may seem less complicated because there are fewer gadgets, such as floppy drive slots and levers, blinking hard disk lights, and so on.

Software Upgrades: Since diskless workstations have no local storage for program files, all programs must reside on the server. When you need to upgrade a program, you copy the new program to the server. You don't have to coordinate upgrading the program in all user machines. It makes the tech support person's life easier knowing that there's only one version of an application on the network.

Size: A diskless workstation can be built smaller than a normal PC. It takes up less space in the user's work area. There are products available with the entire workstation (except for the monitor), built into the keyboard unit. One such product is the EarthStation from Alloy Computer Products.

Power: When you don't have floppy drives, hard disk drives, and the circuitry to support them, your power supply requirements are reduced dramatically. A benefit of lower workstation power requirements is less expensive uninterruptable power. You may be able to connect two or more diskless workstations to one uninterruptable power supply. Ask a user who has been the victim of a power outage about the benefits of uninterruptable power.

Shell and DOS Versions: Diskless workstations must boot from a boot file on the file server since there is no local DOS drive to boot from. This means that network administrators have better control over the versions of DOS and the NetWare shell used. The tech support person's life is easier when you know the version of DOS and the shell being used.

Virus Infection: Since diskless workstations do not boot from a local drive, there is little chance of a virus attack from a boot sector or partition table virus. The workstation boots from a boot image file on the file server. It's not likely that viruses will infect boot image files, even if they have rights to the directory (SYS:LOGIN) where the boot image files reside.

 Note: It's been suggested that the diskless workstation's boot PROM could be infected by a virus. Boot PROMs are not alterable when they're installed in the workstation, so virus infection of the boot PROM is impossible. However, it's possible for a boot PROM to be infected during its manufacture. Always obtain them from a reliable source.

Disadvantages

Diskless workstations have a few disadvantages which are discussed next. Generally, these disadvantages are not difficult to deal with and solutions to potential problems are easy to implement.

Server Failures: Critics of diskless workstations are quick to point out that if the file server fails, the diskless workstations are useless because they rely on the server for their file system. Users can do no work while the file server is down. This is true and may be an issue if file server failures were common. Practically speaking, file server failures occur infrequently and repairs can be made quickly.

 Note: You can maintain a backup file server to take over when your production server is down for repairs. The cost of purchasing and maintaining a backup file server is relatively low compared to the cost of purchasing and maintaining a hard disk at every workstation.

LAN Traffic: Since diskless workstations have no local storage, programs and their overlay files must flow over the network cable. An environment like Windows, for example, could cause significant LAN traffic. This is a legitimate concern that must be considered against the increase in security. One way of dealing with this issue is to reduce the load on your cable segments and file servers so the additional LAN traffic doesn't significantly affect performance.

One way of dealing with this issue is to reduce the load on your cable segments and file servers. This prevents the additional LAN traffic from significantly affecting server performance. You may accomplish this by adding additional LAN cards to your file servers and moving workstations to other cable segments. You can also use faster file servers or install additional file servers. Also, client/server database technology can be used to lessen the LAN traffic.

Note: The impact of Microsoft Windows on LAN traffic is significant when diskless workstations are used. Most people agree that Windows users need local hard disks unless workstations have at least 8 megabytes of memory (RAM).

Emotion: Users who have had local drives in the past and find themselves working with a diskless workstation are often hostile because they feel that they've lost a bit of independence and some of their rights. This is especially true in an environment where users have experienced the "tyranny" of the data processing department in the past. The solution here is to prepare the users for the switch to diskless workstations by pointing out the benefits of the switch well in advance.

Diskless or "Without Disks"

There are two ways to build a diskless workstation. One is to take a standard PC and simply remove the disk drives and controller card. Usually, this type of diskless machine is less expensive than one that has drives. If you change your mind about going diskless or these machines need to be redeployed elsewhere where local storage is needed, you can add drives in the future.

The problem is the ease with which someone can add a controller card and floppy or hard disk drive and circumvent security. While locking devices can be added to PCs to make access to the PCs' internals difficult, this increases your costs.

The second way to build a diskless workstation is to design a machine to be diskless. This means that you cannot add a controller card and disk drives in the future. This type of diskless workstation is more secure, because it is difficult to attach a floppy drive or hard disk drive to circumvent security. It would not be unusual for diskless workstations of this type to be more expensive than similarly-equipped PCs with disk drives.

Justification

If you want to introduce diskless workstations in your organization, but others make the purchasing decision, you're likely to encounter economic justification problems. Typical comments are, "These are more expensive than our other PCs, and these things don't even have floppy disk drives!" or, "For only 200 dollars more, we can have hard disks!" They've missed the point, and you'll need to redirect their attention.

You need to focus everyone's attention on the security benefits of diskless workstations. If economic justification continues to be an issue, you'll need to base your case on the economic benefits of diskless workstations. Estimate the cost of a security breach where data is lost or falls into the hands of the enemy (competitors, a foreign power, the press, and so on). This is surely going to be more than the differential in price between diskless workstations and normal PC workstations.

 Tip: In the event that you haven't read your DOS License Agreement lately, I'd like to remind you that DOS is licensed for use on one machine. Even though all diskless workstations boot DOS from the same NET$DOS.SYS file on the server, you should still purchase one copy of DOS for each workstation. It's easy to forget the cost of the operating system when budgeting for a network involving diskless workstations.

Logically Diskless

Various products can be used to disable a workstation's local drives. This allows the security of a "real" diskless machine while retaining the flexibility of a "disked" PC. The SiteLock product from Brightwork Development allows this, as well as providing software metering and virus protection. The Watchdog product from Fischer International also provides this function in addition to several other security-oriented features.

How Diskless Workstations Boot

Since a diskless workstation has no local disk drives, DOS must be loaded from a network server. A diskless workstation must have enough intelligence to go to the server and download the client operating system, NetWare shell, AUTOEXEC.BAT file, and so on. This intelligence is provided by a device called a Boot PROM or Remote Reset PROM. This PROM is usually mounted on the LAN card, but in some diskless workstations is included on the mainboard.

Boot PROMS are included when you buy diskless workstations. If you want to convert normal PCs into a diskless workstation, you'll need to buy boot PROMs. They are sold by a number of vendors. One of the more popular vendors is LANWorks in Ontario, Canada. Boot PROMs may also be purchased from Novell. A boot PROM needs to know how to communicate directly with the LAN card. Boot PROMs are designed to work with certain LAN cards. For example, a boot PROM that will work with a NE1000 EtherNet card will not work with a NE2000 EtherNet card.

The boot PROM first establishes a connection to a file server on the network. It does this the same way that a NetWare shell establishes a connection:

1. It sends a message, `Get Nearest Server`, over the network.

2. It waits for a `Give Nearest Server` message, which is sent by the file server able to respond first. This tells the boot PROM the file server name and internetwork address of that file server. (The *internetwork address* is a composite of the network address and the node address.)

3. The boot PROM then sends another message called a `Route Request` to that server. The server responds with a message containing the route (network path) the boot PROM should use when sending packets.

4. Now that the boot PROM has a connection to a file server, it can access files in the SYS:LOGIN directory of that server. It then searches for a boot index file called BOOTCONF.SYS. If it finds it, it opens the file and scans it for its internetwork address. If it finds the address, it gets the name of a boot image file it should use for booting. If it doesn't find its internetwork address, it assumes that it will boot from a boot image file called NET$DOS.SYS.

 Note: Older versions of NetWare used a boot image file called IBM$DOS.SYS. A boot PROM will usually search for this filename if it can't find NET$DOS.SYS.

5. The boot PROM next opens the boot image file and boots DOS from it (as if it were booting DOS from a floppy disk). When DOS loads, it sees the boot image file as a local floppy disk (Drive A). It looks for a file called CONFIG.SYS on this "Drive A." If it finds it, it opens it and reads and executes statements it finds there. If the CONFIG.SYS file contains `DEVICE=` statements, device drivers must be loaded. The device driver files must be in the boot image file.

6. DOS now starts its command processor (usually COMMAND.COM). The command processor searches for a file called AUTOEXEC.BAT. If it finds it, it opens the file and reads and executes the statements it finds there.

7. At some point, the command processor will load the IPX.COM program which is contained within the boot file.

8. The command processor will next load a NetWare shell as a result of reading a statement like NETX from the AUTOEXEC.BAT file. When the shell loads and begins running, it tries to establish a connection with a file server using the same procedure the boot PROM used (`Get Nearest Server, Give Nearest Server` and so on).

9. When the connection is made and the shell now has access to the file server's SYS:LOGIN directory, the shell takes control away from the boot PROM. Now, Drive A: is the SYS:LOGIN directory rather than the boot image file.

 Note: At this point, the NetWare shell has established another connection with the file server. The connection that the boot PROM had used is no longer active.

10. The command processor continues to read statements from the AUTOEXEC.BAT file (if there are additional statements in that file), but it is now reading the AUTOEXEC.BAT file located in the SYS:LOGIN directory. Since the NetWare shell is now in control, the boot PROM is no longer functional.

A Simple Installation

You can get a diskless workstation running in a short time with the following procedure. This procedure places a single boot image file on the file server, so it only works if all your diskless workstations boot the same way.

Creating a Boot Diskette

You must first create a bootable diskette for the diskless workstation. Even though your diskless workstation has no floppy disk drive, you need to prepare a boot diskette for it so you can create the boot image file which will reside on the file server. The diskette should contain the following files:

- The DOS system files
- COMMAND.COM
- AUTOEXEC.BAT
- CONFIG.SYS
- SHELL.CFG
- IPX.COM
- NETX.COM

1. Format a bootable diskette by using the /S switch with the FORMAT command:

```
FORMAT A: /S
```

This puts the DOS system files on the diskette. These files are hidden, so you do not see them when you list the files on the diskette with the DIR command. The COMMAND.COM file is also placed on the diskette.

 Note: Old versions of DOSGEN require that this diskette be formatted as a single-sided diskette. This is no longer a requirement beginning with NetWare 2.15.

2. Create the AUTOEXEC.BAT file. A simple AUTOEXEC file might have these statements:

```
PROMPT $P$G
IPX
NETX
```

3. Create a CONFIG.SYS file. A simple CONFIG file might have these statements:

```
BUFFERS=1
FILES=30
```

 Note: You need to include additional statements in your CONFIG.SYS file if you want to load additional device drivers like ANSI, QEMM, or EMM386.

 Tip: The BUFFERS=1 statement reduces DOS buffers to the minimum (one) to save memory space. With a diskless workstation, there is no need for DOS disk buffers since they are only used when accessing local drives. The NetWare shell does its own buffering.

4. Create a SHELL.CFG file. This file is optional because the NetWare shell defaults are usually adequate for DOS workstations. A SHELL.CFG might contain this statement, in the case of a workstation running Windows:

```
SHOW DOTS = ON
```

This statement is necessary for Windows applications to recognize parent directories in NetWare volumes.

5. Create an IPX.COM file for the diskless workstation and copy it to the boot diskette. If you don't know how to create the IPX.COM file, consult your NetWare manuals.

6. Copy the NETX.COM file to the boot diskette.

Tip: If you're still using NetWare shell files called NET3.COM, NET4.COM, or NET5.COM, you should consider using the newer NETX.COM shell. It is MS-DOS or PC DOS version-independent.

Generating the Boot Image File

Now that you've created the boot diskette for your diskless workstation, the next step is to generate the boot image file that your diskless workstation will boot from. This file will reside on your file server in the SYS:LOGIN directory.

Put the boot diskette in drive A of any workstation that has a diskette drive. Log in as Supervisor (or equivalent) and get to the DOS prompt. Then, perform the following steps:

 Creating a Boot Image File

1. Map Drive F: to SYS:SYSTEM. Map Drive G: to SYS:LOGIN.

2. Make Drive G: your current drive.

3. Type **F:DOSGEN** and press **Enter**.

   DOSGEN will display information similar to Figure 3.1 before exiting to DOS. The boot file NET$DOS.SYS now resides in the SYS:LOGIN directory.

4. Type **FLAG NET$DOS.SYS S** and press **Enter**.

You're finished. Your diskless workstation will now boot from your file server.

```
G:\LOGIN>f:dosgen
Floppy Type f9 = 3 1/2 inch, 720 KB
Total Floppy Space 1440 Sectors
Setting Up System Block.
Setting Up FAT Tables.
Setting Up Directory Structures.
Traversing Directory Structures.
Processing IBMBIO   COM
Processing IBMDOS   COM
Processing COMMAND COM
Processing IPX      COM
Processing NETX     COM
Processing CONFIG   SYS
Processing AUTOEXECBAT
Processing SHELL    CFG
Diskette Label = NET$DOS_SYS
Transferring Data to "NET$DOS.SYS"

G:\LOGIN>
```

Figure 3.1   Running DOSGEN.

Multiple File Servers

If your network has more than one NetWare file server, you must
copy the boot image file (NET$DOS.SYS) to the SYS:LOGIN di-
rectory of all of the other file servers. This is because your diskless workstation's boot PROM will not always connect to the
same file server. If the boot PROM connects to a file server which
does not have a boot image file in its SYS:LOGIN directory, it will
complain that it could not find a boot image file and the workstation will freeze.

Multi-Server Boot File Management

Diskless workstations on a multi-server network can be a network
administration nightmare because of the requirement that copies
of BOOTCONF.SYS, AUTOEXEC.BAT and all of the boot image
files must reside on *all* servers. The root of the problem is the
way a boot PROM establishes a connection with a server (`Get
Nearest Server`, `Give Nearest Server`, and so on).

The solution would be for the boot PROM to try to establish
a connection with a *preferred server* first. If it couldn't establish a
connection with a preferred server, it would resort to connecting
to any server. Unfortunately, on a diskless workstation, there's no
place to store the name of the preferred server.

A Simple Installation

Restricting LAN Topology

A simple solution requires that you design your network topology so that diskless workstations are always forced to boot from the same server. If you ensure that there is only one file server connected to the cabling segment that the diskless workstations are connected to, the diskless workstations will always boot from that server. Figure 3.2 illustrates this concept.

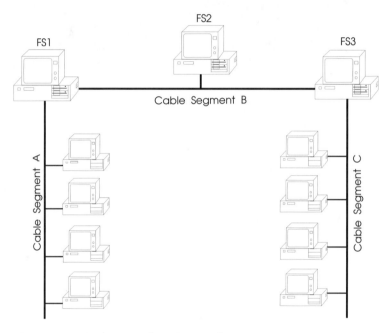

Figure 3.2   Restricting the LAN topology.

If all of the workstations in this diagram are diskless and have boot PROMs, they will attempt to boot from a file server's boot image file. If they must establish a connection with a file server using the `Get Nearest Server/Give Nearest Server` technique, they will always establish a connection with the closest server because the other servers are one router (hop) away. The presence of a router is often described as a "hop" because a router must forward a packet from one cabling segment to another—this takes additional time.

■ The diskless workstations on cable segment A will always connect to FS1.

3 — Diskless Workstations

- The diskless workstations on cable segment C will always connect to FS3.

- If there were diskless workstations connected to cable segment B, they would connect to any one of the three servers.

BootWare/MSD

Another solution is a product called BootWare/MSD from LANWorks. MSD stands for Multi-Server Director. This product consists of a NetWare 3.x NLM and MSD-compatible boot PROMs. Instead of searching for a server with the `Get Nearest Server` technique, the boot PROM establishes a connection with the NLM and reports its internetwork address. The NLM then searches its database for the name of the file server and the name of the boot image file the boot PROM should boot from.

If the BootWare/MSD NLM is not currently running on the network, the boot PROM resorts to the `Get Nearest Server` technique.

A More Complex Installation

The simple installation described above will not work if your diskless workstations:

- Need to boot different versions of DOS.

- Need to use a custom DOS command processor (COMMAND.COM).

- Use different LAN cards that need their own IPX.COM file.

- Need to use different CONFIG.SYS files.

- Need to use different AUTOEXEC.BAT files.

- Need to use different SHELL.CFG files.

Your diskless workstations will need to boot from different boot image files.

Multiple Boot Image Files

The boot image file does not need to be called NET$DOS.SYS in order for the boot PROM to boot from it. Once you generate the NET$DOS.SYS file, you can rename it however you wish. The name must comply with DOS naming conventions. There are no naming restrictions imposed by the boot PROM. This allows you to have as many boot image files in the SYS:LOGIN directory as are needed. Certain workstations will boot from certain boot image files.

 Tip: It's possible that every diskless workstation will boot from its own boot image file. If this is the case, you can choose names for your boot image files which relate to the workstation address or user name.

Rather than generating a file called NET$DOS.SYS and re-naming it, you can tell DOSGEN to produce a boot image file with a name that you choose. The syntax for the command would be:

DOSGEN *D: filename*

where:

D: is the drive letter of the local floppy drive with the boot diskette loaded.

filename is the name of the boot image file to be placed in the SYS:LOGIN directory.

BOOTCONF.SYS

You need some way for a diskless workstation to know which boot image file to boot from. This is accomplished with a boot index file. You create a file called BOOTCONF.SYS and place it in the SYS:LOGIN directory. The file contents specify workstation addresses and the names of the boot files they should boot from. You can use any editor that produces plain-text ASCII files to create this file. The syntax of each line in the file is:

0x*n,w=filename*

where:

> *n* is the network address of the workstation represented as hexadecimal digits.

> *w* is the node address of the workstation represented as hexidecimal digits.

> `filename` is the name of the boot file this workstation should boot from.

> An example of a BOOTCONF.SYS file is shown below.

```
0x1FA,10=WKJOHN.SYS
0x1,12=WKBETTY.SYS
0xB2FFF,1B230124=NE2000.SYS
```

- The first line indicates that the workstation with a node address of 10 connected to the cabling system with a network address of 1FA will boot from the boot image file called WKJOHN.SYS.

- The second line indicates that the workstation with a node address of 12 connected to the cabling system with a network address of 1 will boot from the boot image file called WKBETTY.SYS.

- The third line indicates that the workstation with a node address of 1B230124 connected to the cabling system with a network address of B2FFF will boot from the boot image file called NE2000.SYS.

 Note: Those diskless workstations whose addresses are not included in the BOOTCONF.SYS file will boot from the NET$DOS.SYS file by default.

Multiple AUTOEXEC.BAT Files

It's pretty obvious even to the novice that there cannot be more than one file called AUTOEXEC.BAT located in the SYS:LOGIN directory. Even though you can have numerous boot image files and each of those can have its own copy of AUTOEXEC.BAT, there can only be one AUTOEXEC.BAT file in the SYS:LOGIN

A Simple Installation

directory. While this is certain to be disappointing news to those who are unaware of this, there are techniques to overcome this obstacle.

First look at how AUTOEXEC.BAT is treated by the boot process. For this discussion, assume that there is a copy of AUTOEXEC.BAT in the boot image file and an identical copy in the SYS:LOGIN directory. It contains the following statements.

```
@ECHO OFF
IPX
NETX
LOGIN
```

1. When the boot PROM boots from the boot image file and loads DOS, COMMAND.COM is started.

2. COMMAND.COM looks at the current drive to see if there is an AUTOEXEC.BAT file. The current drive is A:—the boot image file. It finds the AUTOEXEC.BAT file and begins reading it and executes the statements it reads.

3. When it executes the statement NETX, the NetWare shell is loaded. The NetWare shell takes control away from the boot PROM, but this is transparent to COMMAND.COM.

4. When COMMAND.COM reads the next statement from the AUTOEXEC.BAT file, it reads from the AUTOEXEC.BAT file in the SYS:LOGIN directory. This file must be identical to the one in the boot image file because COMMAND.COM keeps track of which statement is read next by a pointer which contains the offset into the file.

So how can each boot image file have it's own AUTOEXEC? A very simple solution is to have two batch files in the boot image file. One batch file is the autoexec.bat file that COM-MAND.COM automatically executes. The contents of AUTOEXEC is one statement that runs a second batch file whose name is the name of the boot image file, but with a .BAT file extension.

An example is in order here. Suppose user GEORGE needs his own AUTOEXEC. We create a boot image file called GEORGE.SYS which contains an AUTOEXEC.BAT file which contains the following statements.

```
@ECHO OFF
GEORGE
```

The boot image file also contains a file called GEORGE.BAT that contains the statements that GEORGE would normally have in his AUTOEXEC.BAT file. An example of these statements follows.

```
IPX
NETX
LOGIN GEORGE
```

 Note: The file GEORGE.BAT must also reside in the SYS:LOGIN directory.

Now when DOS boots, it begins reading the AUTO-EXEC.BAT file (in the boot image file, GEORGE.SYS), and then switches to the GEORGE.BAT file (also in the GEORGE.SYS file). When NETX is run and the A: drive is switched from the boot image file to the SYS:LOGIN directory, the command processor will now be looking for GEORGE.BAT—not AUTOEXEC.BAT.

Other solutions to the multiple AUTOEXEC problem exist, but are a bit more complex and usually involve working with DOS environment variables.

AUTOEXEC Hints

You may be able to take advantage of DOS ERRORLEVEL information when you build your AUTOEXEC.BAT files (or the batch files mentioned above).

- When you load NETX.COM, the ERRORLEVEL variable is set to 0 if all goes well.

- If NETX is unable to find a file server to connect to it, ERRORLEVEL is set to 1.

- If NETX.COM is already loaded, ERRORLEVEL is set to 3.

- Unfortunately, if NETX.COM is unable to connect to the preferred server, the ERRORLEVEL is set to 0.

- When you load IPX, there is little to go wrong except incorrect hardware settings for the IPX driver. If IPX is unable to initialize the LAN card, it sets the ERRORLEVEL to 36.

A Simple Installation

An example of an AUTOEXEC file that takes advantage of ERRORLEVEL information is shown next.

```
IPX
IF ERRORLEVEL 36 GOTO IPXERR
NETX
IF ERRORLEVEL 3 GOTO LOADED
IF ERRORLEVEL 1 GOTO NOSERVER
:LOADED
F:
GOTO DOIT
:IPXERR
ECHO IPX could not initialize your LAN card.
ECHO Call your network administrator.
GOTO EXIT
:NOSERVER
ECHO Could not find a file server.
ECHO Is your EtherNet cable connected?
GOTO EXIT
:DOIT
LOGIN
:EXIT
```

Common Problems

There are a few common problems that occur with almost every installation of diskless workstations. These problems and their solutions are described below.

DOS Version 5

You're likely to have difficulty getting a diskless workstation to boot from a boot image file that was generated from a boot diskette with a DOS version 5 system on it. There are two solutions to this problem:

■ The best solution is to upgrade your boot PROMs to a version that supports DOS 5. Not all vendors have these boot PROMs available.

78

- The second solution is to use a patch program called RPLFIX.COM supplied by Novell. This patches the boot image file so older boot PROMs can boot from it. This patch does not work with all boot PROMs—including older versions of Novell's boot PROMs.

If these two solutions do not work, you may be forced to continue to run with an older version of DOS.

Bad Command or Filename

When the AUTOEXEC.BAT file in the boot image file is different from the one in the SYS:LOGIN directory, the DOS batch file interpreter (COMMAND.COM) does not read commands correctly because its file pointer is incorrect. Each time a line is read from the AUTOEXEC.BAT file, COMMAND.COM keeps a pointer to the location within the file where it last read from. Once NETX is loaded, COMMAND.COM now reads from the copy of AUTOEXEC.BAT in the SYS:LOGIN directory. If this copy is not identical to the AUTOEXEC.BAT file in the boot image file (up to the NETX statement at least), COMMAND.COM will read the next statement incorrectly.

This problem is easily fixed by making sure that the two copies of AUTOEXEC.BAT are identical.

Batch File Missing

A common problem with diskless workstations is the `Batch file missing` error message. This occurs when there is no AUTOEXEC.BAT file in the SYS:LOGIN directory, but there is one in the boot image file. The obvious solution is to put a copy of AUTOEXEC.BAT in the SYS:LOGIN directory.

However, you may have your own reasons for not wanting a copy of AUTOEXEC.BAT in the SYS:LOGIN directory. After all, this is a plain ASCII text file and you may not want it visible to users. The AUTOEXEC.BAT file in the boot image file is not visible to users.

The following solution works only if the last thing you do in the AUTOEXEC.BAT file is load the NetWare shell. The solution is to add a end-of-file character immediately after the shell name. Consider the following batch file:

```
@ECHO OFF
PROMPT $P$G
IPX
NETX
```

Each line in the AUTOEXEC.BAT file usually ends with a carriage return followed by a line feed. The last line (NETX in this example), usually ends with a carriage return, line feed and end-of-file character. If you replace the carriage return with an end-of-file character, this will eliminate the error message.

If your text editor or word processing program lets you edit a file and search for and replace or insert ASCII control characters, you can change the AUTOEXEC.BAT file using your editor. To do this, follow these steps.

1. Find the carriage return character which follows the last line in the file. You may know the carriage return as "decimal 13" or "hex 0D."

2. Replace the carriage return code with the ASCII SUB character. This is the DOS end-of-file character. You may know it as "control Z," "decimal 26," or "hex 1A."

3. Save the file.

If your text editor or word processor will not allow you to do this, you'll need to use the DOS DEBUG program or an equivalent. The following procedure shows you how to use DEBUG to do this:

1. Run DEBUG with the AUTOEXEC.BAT file as the only parameter:

   You'll see the debug prompt, which is the hyphen or dash character.

   ```
   DEBUG A:AUTOEXEC.BAT
   ```

2. To display the contents of the file, type the letter **d** and press **Enter**.

   You'll see the contents of the AUTOEXEC.BAT file in a format similar to that shown in Figure 3.3.

3 — Diskless Workstations

3. Locate the carriage return
   which follows the NETX
   statement.

   Your statement may be
   NET3, NET4, or NET5 instead
   of NETX., The carriage return
   is surrounded with a box in
   Figure 3.3.

4. Determine the address of
   the carriage return
   character.

   The address in the
   Figure 3.3 example is 0126.

5. Type **e** *aaaa* (where *aaaa*
   is the address) and press
   Enter.

   You'll see **0D** appear on the
   screen.

6. Type **1a** and press **Enter**.

   You'll see the DEBUG
   prompt appear.

7. Press **w** and then press **Enter**.

   The modified file is written
   back to disk.

8. Press **q** and press **Enter**.

   You're back at the DOS
   prompt.

```
C:\TEMP>debug autoexec.bat
-d
2259:0100   40 65 63 68 6F 20 6F 66-66 0D 0A 70 72 6F 6D 70   @echo off..promp
2259:0110   74 20 24 70 24 67 0D 0A-63 6C 73 0D 0A 69 70 78   t $p$g..cls..ipx
2259:0120   0D 0A 6E 65 74 78 0D 0A-1A 26 C6 07 C1 C4 1E CC   ..netx...&......
2259:0130   DD 81 C3 11 0E A1 70 DD-26 88 07 EB 31 B8 10 00   ......p.&...1...
2259:0140   50 B8 A6 EF 50 9A 4E 14-7E 20 EB 22 83 FB 07 77   P...P.N.~ ."...w
2259:0150   EC 83 EB 01 73 03 E9 69-FC D1 E3 2E FF A7 50 04   ....s..i......P.
2259:0160   E0 00 1D 01 74 01 02 02-76 02 04 03 92 03 8B E5   ....t...v.......
2259:0170   5D C3 55 8B EC 81 EC 06-00 8B 46 06 89 46 FC 8B   ].U.......F..F..
-e 0126
2259:0126   0D.1a
-w
Writing 00029 bytes
-q

C:\TEMP>
```

Figure 3.3   Modifying the AUTOEXEC.BAT file.

Common Problems

CHAPTER 4

Physical Server Security

This chapter will attempt to convince you that you need to provide physical security for your NetWare file server in order to protect your data. Without physical security, anyone could break into your file server and gain access to all of your files.

■ Access to NetWare Volumes

■ SERV+

■ Breaking into the Server

■ Server Password Protection

■ Hardware Failures

Access to NetWare Volumes

In the past, Supervisors were confident that NetWare volumes were secure because there was no way to access files in a NetWare volume directly by booting the server with DOS. The NetWare file system does not use DOS-formatted volumes—it's more like UNIX. If you booted your NetWare file server with DOS and tried to read the hard disk, DOS would report that the disk was not a DOS disk.

This was a major advantage of NetWare when compared to networks where the server used a DOS file system. Networks based on IBM's PC LAN Program, 3Com's 3Plus, or OS/2, for example, are not secure because anyone who has physical access to the server has access to the files on the server.

Now vendors are selling utility programs for the "Network Administrator" which allow access to files on a NetWare volume without the server running the NetWare operating system. One very popular product is NetUtils from OnTrack Computer Systems. You first boot a NetWare server with DOS and then run NetUtils. You then have access to the files on any NetWare volume. A similar product is SERV+ from Procomp.

So, storing files on a NetWare file server does not necessarily mean they're secure. You need to do other things to secure your data. This chapter covers issues where the universal solution is to physically secure your server.

That can mean putting it in a locked room where nobody can touch the server, but your view of physical security may differ. You may prefer to place the server in the center of the office where everyone can see it.

If you can physically secure your server, the NetWare operating system will provide the security you need to protect your data. If you can't provide physical security, you run the risk that someone can bypass NetWare's security mechanisms and access your data.

In this chapter, you'll learn how to bypass NetWare security. The purpose of this chapter is not to encourage you to break into file servers, but to know how it's done so you can better protect your server.

SERV+

SERV+ is a product from Procomp Inc. This is the company that makes clones of the Novell Disk Coprocessor Boards. SERV+ is a DOS program which lets you look at a NetWare volume as if it were a DOS drive. You can copy files from a directory on a NetWare volume to a DOS device such as a floppy disk. This is useful in the event that a NetWare volume becomes corrupted and you don't want to lose files which haven't been backed up.

> **Caution:** Since SERV+ is a dangerous tool in the hands of the wrong person, you need to specify a password when you run the program. The password is manufactured into the program and cannot be changed. The password is a fairly long arbitrary sequence of characters. As a result, most people write the password on the disk label. This, of course, creates a severe security problem.

When you run the program and specify the password, you find yourself at a DOS prompt. This is a simulated DOS prompt since you are really conversing with SERV+. You enter DOS-like commands to copy files, display a list of files and so forth. The commands are listed below.

CD   This is used to change the current directory of the current drive. The syntax is the same as in DOS. It does not support the NetWare ancestor directory feature where three periods (cd...), switch you to the grandparent directory, four periods (cd....) switch you to the great-grandparent directory and so forth.

COPY   This is used to copy one or more files from the current server drive and directory to the specified DOS drive, such as Drive A:. You cannot copy files to another NetWare volume. This is intended to copy your files from a corrupted NetWare volume.

DDIR	This lists all of the directory names on the current server drive.
DIR	This is used to list all the files in the current directory. It supports the DOS wildcard characters. The attributes of each file are also listed.
DUMP	This displays the contents of the selected disk sector in a typical hex/ASCII dump format.
EXIT	This stops the program and returns to DOS.
GDIR	This lists all of the files and directories on the current server drive in their physical order in the directory.
HELP	This displays a help screen which lists all of the available commands.
INFO	This is used to display the physical parameters of the current server drive. The parameters are: head, cylinder and sector numbers, total storage capacity including Hot Fix area, and the directory and FAT starting sectors.
LIST	Lists all of the server drives and their controller type.
SBACKUP	Back up all or specified files to a DOS drive. If the DOS drive is a floppy drive, you will be prompted to insert a new disk when the current floppy is full.
TYPE	This is similar to the DOS TYPE command. It prints the contents of a file to the screen.
VER	This prints the SERV+ version number to the screen.
XCOPY	This is similar to the DOS XCOPY command, including recursion through subdirectories.

Breaking into the Server

You are about to discover how to break into a NetWare 2.x file server. You might wonder why we're telling you how to do this and you might be angry that this book is helping to train people how to compromise the security of your network.

Actually, your network is already at risk because there is a large number of people who already know how to break into your NetWare 2.x server. As far back as 1988 (and probably further back), Novell would occasionally tell their customers how to break into a file server when the Supervisor password was forgotten. Novell now teaches this technique in their Support and Maintenance course. A few other training companies do the same.

In 1989, M&T Publishing published the NetWare Supervisors Guide which essentially made this information available to anyone. So, you may be the only one who doesn't know how to break into your file server.

Anyone who has physical access to a NetWare file server can easily break into the server and log in using the Supervisor account. This can usually be accomplished in less than five minutes by someone who has done it several times.

The concept is simple. The trick is to make the NetWare operating system believe that it has no Bindery files. When the server boots up, it checks its Bindery files. When it finds no Bindery files, it will assume that this must be a new installation—the first time the server is being brought up. It will then create a new Bindery with a SUPERVISOR and a GUEST account. You then log in as Supervisor and do whatever you like.

The first challenge is to make the server believe that it has no Bindery files when, clearly, they exist. This is best accomplished by taking the server down and booting the server with DOS. Then run a disk sector editor program to access the physical sectors on the server's disk that contains the SYS: volume.

Novell thoughtfully provided a program for doing this with NetWare 2.15 called DISKED. Novell stopped shipping DISKED with NetWare 2.2 and they never shipped DISKED with NetWare 3.x. DISKED is a difficult program to use for those not accustomed to it. Using DISKED is similar in many ways to the DOS DEBUG program.

A far better tool for breaking into a NetWare file server is the NetUtils program from OnTrack. NetUtils has a simpler user interface, so breaking into a file server is easier than using DISKED.

To break into a NetWare 2.x server using NetUtils, do the following:

1. Scan the SYS: volume for the Bindery file names until you find a disk block that appears to be a directory.

2. Once you find the directory, change the names of the Bindery files.

3. Write the changes back to disk.

4. Reboot the server so it will boot the NetWare operating system.

5. Since you renamed the Bindery files in only the first of NetWare's two mirrored directories, NetWare will complain of a directory mirror mismatch and ask if you want to abandon mounting volume SYS. Answer "no."

6. The server will now boot normally.

7. You can log in to the server as Supervisor without specifying a password.

If you'd like to cover your tracks and hide the fact that you broke into the server, you can restore the original Bindery. Follow this procedure.

1. Make the SYS: SYSTEM directory your current directory.

2. Change the renamed old Bindery files so they have normal file attributes.

3. Rename the files to their original names, except use the file extension .OLD.

4. Run the BINDREST program to restore the original Bindery.

5. At this point, you're logged in as SUPERVISOR with the original NetWare Bindery (therefore original security).

Except for a difference in file server up time in FCONSOLE (you had to take the server down), a Network Administrator would not know that this took place.

Note: Breaking into a NetWare 3.x file server involves a similar technique, but the exact procedure used to break in to a NetWare 2.x server does not work with NetWare 3.x. Novell made some changes in NetWare 3.x which makes it a bit more difficult to break in.

While a large number of people know how to break into a NetWare 2.x server, far fewer people know how to break into a NetWare 3.x server. So we'll keep this a secret for the present. I'm sure somebody will publish this information eventually. For the present, you have a good idea how it's done and now you know what you need to do to protect your file server from a break-in.

 Tip: To *fully* protect your file server, you need to lock it away so nobody can touch it.

Disk Drive Hardware

To a degree, servers which use specialized disk drive controller cards or host adapters are more secure than servers which use general-purpose controller cards. If your server uses a disk controller which is register-level compatible with the Western Digital WD-1000 series controllers (which most PCs use), you're at risk because there are many disk sector editor programs which will work with this hardware.

If you use a controller or host adapter which is not compatible with the WD-1000 series, there are fewer disk sector editor programs available. A good example is Novell's Disk Coprocessor Board (DCB). The DCB is not register-level compatible with the WD-1000 series, so most disk sector editors will not work with it.

 Note: Novell's DISKED program *will* work with the DCB. While Novell is no longer shipping DISKED with NetWare, there are enough existing copies of DISKED in the world that it will represent a risk for the foreseeable future.

Server Password Protection

Both NetWare 2.x and NetWare 3.x servers support console commands which can cause severe disruption of the network if exercised with hostile intent. Someone could, for example, take down the server, clear connections, and disable new logins.

One way to help protect against hostile actions is to lock the keyboard of the server when the server is out of view of the Network Administrator. Many machines support this feature with a metal key lock. Most people view keys as a nuisance and prefer to lock the keyboard by entering a password.

 Note: It's especially important to keep the server console locked with a password because there are various products available for controlling the server console from a remote location. With these products, someone could get to the server console without having physical access to the server.

NetWare 2.x Keyboard Lock VAP

Beginning with NetWare 2.1, Novell started shipping a VAP which was used to lock the server keyboard. This was meant to provide keyboard protection for servers which do not have their own keyboard lock mechanism.

Unfortunately, NetWare administrators learned that the keyboard lock VAP caused the server to crash occasionally. Novell solved the problem by no longer shipping the VAP with NetWare. It's unknown if they will fix the VAP and offer it in the future.

NetWare 3.x Monitor Lock

NetWare 3.x comes with an NLM program called MONITOR which is used to lock the keyboard of the server. To lock the keyboard use the following procedure:

Using MONITOR to Lock the Keyboard

1. Type **MONITOR** and press **Enter**.

   The MONITOR screen appears and the `Available Options` menu appears

2. Select `Lock File Server Console`.

   The `Password:` prompt appears.

3. Enter a password and press **Enter.**

   You're informed that the console is now locked. You're not asked to re-enter the password because the console can be unlocked with the Supervisor password as well.

 Note: It's especially important to lock the console of a NetWare 3.x server in a multiserver network because others may be able to access your server console with the RCONSOLE program. Even though you have a password for RCONSOLE as well, it's a good idea to lock the console with a different password.

SACS

The Sergeant Access Control System (SACS) from Pentagon Systems, Inc. is a hardware product that you install in the bus of a PC. That PC can be your NetWare file server—it will work with any version of NetWare. When the server is first turned on and goes through it's Power On Self Test (POST), SACS will take over the machine and prompt you for a user ID and a password. You simply can't get to the DOS prompt unless you satisfy SACS demands.

SACS is a card that plugs into an 8-bit bus slot in a PC-bus (ISA bus) machine. As long as the card is in the bus, SACS will provide security. The card uses an EEPROM device to store up to 10 user IDs and passwords.

One of the User IDs is essentially an administrator ID. When you log in to SACS with that ID, you'll see a menu that you use to create and delete other User IDs and passwords. You can also examine a login history of the 40 most recent SACS logins. If a user tries to break into SACS, that activity is recorded in the login history list.

Memory Requirements

SACS does not consume any conventional memory and does not use any TSRs. Once you've entered the correct user ID and password, SACS lies dormant until the next time you power up your machine.

 Note: SACS does use 16KB of memory at selectable memory locations. These are C8000, CC000, D8000, DC000, E8000, and EC000. You may not be able to use SACS if your LAN and/or disk controller cards already use all of these regions of memory.

If you forget your SACS administrator password, there's no way to get it back. You'll need to pack up the card and send it back to Pentagon Systems for reinitialization. You also cannot defeat SACS security by snooping on the contents of the EEPROM with DEBUG. An encryption technique is used to protect EEPROM contents.

Defeating SACS

The downside of SACS is that it can be defeated in a few ways. The simplest way to defeat it is to remove the card from the bus. If you have some means of securing the cover of your server, this is not a problem.

You can put Loctite (the brand name of a paint-like compound which is normally used to prevent screws from turning), on the card's mounting screw so you can detect tampering. You can also Loctite the card to the socket and/or Loctite a fine piece of wire between the card and the socket to detect tampering. If you do detect tampering, you assume the worst and take whatever action is appropriate.

You can also defeat SACS without removing the card from the bus. Simply remove one of the PROMS from the card (they are socketed). This would allow a break-in with detection. The solution here is to mount the card between two other full-length cards so a PROM can't be removed and reinserted easily. You can also remove the socket and solder the PROM to the card (to heck with the warranty when server security is at stake).

SACS could also be defeated by plugging a card into the bus which occupies the same memory address as the SACS card. When the machine powers up, the workstation's BIOS will not recognize the card. I don't know how to protect against this except to prevent the machine's cover from being removed.

As you can see, there is no bulletproof solution to server security unless you restrict physical access to the server. But SACS helps and would discourage all but the most determined hostile user. Of course, SACS can be used in workstations as well if there are local resources (such as a hard disk) to protect.

Hardware Failures

A security issue that few Network Administrators have ever thought about has to do with hardware failures. To illustrate how failures could compromise security, consider how you would handle the following situation.

Your server is running NetWare 2.x. It has only one drive—a 600 MB SCSI drive connected to a DCB. It is partitioned into two NetWare volumes. Your customer list is on one volume and payroll information is on the other volume.

The drive is warranted for one year and you purchased it just last month. This morning you discover that the server has crashed. You call the local serviceperson who diagnoses the problem as a drive failure. He or she tells you not to worry—the drive will be replaced tomorrow at no charge. You check the vault and discover that your last backup was only a few hours before the failure.

What do you do?

NetWare 2.x Drives

The NetWare 2.x file system does not allow volumes to span physical drives. This means that all files within a volume are contained on one physical disk. If that drive were to fail before you could wipe the disk clean, you would be forced to send in your disk for repair with your files still on the drive.

Surprisingly, disk repair companies claim that the majority of drive failures involve the electronics and not the drive media or read/write heads. While this seems backwards (we expect mechanical problems before electronics problems), the message is that unless you feel that the people who repair drives are apathetic towards your data files, these files are at risk.

You may decide that instead of allowing your drive (and data) to be taken away, you'll scrap it and buy a new drive.

NetWare 3.x Drives

The NetWare 3.x file system allows volumes and the files within those volumes to span physical drives. Novell calls this *disk scattering*. In addition to increasing performance, disk scattering means enhanced security for your files because each file is not wholly contained on one drive. If a scattered drive fails, your files are reasonably safe since each file is not wholly contained on one drive. Anyone who repairs your drive does not have access to the whole of each file.

 Note: This measure of file safety assumes that all of the scattered drives for a volume are of the same capacity. Scattering a 300 MB drive with a 600 MB drive is possible but it's undesirable—at the point where the lesser capacity drive fills up, files will be wholly contained on the larger capacity drive.

CHAPTER 5

Viruses and Trojan Horses

A great deal of publicity in the trade press has sensitized the public to the dangers of computer viruses. The marketplace has responded with many software products used to protect you from viruses. Most products are designed to scan for viruses so you can know when your computers have been infected. Some are designed to prevent virus-infected programs from executing.

Even though Trojan Horse programs don't get the same publicity, you're at risk from these hostile programs as well. In some ways, Trojan Horse programs are a more difficult problem to protect against.

- NetWare Viruses
- Actions You Should Take
- Floppy Disk Libraries
- Virus Scanning
- Scanning Software
- Trojan Horse Programs

NetWare Viruses

There have been few reports of *NetWare-specific viruses*. Most of these have been viruses written to infect a DOS machine. Since NetWare does such a good job of emulating DOS, a NetWare server is affected by DOS viruses in much the same way that a stand-alone DOS machine is affected.

There are few known viruses which make NetWare function calls or exploit characteristics specific to NetWare. One, in particular, has been reported to exist. It is called the GP1 virus and is supposed to capture user passwords as they log in to a file server. A captured user password is broadcast over the network to a workstation running a program to receive these passwords.

GP1 exists in two parts—it has a virus component and a non-virus component. The virus part infects any executable program. When the infected program is run, the virus code (which remains in memory) waits for a login request to occur. When the user enters his or her password, the GP1 virus broadcasts the password over the network in an IPX packet.

The non-virus part of GP1 is a DOS program, called EARS, which listens for the broadcasts and captures the user passwords. While the virus may spread to other locations, the password-capturing (EARS) program won't, since it's not a virus.

Since NetWare dominates the LAN operating system market, most future network-specific viruses will likely be NetWare viruses.

Nondedicated Servers

Viruses have a far easier time infecting a nondedicated server because the server runs both a DOS process and a server process. The user running the DOS process can cause a virus infection, which could easily affect the NetWare server process and the hard disk containing the NetWare partition.

Note: You can only run your nondedicated server with NetWare 2.x because NetWare 3.x does not support nondedicated operation. Since NetWare 2.x is a product line nearing the end of its life, this is becoming a nonissue. Nondedicated servers have no place in a secure environment.

Dedicated Servers

Just as DOS machines can be infected by a virus which changes the hard disk's boot sector, directory or partition table—a NetWare file server could possibly become infected in a similar way.

 Clients cannot infect the operating system of a dedicated NetWare 2.x file server unless they somehow acquire write rights to the SYS:SYSTEM directory and infect the NetWare operating system file (NET$OS.EXE).

 NetWare 3.x does not keep the operating system on the SYS volume so the operating system can't be infected by a client. The operating system for NetWare 3.x is kept on the server's local DOS volume (a DOS partition on the hard disk or a floppy). A virus would need to strike while the server was running DOS (before NetWare is loaded). The DOS process is suspended and the DOS volume is not available to NetWare clients while the NetWare operating system is running.

Most people who run NetWare 3.x have a bootable DOS partition on their server, which makes it easy to bring up the file server. Loading the NetWare 3.x operating system involves running a program called SERVER.EXE, which is a DOS-loadable program. You must first bring up your server with DOS and then run the SERVER program. Once SERVER begins running, the machine is running NetWare and DOS is suspended.

Tip: You may want to consider not having a DOS partition on the hard disk of your file server. This will reduce the chance of virus infection. This also means that your file server will have to boot from a floppy disk. While booting from a floppy is slower and seems antiquated, you can be certain that you're booting from a clean copy of DOS and SERVER.EXE.

Hostile VAPs and NLMs

A virus-infected Value-Added Process (VAP), or NetWare Loadable Module (NLM), running on your server would be disastrous. These server-based processes run at the same privilege level as the operating system itself. The virus could do anything it wants to your server—and NetWare's normal protection mechanisms would be bypassed. To protect against this, you would never give users rights to the SYS:SYSTEM directory.

 VAPs load from this directory on a NetWare 2.x server.

 With NetWare 3.x, you can load NLMs from volumes other than *SYS* in a normal way. You can force the server to load only NLMs from the SYS:SYSTEM directory by running the SECURE CONSOLE command on the server. This prevents NLMs from being loaded from other directories or volumes.

Actions You Should Take

As a Network Administrator, you need to define procedures that will enhance security in your organization and protect against virus attack. A list of suggestions follows.

Secure Your Diskette Library

Most computer viruses are transmitted by modem connections or by floppy diskettes. Since you're likely to have a large number of diskettes in your office, you need a procedure to protect them.

- Write-protect diskettes
- Scan diskettes for viruses
- Label diskettes
- Catalogue your diskettes
- Implement a strict system for receiving new diskettes and software

Scan Your Server and Local Drives for Viruses

Although this strategy will not prevent infection, regularly scheduled scans will minimize potential damage through early detection. The key to remember is that this must be a regular activity to be effective.

- Use a commercial virus-scanning product, like NETSCAN, Norton Anti-Virus, or Dr. Solomon Toolkit.
- Make the virus scan a regularly-scheduled activity, along with backup procedures.

Secure Your Server

The best way to protect from viruses is prevention—not scanning. Here are things you can do to prevent viruses from striking.

- Assign minimal rights to users and groups in "public" directories. (See Chapter 9, "NetWare Rights.")
- Set program files to read-only and execute-only when possible. (See Chapter 8, "File and Directory Attributes.")
- Rethink your EMAIL functions. (Hostile programs may be communicated via EMAIL attachments.)
- Secure the server physically. (See Chapter 4, "Physical Server Security.")

- Use a workstation-based security product like Certus-LAN or Dr. Solomon.

- Use a server-based security product like SiteLock.

Other Strategies

There are other things you can do to protect from viruses which are discussed throughout this book.

- Lengthen your backup cycle. (See the Introduction.)

- Implement an archive strategy. (See the Introduction.)

- Use diskless workstations. (See Chapter 3, "Diskless Workstations.")

- Establish and enforce policies. (See Appendix D, "Sample Policy Statement.")

Floppy Disk Libraries

Most networks support several applications. If these are purchased applications, they are usually supplied on floppy diskette. You should organize these diskettes in a library that is maintained and kept in a physically secure place. If you have more than a few hundred diskettes, consider tracking them (cataloging) with some sort of database application.

Write-Protected Diskettes

Most software vendors ship software on floppy disks that are not write-protected. With the exception of certain copy-protection schemes, there is little reason for this. Software vendors should begin shipping software on write-protected media if they don't already do this.

If your organization purchases software, you should immediately check for write-protection on the diskettes when you open the package. Engage the diskette's write-protect mechanism before you put this diskette in a drive. Figure 5.1 shows the write-protect mechanism on both 5.25-inch and 3.5-inch diskettes.

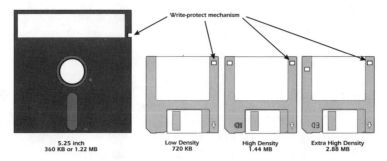

Figure 5.1   Write-protect mechanism on floppy diskettes.

On a 5.25-inch diskette, the write-protect mechanism is engaged when the notch along the right-hand edge of the diskette is
covered with opaque tape. A 3.5-inch diskette is write-protected
when you can see through the square hole along the right-hand
edge of the diskette. The write-protect sensing mechanism may
be optical or physical depending on the manufacturer of the diskette drive. If it's physical, you can be fooled into believing that a
diskette is write-protected if someone places transparent tape
over the write-protect hole.

Is Your Diskette Really Write-Protected?

Is your diskette really protected from viruses if it is write-
protected? Are you sure that a virus cannot write to your diskette
if the write-protect mechanism is engaged? The unfortunate answer is *maybe*.

Most people we (at the Accelerated Learning Center) talk to
say that a virus cannot infect a write-protected diskette. Yet, every few months we encounter someone who claims that a certain
virus can write to a write-protected diskette. Some say they've
seen it but, for various reasons, cannot demonstrate it to us.

To find out, we contacted vendors of floppy disk drives and
controllers to see if write-protection is enforced in hardware. If
the floppy disk drive or controller does not allow you to write to
the floppy diskette when the diskette is write-protected, you don't
have to worry about a virus infecting write-protected diskettes.
Manufacturers of floppy disk drives say that drives only report
the write-protect condition to the controller. It's up to the controller to enforce write-protection.

Manufacturers of floppy disk/hard disk controller cards said that they did not add circuitry to their cards to enforce write-protection. They thought that write-protection was enforced by the floppy disk controller chip on their card.

We then contacted the leading manufacturer of floppy diskette controller chips. Their technical support people eventually decided that their controller chip also did not enforce write-protection. The chip simply reported the write-protect condition in a software-readable register. Now it appeared that it was up to the PC's BIOS to enforce write-protection.

We looked through the BIOS source code listings that IBM provided in their Technical Reference manuals for the XT. We searched for code that appeared to enforce write-protection and found none. We couldn't imagine that it was up to DOS to enforce write-protection. So we started programming to see if we could write to a write-protected diskette.

We were not able to write to the diskette using BIOS function calls. This is what we expected. We then tried to write by addressing the registers of the controller chip directly. Again we were unsuccessful. The controller chip accurately reported a write-protection error. We tried several controller cards, each having a different manufacturer's controller chip. No success.

In summary, I must assume that a virus cannot write to a write-protected diskette. It appears as if the enforcement of write-protection is within the controller chip even though one of the largest manufacturers claimed otherwise. Perhaps there's a way for a virus to disable the write-protection feature of the chip—we couldn't find it. So what do you do when someone tells you that a virus can write to a write-protected diskette? Smile and ask to see proof.

Virus Scanning

When you receive software on diskette, you should immediately scan each diskette for viruses before you install this software. Make certain that the machine that you use to scan diskettes is booted from a write-protected DOS diskette that itself has been scanned for viruses. Yes, this represents a chicken-and-egg problem. You could solve this problem by buying a new copy of DOS. You trust a shrink-wrapped copy of DOS, don't you?

Note: It's best if the machine that you use for scanning is not connected to the LAN. If it is, do your scanning without the NetWare shell files loaded.

 Tip: It's a good idea to scan diskettes twice—each time with a different virus-scanning program.

You may also consider using the McAfee Associates VALIDATE program to compute checksums for all the .EXE, .COM and .OVL files and record the checksums for future reference.

Labeling Diskettes

Once a diskette has been write-protected and scanned, you should immediately label it in some way so you know that it has been checked. Without a label, it's easy to confuse diskettes. You don't want to have to start over when you're scanning several hundred diskettes.

Consider using a label that is unique rather than a plain stick-on dot label available at your stationery store. My office was littered with diskettes and equipment that had colored dots that had lost their meaning to office staff. The Accelerated Learning Center now uses bright yellow labels preprinted with the words *VIRUS FREE.* You may want to use your own unique label with your company logo, security code, or warning message.

A local print shop can arrange to have labels made for you, but be sure to test the label stock first to be sure the resulting labels will stick to your diskettes. Labels meant for paper do not always work well on plastic or vinyl diskette material.

 Tip: Your label should be placed on a 5.25-inch diskette so that a portion of the label covers the write protect tape or sticker as shown in Figure 5.2. If someone removes the write protect tape, the label is also affected, so you'll know that the diskette was tampered with.

5 — Viruses and Trojan Horses

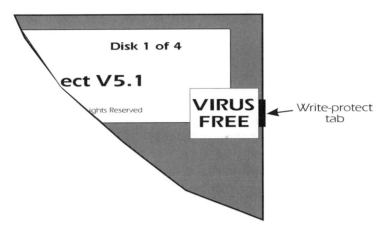

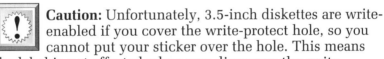

Figure 5.2   Correct placement of a diskette label.

 Caution: Unfortunately, 3.5-inch diskettes are write-enabled if you cover the write-protect hole, so you cannot put your sticker over the hole. This means the label is not affected when you disengage the write-protect mechanism on a 3.5-inch diskette.

Receiving New Diskettes

When new software arrives in your office, don't tear off the shrink wrap and begin working with the diskettes. You need a strict procedure for receiving new diskettes. The diskettes should be checked for write-protection. Most vendors ship diskettes in a write-enabled state.

Next, you need to scan the diskettes for viruses. Do your scanning with a PC that is known not to be infected by a virus itself. This PC should not be connected to your network and should be physically secure. It's best to boot this PC from a floppy diskette which is also kept in a secure location.

Tip: Label the diskettes to show that they've been virus scanned.

Your receiving procedure may include making duplicate copies of the diskettes. The original diskettes can be put in your diskette library and the copies can be given to the appropriate user to work with. Your diskette library should be physically secure. A locked cabinet within a locked room is not too much security.

Additionally, your receiving procedure may include cataloging the new diskettes in your software library database. The database that we developed at the Accelerated Learning Center includes the following fields:

- Vendor name
- Product name
- Product version number
- Serial number
- Diskette number
- Diskette name

You may also want to include information which will tell you where and when the software was purchased. This makes acquiring updates easier.

Virus Scanning

Scanning for viruses should be a regularly scheduled activity just like your backup procedure. Many Network Administrators think virus scanning is unnecessary. It's not unusual to hear comments like, "We don't have computer viruses in this part of the world," and "We used to scan for viruses, but we never found any—so we stopped." Considering that virus scanning can be implemented very easily, it's cheap insurance.

A virus-scanning program searches files for instruction sequences or data patterns that are unique to each known computer virus. Optionally, some can detect unknown viruses in files by appending CRC (Cyclical Redundancy Check) codes to .COM and .EXE files. Then, the program would periodically check the files against their codes to see if any changes were made to the files.

The Price Of Virus-Scanning

Everything has a price—what's the price of virus scanning? The real cost is the time it takes to scan your disks. For example, consider scanning the file server at the Accelerated Learning Center. There are 13502 total files on the server. Of those, 1444 files are executable files (.EXE and .COM), which account for 72.2 MB of server disk space. We wanted to know how long it would take to scan the server daily.

I chose the NETSCAN program from McAfee Associates as my virus-scanning program. The file server is a 80386DX, 40 MHz, 64 KB cache machine with a DCB-based disk subsystem. The workstation normally used for virus scanning is a 80486DX, 33 MHz, 64 KB cache machine. Both have 16-bit NE2000 EtherNet cards. The test was done with no other activity on the EtherNet.

It took 6 minutes and 21 seconds to scan all the executable files. This amount of time is easy to tolerate, especially if this can be part of an automated procedure. NETSCAN can also be told to scan all files by using the /A option (scan All files). When I tested with this option, it took 23 minutes.

 Tip: You can reduce the time it takes to scan for viruses by restricting executable files to certain volumes or directory trees. You can then limit your scan to only those volumes or directory trees.

The Accelerated Learning Center offers a program called FINDEXE which will scan a directory tree for the existence of executable files so you can ensure that certain trees contain data files only.

How Often Should You Scan?

If virus scanning is part of an automated procedure, how often should this procedure run and at what time of day? Scanning for viruses is a procedure similar in purpose to backing up your data files. So, it makes sense to scan as often as you backup data. For most of us, backup is a daily procedure. Virus scanning should be a daily procedure as well.

It's best to scan for viruses at the end of the work day. If you do find a virus, you have several hours to clean up before people report to work in the morning. If, however, virus scanning is part of an automated process that runs unattended, you may not find out about the infection until the morning. You'll need to keep users off the server until you've finished cleaning up.

Keep Scanning Software Current

Many virus-scanning programs are updated by the manufacturer regularly. You need to keep your virus-scanning software updated to detect new viruses. There are a number of ways you can keep the software current:

- Download data files from a bulletin board system.
- Purchase an update subscription from the manufacturer.
- Check monthly updates from vendors.

Scanning Software

There are many virus-scanning products available. This is a result of vendors trying to cash in on the many computer virus scares. During the March 1992 Michelangelo Virus affair, most computer dealers sold their entire inventory of virus protection software products. Some people have speculated that the same people who write computer viruses may also be writing virus protection software. That's one way to guarantee demand for your product.

Some of the better known virus-scanning products are:

- VIRUSCAN and NETSCAN from McAfee Associates
- Virus Tools from Central Point
- Norton Anti-Virus from Symantec

One of the more popular virus-scanning programs on the market is VIRUSCAN. The manufacturer, McAfee Associates, was one of the first to address the issue of computer viruses with virus-scanning products. This chapter will focus on the McAfee products as examples of virus-scanning software.

110

5 — Viruses and Trojan Horses

VIRUSCAN

VIRUSCAN includes a main program file called SCAN.EXE so, in this chapter, I'll refer to it as SCAN.

This program will search for known computer viruses in various locations:

- Memory
- The boot sector
- The partition table
- Files

SCAN can run on a workstation and check for viruses within files that reside on a local disk or on your NetWare file server. It cannot check a NetWare file server's memory, boot sector, or partition table for viruses, since it runs in a workstation.

 Caution: SCAN runs a self-test when it begins running. If it has been modified in any way, a warning message will be displayed, but it will still check for viruses. It's risky to allow SCAN to continue when it has been modified. Stop it and obtain a new copy of SCAN.

 Note: SCAN (version 72 and later) is distributed as a ZIP archive, with PKZIP Authentic File Verification. You'll see the -AV message after every file is unzipped and the message `Authentic Files Verified! # NWN405 Zip Source: McAFEE ASSOCIATES`. When you finish unzipping the files, if you don't see this, obtain a new copy of VIRUSCAN or call McAfee Associates.

SCAN searches files for instruction sequences, or data patterns in files, that are unique to each known computer virus. If a virus is found, a message is displayed with the name of the infected file and the name of the virus.

111

The program will examine files for viruses based on their extensions—checking each file that could be host to a virus. The default file extensions supported by SCAN are:

- .APP
- .BIN
- .COM
- .EXE
- .OVL
- .PGM
- .PIF
- .PRG
- .SWP
- .SYS
- .XTP

Additional extensions can be added to SCAN or all files on disk can be selected for scanning.

SCAN Usage

You can specify numerous options on the command line. Some of the more useful options are listed below.

Table 5.1   SCAN usage options on the command line.

Option	Description
\	Scans root directory and boot area only.
/A	This will cause SCAN to check all files on the specified drive. The /A option will add substantial time to scanning. This option takes priority over the /E option.

Option	Description
/AV	This lets you add validation codes to the files being scanned. If a full drive is specified, SCAN will create validation data for the partition table, boot sector, and system files of the disk as well. Validation adds ten bytes to files; the validation data for the partition table, boot sector, and system files is stored separately in a hidden file in the root directory of the scanned drive.
/CHKHI	This checks any memory between 640KB and 1088KB. This option can not be used with the /NOMEM option.
/CV	The /CV option checks the validation codes inserted by the /AV option. SCAN will notify you that a file has been modified.
/D	This tells SCAN to prompt you to overwrite and delete an infected file when one is found. If you select Y, the infected file will be overwritten and then deleted.
/E .xxx .yyy .zzz	Scan files with extensions of .xxx .yyy .zzz. The /E option allows the user to specify an extension or set of extensions to scan. Extensions should include the period character and be separated by a space after the /E and between each other. Up to three extensions may be specified. For more extensions, use the /A option.
/M	This tells VIRUSCAN to check system memory for all known computer viruses that can inhabit memory. By default, SCAN only checks memory for critical and stealth viruses. If one of these viruses is found in memory, SCAN will stop and advise you to power down and boot the system with a virus-free DOS boot diskette.
/RV	This is used to remove validation codes from files. It can be used to remove the validation code from a diskette, subdirectory, or file(s). Using /RV on a disk will remove the partition table, boot sector, and system file validation.
/SUB	This tells SCAN to scan subdirectories under a subdirectory when scanned.

If you have installed new software or programs on your system, and are running SCAN with the /CV option, you will need to

113

reinstall validation codes to the new files with the add validation codes /AV option of VIRUSCAN. Additionally, the SCANVAL.VAL hidden file containing validation codes for the partition table, boot sector, COMMAND.COM, and system files may have to be replaced.

 Tip: SCAN can perform a quick check for viruses in memory only. This is useful when you want to check workstations for viruses before allowing them to log in to a NetWare file server.

The command to perform a memory-only scan is:

```
SCAN NUL /M /CHKHI
```

The /M and /CHKHI switches were described earlier in this section. By designating NUL as the drive to be scanned, the SCAN program will check system memory for viruses and then return to DOS without scanning any disks. SCAN will set the DOS ERRORLEVEL as described below.

Examples

The following examples may help you understand SCAN's usage.

SCAN C	Scans all files on Drive C:.
SCAN A:WP.EXE	Scans file WP.EXE on Drive A:.
SCAN M:\MAIL /SUB	Scans the M:\MAIL directory and all subdirectories of MAIL.
SCAN C: /A /CV	Scans all files and checks validation codes for unknown viruses on Drive C:.
SCAN C: /D /A	Scans all files on Drive C:, and prompts for erasure of infected files.

`SCAN C: D: /AV /NOMEM`	To add validation codes to files on Drives C: and D:, and skip memory checking.
`SCAN C: D: /M /A /FR`	Scans memory for all known and extinct viruses, as well as all files on Drives C: and D:, and outputs all messages in French.
`SCAN C: /E .VP1 .OV1`	Scans Drive C: and includes files with the extensions .VP1 and .OV1.
`SCAN R: /REPORT` `    H:INFECT.RPT`	Scans all files on Drive R: and creates a report file on Drive H: called INFECT.RPT.

Automating SCAN

SCAN will set the DOS ERRORLEVEL variable when it finishes executing. This makes it possible to run SCAN from a DOS batch file or a NetWare login script, taking a different action depending on whether or not viruses were found during the scan.

Table 5.2   DOS ERRORLEVEL variables.

ERRORLEVEL	Description
0	No viruses found
1	One or more viruses found
2	Abnormal termination (program error)

 Note: If you interrupt SCAN with a **Ctrl-Break** or **Ctrl-C**, SCAN will set the ERRORLEVEL to 0 or 1 depending on whether or not a virus was discovered prior to interruption of SCAN.

115

Tip: The /NOBREAK option can be used to prevent scanning from being stopped with a **Ctrl-C** or **Ctrl-Break.**

Virus Removal

What do you do if a virus is found? That depends on whether or not the virus is found in one of your file server's directories or on your workstation's local drives.

A McAfee program called CLEAN-UP will disinfect the majority of reported computer viruses on local drives by removing the virus code and restoring the infected program to the condition it was in before the infection. CLEAN-UP is updated with each release of the SCAN program to remove new viruses.

If the virus-infected file resides on your NetWare file server, it's best to delete the file entirely and replace it.

 Note: Load the replacement file from your virus-free diskette library.

Formatting Infected Floppy Disks

If you reformat an infected floppy disk with DOS 5.0, be sure to use the /U switch. This tells DOS to do an unconditional format of the disk, and not to save the original (infected) boot sector of the disk. This prevents the virus from reappearing if you unformat the disk.

NETSCAN

NETSCAN is a network version of the McAfee SCAN program. It differs from SCAN in that it will not stop and display an error message when it tries to scan files (such as the Bindery files), that the NetWare operating system holds open continuously. It should be run under a user account with read and file scan rights to the root of any NetWare volume you want to scan. You'll need additional rights if you want to use the /AV, /D, and /REPORT options.

> **Tip:** Run NETSCAN with all users logged out of the server so it can scan all files. If a user has a Nonshareable file open, NETSCAN will either post an error message and stop, or it will skip that file (if the /UNATTEND option is used).

McAfee recommends that NETSCAN should always be run from a write-protected floppy disk to prevent the program from becoming infected. While this is best, it may be desirable to have NETSCAN run automatically as the result of a DOS batch file or a NetWare login script. You can do this, but be aware that it's critical that you protect the NETSCAN.EXE file from virus attack. How do you do this when the NETSCAN file resides on a NetWare volume and you're trying to scan that volume for viruses?

There's no way to be absolutely certain that NETSCAN.EXE won't be infected, but you can reduce the probability to an acceptable level. The following steps are things that you can do to minimize risk:

1. Put NETSCAN.EXE in a directory (such as SYS:SYSTEM), that only the Supervisor account has access to. Only the Supervisor or equivalent can run NETSCAN.

2. Put NETSCAN.EXE in a directory where users have no rights and your administrative account only has READ rights.

3. Set NETSCAN's file attributes to Read Only.

4. You could also take the precautions mentioned in other chapters in this book, such as physical security for your file server.

NETSCAN Usage

If you want to scan more than one NetWare volume, you must have a drive letter mapped to each of the volumes you want to scan. Put a space between each of the drive letters on the command line.

/UNATTEND

The /UNATTEND option is unique to NETSCAN. It allows the program to continue scanning when a Nonshareable open file is scanned. The NetWare operating system normally holds open several files, such as the Bindery files and files related to the print queues. Without the /UNATTEND option, NETSCAN will try to scan these files and the NetWare shell will stop with an error message, as shown in Figure 5.3.

```
R:\SYSTEM>netscan r:
NETSCAN V84 Copyright 1989-91 by McAfee Associates.   (408) 988-3832
Scanning memory for critical viruses.
Scanning for known viruses.
Scanning R:\SYSTEM\RCONSOLE.EXE
Network Error: file in use during OPEN A FILE.   File = R:NET$OBJ.SYS
Abort, Retry, Fail? Fail
Scanning R:\SYSTEM\ATOTAL.EXE
Network Error: file in use during OPEN A FILE.   File = R:NET$PROP.SYS
Abort, Retry, Fail? Fail

Network Error: file in use during OPEN A FILE.   File = R:NET$VAL.SYS
Abort, Retry, Fail? Fail
Scanning R:\SYSTEM\FIRMLOAD.COM
Network Error: file in use during OPEN A FILE.   File = R:Q_0008.SYS
Abort, Retry, Fail? Fail
Scanning R:\SYSTEM\BV3\IBM$LSG.OVL
Network Error: file in use during OPEN A FILE.   File = R:Q_0005.SYS
Abort, Retry, Fail? Fail

Network Error: file in use during OPEN A FILE.   File = R:Q_0009.SYS
Abort, Retry, Fail? Fail
Scanning R:\PUBLIC\MAKEUSER.EXE
```

Figure 5.3   Using NETSCAN without the UNATTEND option.

Nearly all the NETSCAN options are the same as those allowed by SCAN. Refer to the VIRUSCAN section of this chapter for information about these options.

When you use the /UNATTEND option, NETSCAN now skips these open files and continues normally as shown in Figure 5.4.

```
R:\PUBLIC\MCAFEE>netscan r:
NETSCAN V82 Copyright 1989-91 by McAfee Associates.  (408) 988-3832
Scanning memory for critical viruses.
Scanning for known viruses.

Disk R: contains 366 directories and 10913 files.

 No viruses found.

NETSCAN V82 Copyright 1989-91 by McAfee Associates.  (408) 988-3832

    This program may not be used in a business, corporation, organization,
    government or agency environment without a negotiated site license.

R:\PUBLIC\MCAFEE>
```

Figure 5.4   Using NETSCAN with the UNATTEND option.

VALIDATE

A fundamental problem with virus-scanning software is that viruses can only be detected if the scanning software knows what to scan for. A virus-scanning product may not detect a newly-written virus. So, we need a way to see if a file has been infected by a virus without knowing how the file has been modified.

This is accomplished by computing a numeric value for the file which is based on the file's contents. If the contents of the file changes, the numeric value will change. One popular program which does this is the VALIDATE program supplied by McAfee Associates. It is available from their bulletin board and is included on disk when you obtain one of their virus-scanning products such as NETSCAN or VIRUSCAN.

VALIDATE computes Cyclical Redundancy Check (CRC) values—often incorrectly called *checksums.* A technical description of a CRC is beyond the scope of this book.

The VALIDATE program returns two CRC values. Each four-digit hexidecimal value is the result of a different CRC computation. This makes it very unlikely for a modified program file to appear to be correct. Experts claim that a CRC is not foolproof and better results are obtained with a cryptographic checksum.

While this is true, the advantage of VALIDATE is its distribution. Tens of thousands of PC users already have VALIDATE.

VALIDATE can be used to compute CRCs on any file, including data files. If you have data files that are static, you can use VALIDATE to compute a CRC on the file.

 Tip: If you need to ship files to a different location, you can have someone run VALIDATE against that file to see if it's been modified in transit.

Trojan Horse Programs

Viruses are not the only evil programs you have to worry about and protect against. There are programs called Trojan Horse programs which can also make your life miserable. A virus infects a normal program and adds additional functions to it, while a Trojan Horse program is written from the start with hostile intent. Another difference is that viruses propagate by infecting additional programs, while Trojan Horse programs do not replicate themselves.

Authors of Trojan Horse programs know that you probably wouldn't run the program if you knew the program's function in advance. So, these programs often masquerade as other programs that you do use normally.

Trojan Horse programs are difficult to detect because you can't scan for them like you can a virus-infected program. Trojans seem like any other normal program file to a virus scanner. In a sense, Trojans are more of a concern than viruses because you can't easily detect them and you may not know that they've done their evil deed.

We'll give you some examples of various things that Trojan Horse programs can do so you can see that you're at risk from Trojans just like computer viruses.

The ANSI.SYS Trojan

Consider a seemingly innocent DOS feature that can be exploited for hostile purposes—the ANSI.SYS driver. You normally think of ANSI.SYS as a DOS display driver that adds functionality to DOS screen printing. You may forget that ANSI.SYS is also a keyboard remapper. You can redefine keys on your keyboard with it. So how can it be used for hostile purposes?

Consider the following example. A user leaves his or her workstation unattended for a while, and someone creates a text file in that user's home directory. The text file has a provocative name, so the user notices it when he or she returns. If it has an extension of .TXT the user is likely to print the file to the screen with the DOS TYPE command.

Let's suppose that the contents of the file are as follows:

```
←[0;59;"erase *.dbf";13;"purge";13p
```

In the line above, the first character (the left arrow) is really the ASCII character ESCAPE. When this file is typed to the screen, the ANSI.SYS driver intercepts it and interprets it as a keyboard definition command. Nothing appears on-screen, so the user may think that the file is empty and erase it. Meanwhile, the F1 key has been redefined to erase all files with the .DBF extension and to purge all the erased files so they can't be recovered. Pretty nasty—and using nothing more than a text file and the DOS ANSI.SYS driver.

If you're afraid that the user is too cautious and won't type the text file, you can disguise the keyboard definition in a Trojan Horse program. As a demonstration, I designed a simple Trojan Horse program that, when run, redefines the user's F1 key to erase all files in the current directory and purges all salvageable files. I called the program CHESS so the user thinks that he or she is running a chess program, but the program name can be anything that would tempt the particular user.

When the user runs the program, the program complains about incompatible display hardware, so the user won't get too suspicious when a chess game doesn't appear. Figure 5.5 shows the screen output of the CHESS program.

```
H:\>chess

CHESS Version 3.1
Copyright 1992 by Chess Masters, Ltd.

Incompatible display hardware
Program cannot continue normally - Aborting.

H:\>
```

Figure 5.5   The CHESS Trojan.

How would you protect against this type of Trojan Horse? Of course, it's difficult to recommend that you don't load the ANSI.SYS driver, since it may be required to make some of your applications or menus output to the screen correctly. It's too bad that Microsoft didn't put keyboard definition in another device driver.

One solution is to use a replacement for ANSI.SYS called FANSI-Console sold by Hersey Micro Consulting. It lets you load an ANSI.SYS-compatible display driver without including the code that allows keyboard redefinition.

The LOGOUT Trojan

A simple Trojan horse program is a false LOGOUT program. The concept is simple. The false LOGOUT program makes users believe that they are logged out. If they leave the machine unattended, anyone can use the machine to exit the false LOGOUT program and be logged in as the original user.

We wrote a more sophisticated LOGOUT Trojan for demonstration purposes at the Accelerated Learning Center. The Trojan performed a false logout and also emulated the DOS command processor (COMMAND.COM), so the user believed that not only was he or she logged out and also at the real DOS prompt. The Trojan would respond to nearly all the internal DOS commands as well as appear to run SLIST and LOGIN when the user was at the false F:\LOGIN> prompt.

When the user tried to log in, the LOGOUT Trojan prompted for the password. When the user entered his or her password, the Trojan wrote it to a file on the file server and then told the user that they were trying to log in during an unauthorized time period.

122

Getting Supervisor-Equivalence

In a previous chapter, you saw how the SUPERVISOR account could be fooled into granting all rights to a user or group by assigning SUPERVISOR a login script if the account did not already have one. Even if that works, it only gives the user or group rights to directories. It does not give the user or group Supervisor-equivalence. How can you get Supervisor-equivalence?

Perhaps you can trick the Supervisor into granting you equivalence. Once again, call upon a Trojan to help you out. If you have Write and Create rights to the Supervisor's mail directory, you can put a program into this directory that grants rights and gives the Supervisor a login script that calls the program. The program could be stealthy and delete itself after it does the deed.

But what happens if you don't have Write and Create rights in the Supervisor's mail directory? What if the Supervisor already has a login script? Or, what if user login scripts are not allowed to run? In these cases, you could still put the Trojan into your home directory and give it a provocative name like TETRIS. Then tell the Supervisor about the wonderful game program you have. The Supervisor would run the program and the Trojan would grant you Supervisor-equivalence.

If you don't want the Supervisor to get suspicious when your Trojan doesn't play the Tetris game, simply print an "error message" to the screen complaining about incompatible display hardware.

Protecting Against Trojans

As you've seen in this chapter, Trojan Horse programs are easy to write and can destroy a lot of valuable data. What can you do to protect against them?

The most obvious step in avoiding Trojan Horse attack is to prevent the Trojan from being installed on your file server. This is easier said than done, but you can take obvious steps to reduce the chance of the Trojan striking.

In Chapter 8, "File and Directory Attributes," you'll see that file attributes such as Read Only, Delete Inhibit, and Rename Inhibit can be used to prevent files from being deleted and replaced by Trojans. In Chapter 9, "NetWare Rights," you'll see how restricting user rights in directories can prevent someone from storing a Trojan in a directory commonly accessed by other users. Back in Chapter 6, "Server-Based Protection," you saw how a product like SiteLock can prevent virus-infected files as well as Trojan Horse programs from running in workstations. You have quite a number of tools to use in your quest to keep viruses and Trojans off of your file server.

While all this goes a long way toward preventing Trojan Horse attack, there is always the possibility that the Trojan can be installed on a user's local drive. The solutions to this possibility are diskless workstations (see Chapter 3, "Diskless Workstations"), or security products that protect local disk drives (see Chapter 2, "Intruder Security").

Server-Based Protection

This chapter focuses on two areas. The first concerns products re-siding on the file server that protect users from running programs potentially infected by computer viruses or programs that have been replaced by Trojan Horse programs. SiteLock from Brightwork Development is our main example, but other products are men-tioned as well.

The second area concerns products which run on the file server and attempt to tell you when the file server itself has fallen victim to a hostile program. The possibility that viruses may infect a NetWare file server is explored. NET-Check is used as an ex-ample of a program that takes an active role in protecting your file server from hostile programs.

- Software Protection Products
- SiteLock
- LANProtect
- Hostile Server Processes
- MONITOR -p
- NLM-Profile
- NET-Check

Software Protection Products

In this chapter, you'll look at software protection products you can use which reside and run on your file server. The first product is SiteLock from Brightwork Development. This program runs on the file server and scans program files for integrity before it allows users at workstations to run the programs. Fundamentally, SiteLock protects workstations from becoming infected by viruses or from running Trojan Horse programs that may reside on the file server.

Following SiteLock, we'll take a quick look at Intel's new product called LANProtect. Its function is similar to SiteLock.

The remainder of the products featured in this chapter are designed to protect the server in some way. Novell's MONITOR NLM and Nu-Mega's NLM-Profile are programs which display your server's processor utilization so that you can see if a process running in your server is consuming more than its fair share of processor resources. It's possible that an NLM virus could simply consume processing time and impact the performance of your server.

Nu-Mega's NET-Check program is an NLM which solves the controversial Ring 0 problem with NetWare by forcing all processes to run at Ring 3 and prevents any process from writing over the code space of another process. This prevents virus infections of NLMs in server memory. If you're not aware of the controversial Ring 0 and nonpreemption issues, they are described in this chapter as well.

SiteLock

SiteLock provides two basic functions—software metering and virus protection. In this chapter, I will focus on its use as a virus-protection product.

 SiteLock has a server component and a workstation component. This makes SiteLock technically a client-server product. For NetWare 2.x servers, the server component installs as a VAP.

For NetWare 3.x servers, it installs as an NLM. The workstation component is a DOS TSR program called SWATCHER.

Throughout the remainder of this chapter, I'll refer to the server component as SiteLock and the workstation component as SWATCHER.

Basic Operation

When a workstation attempts to run a program, SWATCHER sends a message to SiteLock notifying it of this event. SiteLock then scans the file and computes a checksum for it. If the checksum agrees with a checksum that was generated for the file during installation, SiteLock sends a message to SWATCHER giving it permission to load the program.

If SiteLock computes a checksum that differs from the one generated during installation, it informs SWATCHER that the program may not be loaded. SiteLock will also produce an error message for the user, which is shown in Figure 6.1.

```
>> The file [LOADEXE1.EXE] has been changed, unable to run (CTRL-ENTER to clear)
```

Figure 6.1   SiteLock warning of possible virus infection.

SWATCHER then prevents DOS from running the program, so DOS complains. Figure 6.2 shows the error message from DOS.

```
I:\TEST> loadexe1
Cannot execute I:\TEST\LOADEXE1.EXE
```

Figure 6.2   DOS/SWATCHER error message.

If you set SiteLock not to allow programs to run if they've not been registered (checked for viruses), SiteLock will display the message in Figure 6.3 when you try to run the program.

```
>> File [LOADEXE1.EXE] is not virus checked, unable to run (CTRL-ENTER to clear)
```

Figure 6.3   SiteLock refuses to run a non-registered program file.

6 — Server-Based Protection

The SiteLock "database" of checksums is actually the NetWare Bindery. Anytime that you install a new application on the server, you would run a SiteLock program at a workstation in which you are logged in as Supervisor, which "registers" that application's files in the Bindery.

Anytime that you need to change the way that SiteLock operates or protect additional program files, you need to run a program called SITELOCK.

 Note: Don't confuse this program with the SiteLock VAP or NLM. This administration program is a DOS application that is used to configure SiteLock and to "register" program file checksums.

Installation

Installing SiteLock is simple. Just insert the SiteLock diskette in a floppy disk drive of a workstation, log in as Supervisor or equivalent, and type:

INSTALL a: s: w:

> where:

> **a:** may be any floppy disk drive letter with the SiteLock installation diskette.

> **s:** may be any drive letter which points to the directory you want SiteLock files installed in.

> **w:** may be any non-MAP ROOT drive letter that points to the SYS: volume.

Once the installation program is finished, you'll need to run the SiteLock program which is now installed in the SYS:SYSTEM\SITELOCK directory. When the program first runs, it checks to see if SiteLock-related Bindery objects have been created. If it doesn't find them, it creates them. The SiteLock VAP or NLM requires that these Bindery objects be there before they will load and run correctly. You can now exit the SiteLock program and proceed to load the SiteLock VAP or NLM.

On a NetWare 2.x server, you must take the server down and reboot it in order to load the SiteLock VAP. You'll probably choose to do this at a time when taking down the server will have a minimal impact on users.

On a NetWare 3.x server, you load the SiteLock NLM any time you choose. The NLM has already been installed in the SYS:SYSTEM directory. You simply go to the server console and load the SiteLock NLM as shown in Figure 6.4.

```
:load sitelock
Loading module SITELOCK.NLM
   SiteLock NLM with Virus Protection and SWatcher callback
SiteLock NLM with Virus Protection, v3.10
(c)1991 Brightwork Development, Inc.
:
```

Figure 6.4   Loading the SiteLock NLM.

SiteLock will automatically load STREAMS or CLIB if they are not already loaded, so you may see additional information on-screen. The STREAMS and CLIB modules are NLMs that SiteLock needs to run. They are supplied by Novell and installed in the SYS:SYSTEM directory.

Since NLMs can be unloaded, you can unload SiteLock anytime you choose. Figure 6.5 shows the message you'll see when SiteLock is unloaded.

```
:unload sitelock
Beginning SiteLock Resource Cleanup...Please wait
12/30/91 3:27am: 0.0.0 SITELOCK connection 252 cleared by user ALC on station 0
SiteLock Resource Cleanup complete.
*NOTE: SiteLock Protection Removed. Be careful out there.
Module SITELOCK.NLM unloaded
:
```

Figure 6.5   Unloading the SiteLock NLM.

Setting Up SiteLock

After you install SiteLock, you must set it up for virus checking. This involves:

■ Defining the actions that SiteLock will take.

■ Computing checksums for program files.

When you run the SITELOCK program, you'll see the main menu shown in Figure 6.6.

- **Change Current Server** is used to select another server that SiteLock is installed on.

- **Maintenance** is used to declare that you want SiteLock to enforce the loading of the SWATCHER program, to define users who are excluded from this requirement, and to control access to local drives.

- **Metered Applications** is used to set up SiteLock for software metering.

- **Status** brings up a window which displays SiteLock status.

- **Virus Protection** is used to set up SiteLock for virus checking.

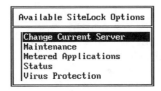

Figure 6.6   SiteLock main menu.

Virus Protection

First, look at how to set up SiteLock for virus protection. When you select the **Virus Protection** item from the main menu, you'll see the submenu shown in Figure 6.7. This submenu is used to define the program files which are to be virus protected and to define how SiteLock will deal with files that it cannot protect directly.

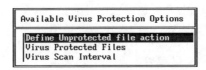

Figure 6.7   Virus Protection submenu.

Non-Virus Checked Files

Some program files cannot be protected by SiteLock because the contents of the program files change occasionally. An example is a program which stores configuration information within the executable program file. If you were to protect this file with SiteLock by computing a checksum on the file, the checksum would change when the contents of the file changed. Then SiteLock would refuse to run the program because it would assume a virus problem.

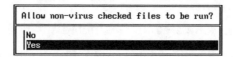

Figure 6.8   Allowing non-virus checked program files to run.

Figure 6.8 shows how to allow non-virus-checked files to always run. If you select No, you'll need to reregister files with SiteLock when they change.

Virus Protected Files

When you select the `Virus Protected Files` item from the menu for the first time, a blank window appears. This window will eventually contain the list of program files which have been virus-checked. This means that SiteLock has computed a check-sum for these files, has created a Bindery record for the file, and has inserted the checksum value in the Bindery.

To begin virus-checking program files, press the Insert key. You'll see a window where you'll enter the name of the current directory. When you press the Enter key, you'll see a screen similar to the one shown in Figure 6.9.

You can now tell SiteLock to virus-check all of the program files in the current directory or in the entire directory tree. The directory tree is the current directory along with all of the subdirectories of the current directory.

As SiteLock computes the checksum for each program file, you'll see the name of the program file and the name of the current directory appear on-screen as in Figure 6.10. These program

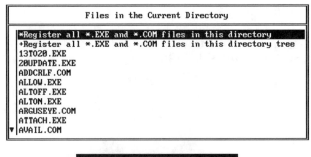

Figure 6.9   *Files to virus check.*

file names will continue to appear on-screen until all of the files in the current directory or in the directory tree have been virus-checked.

Figure 6.10   *Registering program files.*

When all the programs you specified are registered, you'll then see a screen similar to Figure 6.11.

```
                        Virus Protected Files
 SYS:PUBLIC                                          13TO20.EXE
 SYS:PUBLIC                                          20UPDATE.EXE
 SYS:PUBLIC                                          ADDCRLF.COM
 SYS:PUBLIC                                          ALLOW.EXE
 SYS:PUBLIC                                          ALTOFF.EXE
 SYS:PUBLIC                                          ALTON.EXE
 SYS:PUBLIC                                          ARGUSEYE.COM
 SYS:PUBLIC                                          ATTACH.EXE
 SYS:PUBLIC                                          AVAIL.COM
 SYS:PUBLIC                                          AWSH.EXE
 SYS:PUBLIC                                          BCONSOLE.EXE
 SYS:PUBLIC                                          BINDSTAT.COM
 SYS:PUBLIC                                          BIOSFIX.COM
 SYS:PUBLIC                                          BREQUEST.EXE
▼SYS:PUBLIC                                          BROADCAS.COM
```

Figure 6.11   *Files which are registered.*

Execute-Only Program Files

Program files which have their Execute-Only attribute set will present a special problem for SiteLock. An execute-only file cannot be opened for read access. This means that SiteLock cannot compute a checksum for the program file. If SiteLock encounters an execute-only program file while it's computing checksums, you'll see an error message appear in a window as in Figure 6.12.

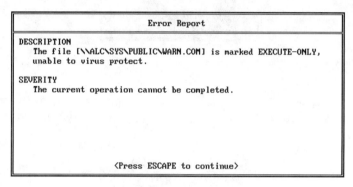

```
                          Error Report

DESCRIPTION
     The file [\\ALC\SYS\PUBLIC\WARN.COM] is marked EXECUTE-ONLY,
     unable to virus protect.

SEVERITY
     The current operation cannot be completed.




                    <Press ESCAPE to continue>
```

Figure 6.12   Execute-only program file error message.

The trick is to have SiteLock compute it's checksum on the program files *before* you set them to execute-only. Once SiteLock has computed its checksum on all of your program files, you can set your program files back to execute-only.

Tip: You can't easily remove the Execute-Only attribute from program files. So, if you have existing program files set to execute-only, it's best to replace them with new copies from your diskettes. Be sure to use the virus-free disks from your library.

Note: If execute-only files cannot be opened and read, how can the SiteLock VAP or NLM compute checksums for these files when a user attempts to run one of these programs? The answer is—it can't! SiteLock assumes that if an execute-only program appears in the Bindery, it has already been error checked. Since a virus cannot infect an execute-only file, SiteLock is safe just letting SWATCHER run the program.

So, if you can mark most (or all) of your program files as execute-only, SiteLock will not have to take the time and server resources to compute checksums on these files. If you can make all of your program files execute-only, what's the point of having SiteLock? Well, SiteLock will still prevent programs from running if they haven't been virus-checked. So, if someone puts a new program on the server, it cannot run until the administrator registers it with SiteLock.

Overlay Files

SiteLock only virus-checks executable files (.COM and .EXE). Many people ask whether a virus can infect overlay files and whether SiteLock will protect against this. Yes, a virus can infect an overlay file, although this is a bit more difficult for the virus, since it would need to know the structure of the overlay file.

SiteLock does not currently protect against this because there are significant technical issues. The most important of these is what to do if the overlay file is infected. If the overlay file is scanned for viruses when it is accessed, this is likely to occur sometime after the main executable program has been running awhile. You don't want to abort a program when it has data files open and some of the data has changed.

There is also the issue of performance. You don't want to scan the overlay file for viruses each time it is accessed. It may be accessed every few seconds by multiple users.

Tip: One solution to the problem of overlay files is to periodically scan them. This would occur at a period defined by the administrator—when the overlay files are not being accessed.

Products like SiteLock need to address the problem of overlay files in the future and here I have a suggested approach for those vendors. Do not check an overlay file when it is accessed by its application—it's too late to do anything about it at that point. Rather, check an application's overlay files at the time a user runs the application. If you're going to deny the reading of an overlay file, do so before the application begins running. Yes, this means keeping a list of overlay files for each application.

Virus Scan Interval

You can have SiteLock scan a program file for virus infection every time a program is run, or you can have SiteLock scan a program file only periodically. For example, if most users on the network run WordPerfect, do you want SiteLock to scan the WordPerfect program file for virus infection every time a user loads the WordPerfect program?

Figure 6.13 shows how to select an interval between virus-checks of the same file. If you enter **0** as in the example screen, you're telling SiteLock to scan a program file for virus infection every time any user loads a program. The disadvantage of this is the additional workload on the server and the time it takes to scan a file for virus infection. If you enter **10**, for example, SiteLock will not check a certain program file for virus infection more often than every ten minutes. This reduces the burden on the server, but increases the opportunity for a virus-infected file to run. While the "correct" setting for this is a matter of personal choice, I'd recommend no less often than every five minutes.

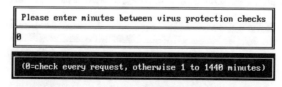

Figure 6.13   Setting the SiteLock Virus Scan Interval.

6 — Server-Based Protection

Maintenance

When you select Maintenance from the main menu, you'll see the submenu shown in Figure 6.14. These options allow you to define the action that takes place when the SWATCHER program is not loaded at workstations. You can also define those users who do not need to load SWATCHER.

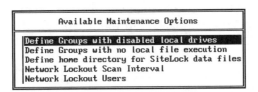

```
                Available Maintenance Options

  Define Groups with disabled local drives
  Define Groups with no local file execution
  Define home directory for SiteLock data files
  Network Lockout Scan Interval
  Network Lockout Users
```

Figure 6.14   SiteLock Maintenance menu.

SiteLock lets you control users' ability to access their local drives by including them in a group. If a user is a member of that group and the user has SWATCHER loaded, local DOS drives will be disabled. You can also control whether users can run programs from their local drives in a similar way.

Groups with Disabled Local Drives

If you include groups here, SWATCHER will disable local drives for users who are members of those groups. You may want to do this to lessen the likelihood that a virus-infected workstation could spread the virus to the file server. If a user tries to access a local drive, they will receive an `Invalid drive specification` error message from DOS. Figure 6.15 shows two groups with disabled local drives.

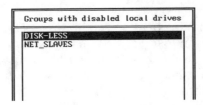

```
  Groups with disabled local drives

  DISK-LESS
  NET_SLAVES
```

Figure 6.15   Groups with disabled local drives.

Groups with No Local File Execution

The SiteLock VAP or NLM which runs on the file server computes checksums for program files. If a workstation attempts to load a program file from a local disk drive, SiteLock cannot compute a checksum for that file, so files on local disk drives cannot be checked for viruses. Figure 6.16 shows how you control this.

If you want to disable a user's ability to execute program files from a local disk, make them members of a designated group, as shown in Figure 6.16.

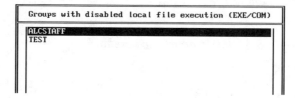

Figure 6.16   Groups with no local drive access.

Define Home Directory

You can define the directory where SiteLock stores its data files which relate to software metering and virus protection reporting. This directory defaults to SYS:SYSTEM\SITELOCK but you can change it by selecting the `Define home directory for SiteLock data files` from the Maintenance menu. You're then prompted for a directory.

Network Lockout Scan Interval

You can have SiteLock check to see that users have the SWATCHER program loaded. If SWATCHER is not loaded in their workstation, SiteLock will clear their connection with the server. This forces users to check for viruses. You may want virus checking to be voluntary, in which case you will not have SiteLock enforce the loading of SWATCHER.

Figure 6.17 shows how to change the time interval between SWATCHER checks. If you enter `0`, SiteLock will never check for

SWATCHER loaded at any user's workstation. The example in Figure 6.17 shows SiteLock checking every ten minutes.

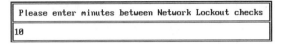

| Please enter minutes between Network Lockout checks |
| 10 |

Figure 6.17   Checking for the presence of SWATCHER.

Network Lockout Users

If you decide to have SiteLock enforce the loading of SWATCHER, you can declare that certain users are excluded from the check. The example in Figure 6.18 shows that a user called BACKUP is excluded from the check.

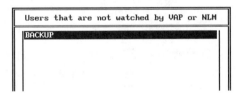

Figure 6.18   Excluding a user from SWATCHER checks.

Caution: It's not a good idea to exclude anyone from SWATCHER checks since the purpose of having SWATCHER loaded is to detect possible virus infections or Trojan Horse programs.

LANProtect

Intel recently released a product called LANProtect. This is a product which is similar to SiteLock in purpose, but somewhat different in implementation. We had time to include the highlights of LANProtect before this book was published.

Like SiteLock, LANProtect runs on a NetWare 3.x file server as a NLM. Unlike SiteLock, there is no VAP version available for NetWare 2.x file servers—there will probably never be one because of the way LANProtect ties into the NetWare 3.x file system.

LANProtect runs entirely on the file server. There is no TSR located on the workstation, as is the case with SiteLock. As a result, there is little or no network traffic associated with virus-checking files. While SiteLock checks for changes made to files using a Cyclical Redundancy Check, LANProtect scans files for viruses.

LANProtect checks for viruses in a few ways. You can check your entire file server for viruses by manually starting a file server scan anytime you wish. This scan may also be scheduled to run anytime you wish. For example, you can set it to run every 24 hours at midnight. Additionally, when the LANProtect NLM is loaded, LANProtect scans for viruses in real-time anytime a file is accessed.

It appears that the tradeoff between LANProtect and SiteLock can be summarized as follows. Since SiteLock can detect any changes made to a program file, it can find new viruses and detect Trojan Horse programs while LANProtect cannot. However, SiteLock cannot protect program files which change in the normal course of usage, such as a program which stores configuration information within its program file. LANProtect can protect program files which change, since it is scanning for viruses—not simply detecting changes to the file.

LANProtect is easier to install and configure. Since LANProtect has no workstation TSR, it doesn't have to check the workstation periodically to see if the TSR is still loaded. However, SiteLock's TSR provides the additional feature of locking out local drives.

Like SiteLock, LANProtect does not handle the problem of overlay file virus infection mentioned earlier in this chapter. In this regard, both products are on equal footing.

Hostile Server Processes

During the last few years, NetWare has been the subject of controversy because of the way it was designed. The NetWare design makes it susceptible to attack from hostile processes and, therefore, is a security concern. There are those (mostly Novell's competitors), who claim that NetWare is less secure than traditional operating systems because a hostile or runaway process can cripple the machine.

NetWare is an operating system specifically designed for a file server. It is not considered a general-purpose operating system and should not be compared to those that are. A NetWare file server is an *I/O engine*—not a platform for running CPU-intensive applications (NLMs and VAPs aside). People who compare NetWare to general-purpose operating systems often criticize NetWare for not implementing traditional protection mechanisms. These protection mechanisms are called *preemption* and *rings*.

Preemption

NetWare is a multitasking operating system because it has a system scheduler (often called the *kernel*), that schedules various processes to run. Many of these processes were written by Novell and are part of NetWare. There are processes that have been written by other companies and are separate products.

Most general-purpose multitasking operating systems will control processes so they don't run longer than the operating system allows. If a process were allowed to run too long, other processes wouldn't get their fair share of the machine and their users may suffer performance problems. To prevent this, the operating system's kernel can stop a process at the end of its *time-slice*. An operating system with the ability to grab control back from a process is called *preemptive*.

NetWare designers decided not to implement preemption in order to reduce overhead and optimize the server for servicing I/O requests. Most server processes are not CPU-intensive. They are performing I/O and waiting most of the time (this will change somewhat as client-server computing becomes popular). Preemptive scheduling wastes CPU cycles in a file-server environment.

The dark side of nonpreemption is the possibility that processes may not play by the rules, and use more CPU time than they need. In order for nonpreemption to work well, it is critical that processes give up control to the kernel periodically so that other processes can run. Novell designers call this *running in a nice-guy environment.*

A hostile process may be designed to steal CPU time from the server. This could seriously affect server performance and prevent other processes from carrying out their tasks properly. A network administrator needs to protect his or her server from processes that abuse the nonpreemptive nature of NetWare. What you need are tools to monitor and detect this. Later in this chapter, tools of this sort—such as Novell's MONITOR program and Nu-Mega's NLM-Profile—will be presented.

Ring 0

Another issue has to do with the ability of the Intel 80286, 80386, and 80486 processors to run processes at a privilege level lesser than the kernel. When these processors run in protected mode, processes may run at various privilege levels which give them more or less access to resources of the processor. Intel calls these privilege levels *rings.* A process running at Ring 0, for example, has the highest privilege level and has full access to anything running on the processor.

The concern is that a hostile process has access to the entire file server and can overwrite or destroy other processes. NetWare cannot protect itself from a hostile process when the process is running at the same privilege level as the operating system itself.

Tip: You can lessen the problem of loading hostile NLMs by using the SECURE CONSOLE command. When you enter this command at the file server console, NLMs can only be loaded from the SYS:SYSTEM directory. This command is only available with NetWare 3.x because NetWare 2.x VAPs only load from the SYS:SYSTEM directory.

6 — Server-Based Protection

Testing VAPs and NLMs

You should take steps to be sure that the VAP or NLM that you load on your file server is genuine and not a Trojan Horse or other form of hostile program. Since these are not .EXE or .COM files, you cannot easily scan them with popular virus-detection software. You can check them with software that computes checksums (CRCs) on the files and compares those checksums to published checksums. One such product is Accelerated Learning Center's V^2 Scan.

> **Tip:** It's a good idea to test your new VAP or NLM on a test server before putting it "into production." The notion of another file server used for testing may seem unusual to some people, but it's common practice in many companies. The additional server is often used for software development as well.

 If you're running NetWare 2.x, you'll be disappointed to learn that there are few tools that you can use to accurately monitor VAPs.

 If you're running NetWare 3.x, you'll be happy to learn that there are usable tools for monitoring the operation and the performance-impact of a new NLM. The remaining pages in this chapter describe tools you can use for NetWare 3.x.

MONITOR -p

NetWare 3.x has an NLM called MONITOR that allows you to monitor file server activity and status. An undocumented feature is the *-p* switch that lets you look at processor utilization during each sample period. This feature can be used to monitor the CPU time that any or all processes consume. A Network Administrator can detect NLMs that consume too much CPU time.

Note: The menu item called Processor Utilization appears only if you use the *-p* switch when you load MONITOR.

When you load the MONITOR NLM, you'll see the main menu shown in Figure 6.19.

Figure 6.19   MONITOR NLM Main Menu

When you select Processor Utilization, the next screen is a list of server processes that you can choose to view. The screen, shown in Figure 6.20, shows a list with the cursor highlighting the server's Polling process. The up and down arrowheads indicate that there are more processes in the list both above and below the visible list. You can use your ↑ and ↓ keys to view them.

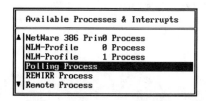

Figure 6.20   List of server processes to monitor.

To display processor utilization:

- For the highlighted process only, press **Enter**.
- To view multiple processes at the same time, mark them with the **F5** key and then press **Enter.**
- To select and view all processes at the same time, press the **F3** key.

144

If you press the F3 key to display all processes, you'll see a screen similar to Figure 6.21. The column labeled Name is the name of the process running on the server. If you use the PgDn key, you'll start to see names that begin with Interrupt. These are the interrupt service routines. The process names are sorted alphabetically and are followed by the interrupt service routines listed numerically in order.

Name	Time	Count	Load
▲ Cache Update Process	1,191	5	0.10 %
Console Command Process	0	0	0.00 %
Directory Cache Process	1,049	5	0.09 %
FAT Update Process	2,453	10	0.21 %
HOTFIX Process	0	0	0.00 %
Monitor Main Process	0	0	0.00 %
NetWare 386 Prin0 Process	2,736	18	0.23 %
NLM-Profile 0 Process	0	0	0.00 %
NLM-Profile 1 Process	8,788	7	0.76 %
Polling Process	1,028,801	208	89.11 %
REMIRR Process	0	0	0.00 %
Remote Process	6,031	12	0.52 %
RSPX Process	0	0	0.00 %
Server 01 Process	50,047	92	4.33 %
Server 02 Process	0	0	0.00 %
Server 03 Process	0	0	0.00 %
STREAMS Q Runner Process	0	0	0.00 %
▼ TTS Finish Process	0	0	0.00 %

Figure 6.21   Display of server processes.

- The Time column is the amount of time (in microseconds) the server's processor spent running that process during the sample period.

- The Count column is the number of times the process ran during the sample period.

- The Load column represents the percentage of the processor's time spent on this process or interrupt.

 Note: Keep in mind that these values are a snapshot of file-server activity during the most recent sample period. The values from sample periods in the past are lost. This means that this information is presented in real time, and there is no way to average these values over time. If you're not watching the screen when a momentary burst of processor utilization occurs, you won't know that it occurred.

Figure 6.22 shows the interrupts. This screen was captured while the server was servicing an EtherNet-connected workstation, which was copying files to the server's SCSI hard disk (connected to the Disk Coprocessor Board). The server's EtherNet card used `Interrupt 3` and the Disk Coprocessor Board used `Interrupt 11`.

Name	Time	Count	Load
▲ Interrupt 0	2,291	18	0.19 %
Interrupt 1	0	0	0.00 %
Interrupt 2	0	0	0.00 %
Interrupt 3	15,087	164	1.30 %
Interrupt 4	0	0	0.00 %
Interrupt 5	0	0	0.00 %
Interrupt 6	0	0	0.00 %
Interrupt 7	0	0	0.00 %
Interrupt 8	0	0	0.00 %
Interrupt 9	0	0	0.00 %
Interrupt 10	0	0	0.00 %
Interrupt 11	30,082	23	2.60 %
Interrupt 12	0	0	0.00 %
Interrupt 13	0	0	0.00 %
Interrupt 14	0	0	0.00 %
Interrupt 15	0	0	0.00 %
▼ Total Sample Time:	1,178,034		

Figure 6.22   Display of hardware interrupt activity.

NLM-Profile

Server processes that take more than their fair share of server CPU time can be detected with a product called NLM-Profile from Nu-Mega Technologies. It is an NLM that runs on a NetWare 3.x server. It monitors kernel task-switching and maintains timing tables. You can view the information in the timing tables on the screen of the server.

 Tip: You can also view the server screen, and hence the NLM-Profile information, from a workstation by using RCONSOLE.

The main NLM-Profile screen is shown in Figure 6.23.

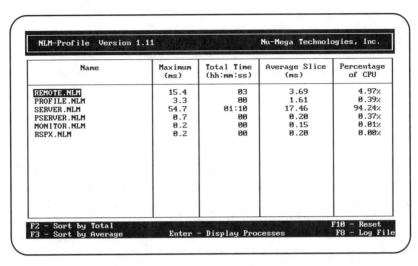

Name	Maximum (ms)	Total Time (hh:mm:ss)	Average Slice (ms)	Percentage of CPU
REMOTE.NLM	15.4	03	3.69	4.97%
PROFILE.NLM	3.3	00	1.61	0.39%
SERVER.NLM	54.7	01:10	17.46	94.24%
PSERVER.NLM	0.7	00	0.20	0.37%
MONITOR.NLM	0.2	00	0.15	0.01%
RSPX.NLM	0.2	00	0.20	0.00%

NLM-Profile Version 1.11 — Nu-Mega Technologies, Inc.

F2 — Sort by Total
F3 — Sort by Average   Enter — Display Processes   F10 — Reset
                                                                 F8 — Log File

Figure 6.23 NLM-Profile main screen showing server processes.

This screen shows a list of NLMs that are currently running on your server. NetWare device drivers such as disk and LAN card drivers, as well as library NLMs such as CLIB, do not show up on-screen because they are not scheduled by the kernel. They run in the context of the calling program. For disk and LAN card drivers, the calling program is the NetWare operating system. For a library such as CLIB, any NLM may call it.

■ The Maximum column shows the longest time-slice that a process has consumed since NLM-Profile tracking began.

■ The Total Time column shows simply an accumulation of time the process has consumed since tracking began.

■ The Average Slice column shows the average time that the process has consumed since tracking began.

■ The Percentage of CPU column shows the percentage of total CPU time the process has consumed since tracking began.

As NLMs are loaded and unloaded, NLM-Profile does not recompute the percentages. If it did, it would consume more CPU resources than it does normally. This means that if NLMs are loaded or unloaded after NLM-Profile begins tracking, the percentages are no longer valid.

Tip: You can manually recompute the percentages by pressing the F10 key. This resets the tables.

Server OS Processes

Figure 6.24 shows the server operating system processes. This screen was captured from a server that was lightly loaded, so most of the CPU time was spent in the Polling process. Under heavy load, you will be able to see which server processes account for most of the server's CPU utilization. The NLM-Profile screens are updated at two-second intervals.

```
NLM-Profile  Version 1.11                     Nu-Mega Technologies, Inc.

        Name          Maximum    Total Time   Average Slice   Percentage
                        (ms)      (hh:mm:ss)       (ms)          of CPU

Polling                 55.0        04:07         15.42          91.74%
FAT Update               3.8          00           0.23           0.25%
AES No Sleep             0.4          00           0.11           0.11%
Cache Update             1.3          00           0.11           0.05%
Directory Cache          3.1          00           0.17           0.08%
AES Sleep               22.5          00           0.88           0.06%
Server 01               18.6          04           0.53           1.87%
TTS Finish               0.2          00           0.15           0.00%
Server 03                0.1          00           0.08           0.00%




NLM:SERVER.NLM                                Esc - Return to NLM screen
```

Figure 6.24   Display of NetWare operating system processes.

Reports

The F8 key creates or updates a file called PROFILE.LOG that contains a report of the table contents at the time the key was pressed. This report is saved in the root directory of the SYS: Volume. Even though your current directory may be SYS:SYSTEM, NLM-Profile's current directory is the root. A sample report is shown in Figure 6.25.

```
NLM-Profile Log File - created 06:52 PM   Sunday January 19

NLM/Process        Maximum   Total   Average   Percent
REMOTE.NLM         13.4      12      3.43      4.50%
Remote             13.4      12      3.43      4.50%


NLM/Process        Maximum   Total   Average   Percent
PROFILE.NLM        15.2      00      1.26      0.25%
NLM-Profile 1      3.1       00      1.07      0.20%
NLM-Profile 0      5.2       00      7.34      0.04%


NLM/Process        Maximum   Total   Average   Percent
SERVER.NLM         54.9      04:21   14.84     95.05%
Polling            54.9      04:19   31.95     94.60%
AES No Sleep       0.2       00      0.0       0.09%
FAT Update         0.6       00      0.05      0.05%
Cache Update       2.0       00      0.06      0.02%
Directory Cache    1.8       00      0.06      0.02%
AES Sleep          1.2       00      0.36      0.00%
Server 03          12.5      00      0.36      0.24%


NLM/Process        Maximum   Total   Average   Percent
PSERVER.NLM        0.6       00      0.10      0.18%
NetWare 386 Prin0  0.6       00      0.10      0.18%


NLM/Process        Maximum   Total   Average   Percent
RSPX.NLM           0.1       00      0.10      0.00%
RSPX               0.1       00      0.10      0.00%
```

Figure 6.25   Example of NLM-Profile report.

NLM-Profile adds little overhead to the server in terms of memory required and processor time. My tests show about 53 KB of memory required and about 0.3 percent of CPU utilization.

NET-Check

The threat of hostile server processes attacking a NetWare 3.x file server can be diminished with a product called NET-Check, from Nu-Mega Technologies. NET-Check runs as an NLM and protects the NetWare operating system from being overwritten in memory by another process, such as a hostile NLM. NET-Check sets all NLMs, including the server operating system and NET-Check itself, so that they run in Ring 3 of the processor.

Figure 6.26 shows NET-Check being loaded. We then load a demonstration NLM program, supplied by Nu-Mega, called CRASH.NLM which tries to write to the server memory space containing the NetWare operating system code. Even though the next line in this demonstration says SERVER.NLM overwritten, NET-Check has protected SERVER.NLM from being overwritten.

```
:load netcheck /w
Loading module NETCHECK.NLM
  Nu-Mega Technologies NetWare 386 Protection

NET-Check  Version 1.11  3/29/91
(c) Copyright Nu-Mega Technologies, Inc. 1991

NET-Check: Including memory mapped device at d0000-d0fff
:load crash
Loading module CRASH.NLM
  NLM crash
NET-Check: SERVER.NLM overwritten at 00145A63
        Current Process: Server Crasher  0    Owned by CRASH.NLM
        Current EIP=006DB22B   Owned by CRASH.NLM
  :
```

Figure 6.26   Loading NET-Check and running demo program.

Figure 6.27 shows an example of what a virus-infected NLM would look like when NET-Check catches it trying to do its evil deed. In this case, the infected NLM's hostile process is called Die you Server and the NLM's filename is FRI13.NLM for dramatization.

```
:load fri13
Loading module FRI13.NLM
  NLM crash
NET-Check: SERVER.NLM overwritten at 00144A61
        Current Process: Die you Server  0    Owned by FRI13.NLM
        Current EIP=0076A5AB   Owned by FRI13.NLM
:
```

Figure 6.27   Example of virus-infected NLM.

While there have not yet been any reported cases of virus-infected NLMs, it's comforting to know that a product is available now to help protect against them.

NetWare Bindery

It's critical that you understand the NetWare Bindery to grasp the security features and problems of NetWare. The Bindery is the database that NetWare uses to identify users, groups, servers and so forth. These are all called objects. The Bindery contains various information about these objects.

This chapter tells you how NetWare uses the Bindery to ensure security as well as how application programs may use the Bindery for their own purposes. I speculate about possible future NetWare-specific viruses or Trojan Horse programs which attack the Bindery. You'll read about a product called BVDEBUG which lets you view the contents of the Bindery and how Novell's SECURITY program will tell you about possible security problems.

- Bindery Overview
- Bindery Files
- How SYSCON Uses the Bindery
- How PCONSOLE Uses the Bindery
- Applications Usage of the Bindery
- Programs which Attack the Bindery
- BVDEBUG
- SECURITY

Bindery Overview

You can think of the Bindery as a simple database. Each record of the database represents a unique Bindery object. The record is divided into fields, which are called properties in Bindery terminology. Each field contains information called values.

In a simple database, each record can be identified by its record number. The NetWare Bindery identifies each object with a Bindery Object Identifier (often abbreviated Object ID). This identifier is a 32-bit value usually represented in hexidecimal notation.

When you create a new user with SYSCON, for example, you're adding a new object to the Bindery (a new record to the database). The object name is the new user name. Later in this chapter you'll see the properties which are created when you add a new user with SYSCON.

Bindery Files

The Bindery is implemented as files that reside in the SYS:SYSTEM directory. NetWare 2.x uses two files to store the Bindery information:

- NET$BIND.SYS
- NET$BVAL.SYS

NetWare 3.x uses three files to store the Bindery information:

- NET$OBJ.SYS
- NET$PROP.SYS
- NET$VAL.SYS.

Note: These files are not available to users because users should never have rights in the SYS:SYSTEM directory. The files are also not normally accessible to anyone because they are nonshareable and are constantly held open by the operating system (therefore they're constantly locked).

Since it is important to access the Bindery files at times to copy them to a backup device, there are NetWare function calls to open and close the Bindery. When the Bindery is closed, the files can be opened by your backup software and copied to the backup device. While the Bindery is closed, the server cannot provide any services (there are many) which rely on access to the Bindery. During a backup session, the Bindery files should be copied quickly so the Bindery can be opened again quickly.

Objects

Any person, process, or device which must connect to a NetWare file server must be represented by an object in the Bindery. A FAX server, for example, which stores its files in a NetWare directory, must be a Bindery object. Even some things which do not "connect" to a file server are represented in the Bindery. A print queue is an example of a Bindery object that doesn't "login."

Names and Types

Bindery object names may be up to 48 characters long. Since the name must be zero-terminated, that leaves 47 characters for the actual name. Invalid characters for Bindery object names are the same as those for user account names, as described in Chapter 1, "NetWare Accounts."

Objects in the Bindery have type numbers associated with them. There is a "field" in the Bindery for the object type. This makes it possible to have objects with the same name but different object types. For example, you could have a user called

LASER as well as a print server called LASER. The Bindery knows that they're not the same object because their object types are different.

Novell administers Bindery object types. Table 7.1 lists several of the currently defined Bindery object types. New object types are defined as developers. Ask Novell to assign them.

Table 7.1   The currently defined Novell object types.

Object Name.	Type (hex)	Type (decimal)
Unknown	0	0
User	1	1
User Group	2	2
Print Queue	3	3
File Server	4	4
Job Server	5	5
Gateway	6	6
Print Server	7	7
Archive Queue	8	8
Archive Server	9	9
Job Queue	A	10
Administration	B	11
Remote Bridge Server	24	36
Advertising Print Server	47	71

Properties and Values

Bindery *properties* are names for information related to a Bindery object. Using the database analogy, a property is like the name of a field in a database record. The property contains a *value*. The Bindery allows a property to contain one value (an *item*), or many values (a *set*).

Table 7.2 contains examples of the names of current properties. This list is necessarily incomplete, since the list expands as Novell and third-party developers require new types of information to store.

Table 7.2 Current properties.

BLOCKS_READ	OLD_PASSWORDS
CONNECT_TIME	OPERATORS
GROUP_MEMBERS	PASSWORD
GROUPS_I'M_IN	Q_DIRECTORY
IDENTIFICATION	Q_OPERATORS
LOGIN_CONTROL	Q_SERVERS
NET_ADDRESS	Q_USERS
NODE_CONTROL	SECURITY_EQUALS

Property Names

Property names are limited to 15 characters and are case-insensitive. Invalid characters are the same as those described for account names in Chapter 1, "NetWare Accounts."

Static vs. Dynamic

Objects and properties in the Bindery may be declared as either *dynamic* or *static*. A *dynamic object* is one that exists in the Bindery until explicitly removed or until the server is powered down and brought back up. When the server initializes, it scans the Bindery for dynamic objects and deletes them. An example of a dynamic object is a file server (other than the file server that the Bindery resides in). You don't want a file server to remember the names of other file servers after you've taken down the server. A file server should "learn" the names of other servers on the network after it initializes.

A *static object* is one that exists in the Bindery forever or until it is explicitly removed. A static object may be deleted by a Supervisor but survives a server reinitialization. Examples of static objects are user and group accounts. You don't want user and group accounts to disappear just because you take down the server.

Item vs. Set

A property may be an item or a set. For example, the *item* property called PASSWORD contains a single value—the password for the object. It's an item property because at any time, an object only has one password.

The *set* property called GROUPS_I'M_IN, for example, contains object IDs of user groups. A user may belong to many groups so the GROUPS_I'M_IN property must handle more than one Object ID.

Object Security

The Bindery provides a security mechanism to allow access to only certain objects. That is, the Bindery can determine who has access rights to Bindery information. There are separate access rights for reading from the Bindery and for writing to the Bindery. There are five levels of security:

- Anyone
- Logged
- Object
- Supervisor
- NetWare

Anyone

The security level *Anyone* means that any program may call a Bindery function regardless of who is logged in to the server. The user running the program does not even need to be logged in to the server. All that's required is a workstation shell connection to the server. You may recall that when you load a NetWare shell, you have a connection to a server and visibility of its SYS:LOGIN directory. You can run SLIST, for example, without being logged in to the server. SLIST gets its information from the Bindery.

Logged

The security level *Logged* means that a program can only access this Bindery information if the user running the program is logged in to the file server. For example, you can only read a user's Full Name from the IDENTIFICATION property if you're logged in to the file server.

Object

The security level *Object* means that only the object itself may access its own Bindery information. For example, when you log in, the LOGIN program can read your account restrictions in the LOGIN_CONTROL property, but the program cannot read anyone else's account restrictions because the property's read security is set to Object.

Supervisor

The security level *Supervisor* means that the user running the program must be the Supervisor or equivalent. The Bindery does not distinguish between the Supervisor account and an equivalent. If you want that additional discrimination, it needs to be built into the application.

ACCOUNT_LOCKOUT property is an example of this security level. You must be a Supervisor to set Intruder Detection and Account Lockout parameters which are stored in the property.

NetWare

The security level *NetWare* means that only the operating system can access the Bindery information. For example, the PASS-WORD property can only be read by and written to by the operating system. Nobody, including the Supervisor, can access the PASSWORD property directly. Since passwords are encrypted in the Bindery using a one-way encryption algorithm, there's no need for anyone to access the PASSWORD property directly.

> **Note:** Since only the operating system can read the PASSWORD property, Bindery viewer products like BVDEBUG (described later in this chapter), do not list the PASSWORD property.

How SYSCON Uses the Bindery

SYSCON can be thought of as a user-friendly editor program for the Bindery. Most SYSCON operations affect the Bindery in some way. This section will show you the Bindery functions that occur when you perform various SYSCON tasks.

Adding a User

When you run SYSCON and select User Information in the main menu, a list of user account names is displayed. If you press the Insert key, you're asking SYSCON to create a new user account. Let's see what SYSCON does to the Bindery when you add a user called *FRED*.

1. Create a user object called FRED.

2. Add a property called SECURITY_EQUALS to the FRED object.

3. Add a property called GROUPS_I'M_IN to the FRED object.

4. Add the EVERYONE group to the SECURITY_EQUALS property of the FRED object.

5. Add the EVERYONE group to the GROUPS_I'M_IN property of the FRED object.

6. Add the user FRED to the GROUPS_I'M_IN property of the EVERYONE object.

7. Add a property called LOGIN_CONTROL to the FRED object.

8. Write the account restrictions values to the LOGIN_CONTROL property of the FRED object.

9. Add a property called OLD_PASSWORDS to the FRED object.

10. Write a value to the OLD_PASSWORDS property of the FRED object.

11. Add a property called ACCOUNT_BALANCE to the FRED object.

12. Write the account balance values to the ACCOUNT_BALANCE property of the FRED object.

13. Add a property called MISC_LOGIN_INFO to the FRED object.

Quite a bit of activity occurs when you create a new user account. Each of these steps involves at least two packets flowing over the network cable. On a busy network where there is already substantial numbers of packets flowing, adding a user may take perceivably longer.

Creating a Group

To use SYSCON to create a group called *SYSOPS*, do the following:

1. Create a group object called SYSOPS.

2. Add a property called GROUP_MEMBERS to the SYSOPS property.

As you can see, very little happens when you create a group.

Adding Members to a Group

When you add a user to a group, SYSCON makes changes to both the user object and the group object. The following shows you how to add a user called GEORGE to the SYSOPS group:

1. Add the user object GEORGE to the GROUP_MEMBERS property of group SYSOPS.

2. Add the group object SYSOPS to the GROUPS_I'M_IN property of user object GEORGE.

3. Add the group object SYSOPS to the SECURITY_EQUALS property of user object GEORGE.

Removing a Member of a Group

To delete user GEORGE from the SYSOPS group, do the following:

1. Remove the group SYSOPS from the SECURITY_EQUALS property of object GEORGE.

2. The group SYSOPS was removed from the GROUPS_I'M_IN property of object GEORGE.

3. The user GEORGE was removed from the GROUP_MEMBERS property of group SYSOPS.

 Note: When you delete a user or a group, SYSCON simply makes one function call to delete the object. When the object no longer exists, all of its properties and values are inaccessible.

Giving a User or Group a Full Name

To use SYSCON to give a user or group a full name, do the following:

1. Add a property called IDENTIFICATION to the object if it does not already exist.

2. Write the full name string to the IDENTIFICATION property.

Adding a Console Operator

When you use SYSCON to define a user or group as a console operator, the file server object is modified. For example, on file server FS1, here is how the Supervisor adds the user GEORGE to the list of console operators:

1. If the property called OPERATORS for file server FS1 does not exist, create it.

2. Add the user GEORGE to the OPERATORS property of file server FS1.

How PCONSOLE Uses the Bindery

Like SYSCON, PCONSOLE's primary function is to allow modification to the Bindery. However, PCONSOLE is used for printing-related Bindery objects, while SYSCON was used primarily for users and groups. Here, consider a few of the operations that PCONSOLE can perform and what actually happens to the Bindery.

 Note: I've long felt that the functions of SYSCON and PCONSOLE should be combined into one network administration program. It seems silly to have these functions separate.

Creating a Print Queue

In the following example, you'll use PCONSOLE to create a print queue called INVOICES:

1. Create a print queue object called INVOICES. When the NetWare OS creates a print queue object, it automatically creates the properties called Q_OPERATORS, Q_USERS, Q_SERVERS, and Q_DIRECTORY. NetWare uses the Bindery object identifier to create a print queue directory for the INVOICES queue (below SYS:SYSTEM), and places the directory name in the Q_DIRECTORY property.

2. Add the user SUPERVISOR to the Q_OPERATORS property of the INVOICES object.

3. Add the group EVERYONE to the Q_USERS property of the INVOICES object.

Creating a Print Server

To create a print server called PS1, do the following:

1. Create a print server object called PS1.

2. Add a property called PS_USERS to the PS1 object.

3. Add a property called PS_OPERATORS to the PS1 object.

4. Add a property called ACCOUNT_BALANCE to the PS1 object.

5. Write unlimited credit limit and zero account balance values to the ACCOUNT_BALANCE property of object PS1.

6. Add user SUPERVISOR to the PS_OPERATORS property of object PS1.

7. Add group EVERYONE to the PS_USERS property of object PS1.

8. Create a directory below SYS:SYSTEM for print server PS1. The name of the directory is the Bindery object Identifier for object PS1.

Adding a Print Queue to a Print Server

If you want print server PS1 to service the INVOICES print queue, do the following:

1. Add print server PS1 to the property called Q_SERVERS of print queue INVOICES.

2. Create a file called QUEUE.000 in the Print Server directory.

Applications Usage of the Bindery

The NetWare Bindery is normally used for NetWare-related information, but it can be used by application programs as well. An application program can access the Bindery through NetWare function calls.

Note: Applications cannot create Bindery objects unless they have Supervisor access. However, once a Supervisor creates a Bindery object, any application can create properties and assign values to those properties. So, an Install program supplied by the application vendor and run by the Supervisor can create the objects and properties prior to the users running the application.

The Bindery can be used by programmers to store any information that does not need to exist in a file. The following suggestions show you ways that the Bindery can be used.

Configuration Information

The Bindery can store configuration information for applications for each user. Rather than storing user configuration information in a file somewhere, it can be placed in the Bindery. An application would not need to know where to find its configuration file—it would simply make Bindery function calls.

Internodal Communications

The Bindery can be used as a communications mechanism between workstations, where the messages passed could survive a network outage, such as a server crash. This would work very well for a NetWare 3.x server where Bindery objects are found in the Bindery very quickly. A NetWare 2.x server takes more time in searching the Bindery, so alternatives to the Bindery are more attractive to the programmer. One alternative to the Bindery is to use a *semaphore*—a Netware programming tool that is often used for software metering applications.

Copy Protection

Network versions of popular application programs often are protected from piracy in some way. A common technique is to place a *key file* in a server directory. If a user tries to run the application but the key file can't be found, the program will terminate.

Note: Many vendors will not admit that key files are for copy protection. They'll point out that key files serve other purposes as well—usually as a user benefit.

The application program often needs to have a certain drive letter point to the directory containing the key file. So, copy-protected network applications may not run if the drive letter is not right. This can be very frustrating for a Network Administrator who makes a change to user menus where the drive letters change.

A better approach (for the Network Administrator), would be for the application program to look to the Bindery for key-file-like information. Since only a Supervisor can create Bindery objects and Bindery security can be set to allow only Supervisors to make changes, this should satisfy most vendors.

Programs Which Attack the Bindery

Since the Bindery is central to NetWare security, you need to be concerned about how well the Bindery could survive attack. Hostile programs can damage the Bindery or fill the Bindery with confusing objects, properties, and values.

Currently, Novell does not offer any tools that a network administrator can use to see if the Bindery has been modified improperly. The tools supplied with NetWare, such as SYSCON and PCONSOLE, only allow you to edit the Bindery. However, there are third-party products, described in this chapter, that you can use to view the contents of the Bindery. In Chapter 13, "Audit Trail," you'll see how audit trail packages can be used to record Bindery changes and trace those changes to a user.

As this book goes to press, there are no known viruses or hostile programs that seek to attack the NetWare Bindery. Since altering the Bindery is so easy, it's likely that these types of programs *will* appear in time.

"Bindery Stuffers"

It's possible for a hostile program to fill the Bindery with objects. When a program fills up the Bindery with objects, problems are created. These problems are:

- No more objects can be added to the Bindery.
- It takes NetWare 2.x a long time to search a large Bindery.
- Larger Binderies consume more disk space.

    There is a limit to the size of the Bindery:

- For NetWare 2.x, the limit is 65,536 objects.
- For NetWare 3.x, the limit is 16,777,216 objects.

A program written to deliberately sabotage the Bindery would fill the Bindery with unique names of unknown object types and give them a lifetime of *static*. The static lifetime means that powering down the server and bringing it back up does not get rid of the Bindery objects. Creating unknown object types makes it stealthy. You won't be able to see the object with SYSCON, PCONSOLE, and so forth.

A NetWare 2.x server would suffer significant performance degradation due to a large Bindery, because it does not use an efficient method of finding Bindery objects quickly. NetWare 3.x can find them quickly regardless of the Bindery size. The only danger to a NetWare 3.x server is consumption of disk space. Filling a NetWare 3.x Bindery is unlikely since it can handle up to 16 million objects.

A Demonstration of Bindery Stuffing

At the Accelerated Learning Center, I developed a simple program called BINDFILL to demonstrate how a Bindery could come under attack. The program creates Bindery object names that are strings of hex characters. A counter increment and an ASCII string is created from the value. The first "user" is called "0000" and the last user would be "FFFF." BINDFILL used these "names" to create user accounts in the Bindery. I chose user objects because I wanted to be able to see them with SYSCON's User Information.

I ran this against a NetWare 2.x server. The program stopped after about six hours when the limit of the Bindery was reached. This tells us that changes to the NetWare 2.x Bindery do not occur very quickly. You'll have a little bit of time to react if you see unusual server behavior.

I then tried to run SYSCON to view these user objects. When I selected User Information, the Please Wait message appeared, and it persisted for about three minutes. I then saw the screen in Figure 7.1.

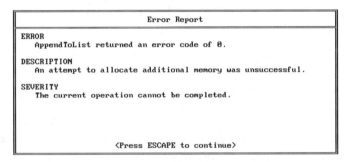

```
┌──────────────────────────────────────────────────────────────────┐
│                          Error Report                              │
├──────────────────────────────────────────────────────────────────┤
│ ERROR                                                              │
│     AppendToList returned an error code of 0.                      │
│                                                                    │
│ DESCRIPTION                                                        │
│     An attempt to allocate additional memory was unsuccessful.     │
│                                                                    │
│ SEVERITY                                                           │
│     The current operation cannot be completed.                     │
│                                                                    │
│                                                                    │
│                   <Press ESCAPE to continue>                       │
└──────────────────────────────────────────────────────────────────┘
```

Figure 7.1   The User Information Screen.

The problem is memory space. SYSCON does you a favor by sorting the user account names into alphabetical order by doing an in-memory sort. In this case, there were so many names that they couldn't fit in available memory for the sort.

The most significant problem with a large Bindery is performance. Whenever I ran a program that made Bindery function calls, there was at least a three-minute delay before the program went on beyond that point. A NetWare 3.x file server with the equivalent size Bindery runs far faster.

Once a Bindery grows in size, there appears to be no way to shrink it. Even if you get rid of Bindery objects, there seems to be no way to shrink the size of the Bindery files. The physical size of the Bindery files affects the performance of a NetWare 2.x file server.

Programs Which Attack the Bindery

Note: The only way to restore the Bindery files to their original size is to restore from a tape backup.

Counterfeit Bindery Objects

It's entirely possible for a program to insert a counterfeit Bindery object that is not what it claims to be. For example, a program could insert a file server object in the Bindery. A user could run the NetWare 2.x LOGIN program and try to log in to this nonexistent server. The user would not be able to log in to the server, causing much confusion and causing the Network Administrator to spend time troubleshooting a problem that does not really exist.

Detecting Corruption of the Bindery

How would you know that your Bindery was being filled or that counterfeit objects were being placed in it? Novell doesn't provide you with any tools to look inside the Bindery. There are a few third-party products available which can help. The best program I've used is BVDEBUG, described in the next section.

BVDEBUG

The BVDEBUG program is part of the BindView Plus 3.x product sold by the LAN Support Group. It is used to examine the contents of the NetWare Bindery. BVDEBUG was called BINDVIEW in earlier versions of the Bindview product. The LAN Support Group changed the focus of the overall product when they went to version 3.0.

BVDEBUG is a passive program. It can be used to view the contents of the Bindery, but it cannot change the Bindery. The Network Administrator can discover Bindery corruption as a result of using BindView.

It is menu-oriented and displays screens showing the names of Bindery objects. If you select a certain object, you can see the names of the object's properties and the values associated with those properties. If the object type is well known, the object's values are displayed in a user-friendly format. If the object is not well known, a hex/ASCII dump format is used.

When you run BVDEBUG, you see the main menu shown in Figure 7.2. You'll be working mostly with the View Bindery Objects menu item.

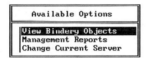

Figure 7.2   BVDEBUG Main Menu.

 Tip: BINDVIEW does a much better job of producing management reports, so you'll probably not use the Management Reports menu item much.

When you select View Bindery Objects, you'll see a list of the types of objects in the Bindery of your current server, plus a menu item called All Objects. You can see this in Figure 7.3. Notice that the Bindery for this server contains users, groups, print queues, file servers, print servers, and advertising print servers. If there were objects in the Bindery that were not well known, there would also be an item in the menu called Unknown.

Figure 7.3   BVDEBUG List of Object types.

If you select the All Objects menu item, you'll see a screen similar to Figure 7.4, which lists all the objects in the Bindery. If you select any other menu item, you'll only see a list of items of that specific object type. Notice that in Figure 7.4, the objects in the list are sorted by the name of the object type first, and then sorted by the name of the Bindery object name.

Bindery Object Name	Object Type	Object ID
ALCPRT	Adv Print Server	1100005D
ALC	File Server	3000001
LABELS	Print Queue	8000004
PAPER	Print Queue	5000024
POSTSCRIPT	Print Queue	9000004
ALCPRT	Print Server	F000003
ACCT	User	D000003
ADAMS	User	1E000008
ADMIN	User	1B000001
BACKUP	User	6000003
BETTS	User	32000005
BRAMMEIE	User	29000001
BUTLER	User	19000002

Figure 7.4   List of Bindery Objects.

You can then use the up and down cursor keys (as well as the PgUp, PgDn, Home and End keys), to highlight the object that you'd like more information about.

You then press the Enter key to select the object. Figure 7.5 shows what happens when you select the file server called ALC. Notice that another menu appears which lets you select from all the properties of the object.

Bindery Object Name		Object Type	Object ID
ALCPRT		Adv Print Server	1100005D
ALC		File Server	3000001
LABELS	ALC	Print Queue	8000004
PAPER		Print Queue	5000024
POSTSCRIPT	NET_ADDRESS	Print Queue	9000004
ALCPRT	ACCT_LOCKOUT	Print Server	F000003
ACCT	ACCOUNT_SERVERS	User	D000003
ADAMS	CONNECT_TIME	User	1E000008
ADMIN	DISK_STORAGE	User	1B000001
BACKUP	BLOCKS_READ	User	6000003
BETTS	Other Information	User	32000005
BRAMMEIE		User	29000001
BUTLER		User	19000002

Figure 7.5   Properties List of a selected Object

172

At this point, you can select any of the properties to see the values of those properties. You can also select Other Information to see additional file server information.

Figure 7.6 shows the additional menu that appears when you select Other Information. This lets you get a variety of information about that file server.

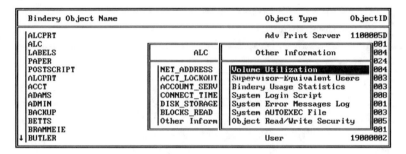

Bindery Object Name			Object Type	ObjectID
ALCPRT			Adv Print Server	1100005D
ALC				001
LABELS	ALC	Other Information		004
PAPER				024
POSTSCRIPT	NET_ADDRESS	Volume Utilization		004
ALCPRT	ACCT_LOCKOUT	Supervisor-Equivalent Users		003
ACCT	ACCOUNT_SERV	Bindery Usage Statistics		003
ADAMS	CONNECT_TIME	System Login Script		008
ADMIN	DISK_STORAGE	System Error Messages Log		001
BACKUP	BLOCKS_READ	System AUTOEXEC File		003
BETTS	Other Inform	Object Read/Write Security		005
BRAMMEIE				001
BUTLER			User	19000002

Figure 7.6   Additional Information about a file server object.

Note: Much of the information in Other Information does not come from the Bindery.

BindView Plus is a useful program for the network administrator. The BVDEBUG program that comes with it is invaluable for anyone concerned with the Bindery contents. This might include a Network Administrator concerned with Bindery attack or a programmer writing a program which makes Bindery function calls.

SECURITY

The SECURITY program has been supplied with NetWare for many years as a way to determine security "holes." The function of SECURITY has changed over the years, but the focus here will be on the latest version of SECURITY (at the time of printing).

```
SECURITY [/C]
```

The optional command-line switch /C will cause SECURITY to continuously display information to the screen. Without this switch, the program will pause when the screen becomes full and will continue with another pageful of information when you press any key to continue.

 Note: Since SECURITY interacts with the Bindery, you must be a Supervisor or equivalent to run this program.

SECURITY reports on the following security issues. Some of these, such as insecure passwords, are security problems or "holes," while others, such as Supervisor equivalence, are just there for your information.

- No password assigned
- Insecure passwords
- Password too short
- Supervisor equivalence
- Workgroup manager
- Root directory privileges
- No login scripts
- Excessive rights in certain directories
- User has not logged in for a certain time

Some of the security problems reported by the SECURITY program are obvious (in other words, No Password Assigned), while others are more subtle (in other words, Insecure Passwords). The following list presents some of the potential breeches in security that might be reported by SECURITY.

Insecure Passwords   This indicates that the password is the same as the user account name. For example, user BETTY has a password of BETTY. While current versions of SYSCON and SETPASS do not allow you to set your new password to your account name, older versions did.

Supervisor Equivalence   This is not saying that it is a mistake for a user to be equivalent to the Supervisor. It's simply reminding you that the user is equivalent to the Supervisor, in case you forgot and no longer want that user to be equivalent.

Root Directory Privileges   This means that the user has one or more rights in the root of the indicated volume. This is usually considered to be a serious security problem, because those rights tend to flow to all subdirectories of the root directory.

No Login Script   If a user does not have a login script, it is possible for another user to create a hostile login script for the user.

Excessive Rights In Certain Directory   You'll see this message when the user has more rights in a directory than are normally assigned. For example, if a user has write rights in SYS:PUBLIC, this is considered to be a security problem.

File and Directory Attributes

You can take advantage of file and directory attributes to protect files on your NetWare file server from deletion or unauthorized modification. If you're concerned about computer viruses or hostile users, this chapter is mandatory reading.

You should pay particular attention to the new attributes available in NetWare 3.x. If you're still running NetWare 2.x, the new attributes alone are a compelling reason to upgrade.

- File Attributes
- DOS Attributes
- NetWare Attributes
- Execute Only Files
- Hidden Files
- Setting Attributes
- Recommendations

File Attributes

A NetWare file server works in concert with the NetWare shell running in a workstation. Together, they look like a DOS file system to a DOS workstation user, an OS/2 file system to an OS/2 workstation user, and so on.

Operating systems, such as DOS, allow you to assign *attributes* to files and directories. The attribute specifies the actions that are either allowed or prohibited.

For example, a file with a *Read-Only* attribute can be read from but cannot be written to. Whether a user has the *rights* to open the file is another matter and is covered in Chapter 9, "NetWare Rights."

Even though attributes are linked to the rights that users have in directories, in this book these concepts are in different chapters so the distinction is kept clear. In this chapter, it is assumed that you have the needed rights to operate on a file or directory.

DOS Attributes

DOS supports all the following attributes:

- Archive Needed
- Hidden
- Read-Only
- System

Archive Needed (Files Only)

The *Archive Needed* attribute indicates that the file was modified since the last time it was backed up. Whenever a file is opened for write access, written to, and closed, DOS sets the Archive Needed attribute for that file. Your backup software clears this attribute once the file is backed up.

Hidden (Files and Directories)

Set the *Hidden* attribute when you don't want files and directories to be visible to the DIR command or any other program that searches for "normal" files or directories. An executable file whose Hidden attribute is set can still execute.

Read-Only (Files Only)

You can only read from a file whose *Read-Only* attribute is set. You cannot write to the file. Also, you cannot delete or rename a Read-Only file.

System (Files and Directories)

Set the *System* attribute when you do not want files and directories to be visible to the DIR command—or any other program that searches for "normal" files or directories. An executable file whose System attribute is set cannot be executed.

NetWare Attributes

NetWare has additional file and directory attributes that don't exist in DOS. However, NetWare 2.x and NetWare 3.x have dramatically different file systems, so some of their attributes are different.

NetWare 2.2 shares many of the same attributes with NetWare 3.x. Table 8.1 lists the attributes of files and directories that can be set by NetWare 2.15 and NetWare 2.2 or 3.x file systems.

Table 8.1 Attributes which different NetWare versions can set.

Attribute	NetWare 3.x Files	Dirs	NetWare 2.2 Files	Dirs	NetWare 2.15 Files	Dirs
Archive Needed	✓		✓		✓	
Copy Inhibit	✓					
Delete Inhibit	✓	✓				
Execute Only	✓		✓		✓	
Hidden	✓	✓	✓	✓	✓	✓
Index			✓		✓	
Purge	✓	✓				
Read Audit	✓		✓			
Rename Inhibit	✓	✓				
Shareable	✓		✓		✓	
System	✓	✓	✓		✓	
Transactional	✓		✓		✓	
Write Audit	✓		✓			

Copy Inhibit (3.x Files Only)

This attribute has significance to users who are using Macintosh workstations. It does not affect users at DOS or OS/2 workstations. It prevents a Macintosh user from copying a file.

It's unfortunate that this attribute does not apply to DOS users. This could be a nice way to prevent nonexecutable files from being copied. Unfortunately, if you can open and read a file, you can copy it.

Delete Inhibit (3.x Files and Directories)

This attribute prevents a user from erasing a file or directory. While you can accomplish the same thing (for files) by assigning the file a Read-Only attribute, the file cannot be opened for write access. *Delete Inhibit* allows you to prevent any file from being deleted—regardless of other file attributes.

Execute Only (3.x, 2.2, and 2.15 Files Only)

This attribute applies only to files with the .COM and .EXE extensions. It prevents the file from being copied, but allows the file to be executed. This attribute is explained in more detail later in this chapter.

Index (2.2 and 2.15 Files Only)

The index attribute is used to improve the performance of random access to large data files. The NetWare operating system uses a "Turbo FAT" to more quickly determine the location of the file on disk. This attribute has little to do with security, so it will not be explained in detail here. Refer to your NetWare manuals for more information.

This attribute is set in a NetWare 2.x file system with the FLAG command or with FILER. The notion of an indexed file also exists in NetWare 3.x, but it handles this attribute automatically. Whenever a file grows so large that it requires over 64 FAT entries, the NetWare 3.x file system automatically makes it an indexed file. This attribute has no known impact on NetWare security.

Purge (3.x Files and Directories)

When this attribute is assigned to a file, the file is purged as soon as it is deleted. These files cannot be salvaged by the NetWare SALVAGE utility.

This attribute is useful when a program needs to create temporary files that are deleted before the program terminates. The program can set the purge attribute so that the erased files are automatically purged. It is up to the program developer to put in this capability.

When a directory has the *Purge* attribute, any file within that directory is purged when it is deleted.

Read Audit (3.x and 2.2 Files Only)

This attribute first appeared in NetWare 3.0 documentation, but has not been implemented yet as this book goes to press. It is intended to be used for future audit trail purposes.

Rename Inhibit (3.x Files and Directories)

This attribute prevents you from renaming a file or directory. When a directory has the *Rename Inhibit* attribute, this only restricts you from renaming the directory. You can still rename files within the directory.

Shareable (3.x, 2.2, and 2.15 Files Only)

This attribute allows more than one user to open a file at the same time. If a file is not *Shareable,* it is called *Nonshareable.* A DOS application normally creates files that are Nonshareable. You must assign the Shareable attribute to the file to allow multiuser access.

Transactional (3.x, 2.2, and 2.15 Files Only)

This attribute signals the Transaction Tracking System that the file should be protected by TTS functions. This attribute also prevents the file from being deleted.

The Transaction Tracking System protects data file contents from corruption if a workstation or file server failure occurs while an application program was in the midst of a "Transaction." A transaction is generally regarded as an update of two or more files.

Write Audit (3.x and 2.2 Files Only)

This attribute first appeared in NetWare 3.0 documentation, but has not been implemented as this book goes to press (see *Read Audit*).

Execute Only Files

NetWare has supported a file attribute called *Execute Only* since early versions of Advanced NetWare. Many Network Administrators have never heard of this attribute because the description is usually buried in the manuals (which few people read). In the past, you could only set this attribute from a submenu in the

FILER utility. Modern versions of FLAG will also allow you to set this attribute.

The Execute Only attribute is supposed to prevent someone from copying the file from the file server to a local drive. The usual intention is to prevent someone from pirating software. When a file is marked as Execute Only, it cannot be opened, so it can't be copied. It can only be executed. You cannot remove the Execute Only attribute even if you are the Supervisor.

While Execute Only appears to be a useful attribute for security purposes, there are two cases when you should not use this attribute—when program overlays and configuration information are contained within the EXE file.

Overlays

When a programmer writes a program that requires more memory than can be safely assumed to be available in a computer, the programmer can use a technique called *overlaying*. The program loads only a portion of itself into memory. We'll call this portion the base program. When the program needs to execute program code that is not in memory, it loads that overlay code from disk.

Normally, overlay code is contained in a file called an overlay file. By convention, overlay files have a file extension of .OVL, though other extensions are possible. A base program called WP.EXE, for example, could fetch its overlay code from a file called WP.OVL. If you set WP.EXE to Executable Only, the program could still access its overlay code in WP.OVL.

Some programmers, who use overlays, put the overlay code in the program's .EXE file. If you set that .EXE file to Execute Only, the program cannot access its overlay code. As a Supervisor, there is nothing you can do to protect an .EXE file containing overlays from being copied. The solution must come from the programmer.

Configuration Information

Some programs store configuration information within the executable (.EXE) file. If the file is Execute Only, configuration information cannot be read from the file because the file cannot be opened. Also, configuration information cannot be written to the file because the file can't be opened for update. An example of this can be seen in older versions of WordPerfect. These programs stored configuration information within the main WordPerfect .EXE file.

There is nothing you can do about this, except to avoid setting the Execute Only attribute. Current versions of WordPerfect have solved the problem by writing configuration information to a separate file.

> **Tip:** In NetWare, you cannot undo the Execute Only attribute, but you can delete an Execute Only file— if you have delete rights in the directory and the file is not marked as Read-Only. You can then replace the Execute Only file with another file by the same name.

You can remove the Execute Only attribute by modifying the program's entry in the NetWare directory. This requires that you take down the server and access the NetWare directory directly with a disk sector editor program such as DISKED supplied with NetWare 2.x or NetUtils from Ontrack. This technique is beyond the scope of this book.

Hidden Files

Hidden files may seem like a good way to keep files away from those who shouldn't access them, but there are drawbacks to this approach. For example, anyone with search rights in a directory can run Novell's NDIR program to see all files—including hidden files. You could simply remove user access to the NDIR program, but it's easy for users to get their own copy of NDIR or to buy or write a program to list hidden files.

To truly "hide" hidden files, you'd have to remove a user's search rights in the directory. A user can't scan for hidden files if they do not have the search right in that directory.

Editing Hidden Files

A hidden file can still be opened, which could be confusing and may create a security problem. Suppose you edit a hidden text file. You know the name of the file so you type **EDIT** *filename* (where EDIT is the name of your editor program). NetWare will allow you to open the file and read it, even though it is hidden. This is normal and does not (by itself) represent a security problem.

When you save this text file, the editor may create a backup file by renaming the original file—usually by changing the file extension (FILENAME.BAK, for example). It will also create a new file with the original name. With most editor programs, the renamed old file still has the hidden attribute and the new file doesn't. Most editor programs do not preserve a file's attributes. The new file will appear in a DIR listing and anyone will be able to open it and see its contents.

 Caution: Hidden files are not a way to prevent users from displaying files or accessing them. The Hidden file attribute adds little to file security.

Setting Attributes

You can set file and directory attributes in NetWare using one of three programs that are supplied with NetWare. These are:

- FILER
- FLAG
- FLAGDIR

In addition to these Novell-supplied programs, there are third-party programs such as XTreeNet from XTREE Company. I'll focus on the Novell-supplied command-line programs here since they do the job well and are easy to use.

FILER

While the FLAG and FLAGDIR programs can be used to quickly view and set attributes from the command line, some people prefer a user-friendly, menu-oriented way of doing things. Novell provides this in the FILER program. The use of FILER is fairly intuitive. Help is always available by pressing the F1 key.

FLAG

The FLAG program is used to display or change the attributes of files in NetWare directories.

 Caution: Recent versions of the FLAG program supplied with NetWare 2.2 and 3.x have had minor differences in command-line syntax. Your version may not operate exactly as described here.

Viewing File Attributes

To display existing file attributes:

FLAG *directory|filespec* [SUB]

- *directory\filespec*: Specifies the directory and/or files that FLAG will display attributes for. If this is not specified, FLAG will show all files in the current directory.

- SUB (optional): Shows the attributes for the indicated files in the current directory as well as all subdirectories which are below the current directory.

  Figure 8.1 shows the results of entering **FLAG**.

 Tip: If you want the output of FLAG directed to a disk file, you can use the DOS redirection operator (>).

187

```
┌─────────────────────────────────────────────────────────────────────┐
│                                                                       │
│     RIGHTS.TXT              [ Rw S A - - -- - - - -- -- -- DI -- ]     │
│     IPX.TXT                 [ Rw S A - - -- - - - -- -- -- DI -- ]     │
│     ARTICLES.WRD            [ Rw - - - - -- - - - -- -- -- -- -- ]     │
│     LTR.TXT                 [ Rw S A - - -- - - - -- -- -- DI -- ]     │
│     TEST.DOC                [ Rw - - - - -- - - - -- -- -- -- -- ]     │
│     LAU.XLS                 [ Rw - - - - -- - - - -- -- -- -- -- ]     │
│     DUALPASS.TXT            [ Rw S A - - -- - - - -- -- -- DI -- ]     │
│     WATCHDOG.TXT            [ Rw S A - - -- - - - -- -- -- DI -- ]     │
│     WP.TXT                  [ Rw S A - - - - - - -- -- -- DI -- ]     │
│     FCC.TXT                 [ Rw S A - - -- - - - -- -- -- DI -- ]     │
│     TEST.SEC                [ Rw - - - - -- - - -- -- -- -- -- ]     │
│     TEST.TXT                [ Rw S A - - -- - - - -- -- -- DI -- ]     │
│     BIRTH.TXT               [ Rw S A - - -- - - - -- -- -- DI -- ]     │
│     WP.SEC                  [ Rw - - - - -- - - - -- -- -- -- -- ]     │
│     ED.TMP                  [ Rw - - - - -- - - -- -- CI -- -- ]     │
│     ED                      [ Ro S - - H Sy - P -- -- -- DI RI ]     │
│     LAU.TXT                 [ Rw S A - - -- - - - -- -- -- DI -- ]     │
│     486.TXT                 [ Rw S A - - -- - - - -- -- -- DI -- ]     │
│     ROLODEX.ASM             [ Rw - - - - -- - - - -- -- -- -- -- ]     │
│     FOOLPASS.BAT            [ Rw - - - - -- - - - -- -- -- -- -- ]     │
│     LIST.TXT                [ Rw S A - - -- - - - -- -- -- DI -- ]     │
│     FCC                     [ Ro - - - - -- - - -- -- -- DI RI ]     │
│     INIT.BAT                [ Rw - - - - -- - - - -- -- -- -- ]     │
│                                                                       │
│   H:\>                                                                │
│                                                                       │
└─────────────────────────────────────────────────────────────────────┘
```

Figure 8.1   An example FLAG listing.

Here are some examples of using the FLAG program.

FLAG *.DOC

Lists the attributes of all files with the DOC extension in the current directory.

FLAG *.TXT SUB

Lists the attributes of all files with the TXT extension in the current directory as well as the subdirectory tree.

FLAG *.EXE SUB > LPT1

Lists the attributes of all files with the .EXE extension in the current directory, as well as the subdirectory tree. Sends the output to the LPT1 port (which you may have captured).

8 — File and Directory Attributes

FLAG R:*.EXE SUB > H:FLAG.LST Lists the attributes of all files with the .EXE extension in the entire directory tree, starting with the directory that drive R: points to. That list will be written to a file called FLAG.LST in the directory that drive H: points to.

Changing File Attributes

To change file attributes:

FLAG *directory\filename* [+|- *options*] [SUB]

- *directory\filename*: Specifies the directory and/or files that FLAG will change attributes for. If this is not specified, FLAG will change the attributes for all files in the current directory or directory tree (if SUB is used).

- [+|- *options*]: Specifies which attributes to change. You can include as many options as you like on the command line. Optionally, each attribute may be preceded by a minus sign to subtract the specified attribute from the attributes that are already there. You may also use a plus sign to add an attribute, but this has the same effect as not using a plus sign.

- SUB: Changes the attributes for the indicated files in the current directory as well as all subdirectories which are below the current directory.

The options for setting attributes can be one or more of the following.

Table 8.2 File attribute options for FLAG.

Option	Attribute
ALL	(sets all except RA and WA)
CI	Copy Inhibit
A	Archive Needed
DI	Delete Inhibit
H	Hidden
N	Normal (The absence of all attributes)
P	Purge
RA	Read Audit
RI	Rename Inhibit
RO	Read-Only
RW	Read Write (The absence of Read-Only)
S	Shareable
SY	System
T	Transactional
WA	Write Audit
X	Execute Only

 Note: If you specify only an R option, FLAG interprets this to mean *Rename Inhibit*.

The following examples should give you a good idea about how the FLAG command can be used to change file attributes.

FLAG WP.EXE SRO — Sets the Shareable and Read-Only attributes of file WP.EXE in the current directory.

FLAG Z:*.* -A — Removes the Archive Needed attribute from all files in the directory that drive Z: points to (usually SYS:PUBLIC).

FLAG SCAN.EXE SRODIRI-A	Sets the Shareable, Read-Only, Delete Inhibit and Rename Inhibit attributes of file SCAN.EXE in the current directory and removes the Archive Needed attribute.
FLAG *.EXE X SUB	Sets the Execute Only attribute of all files with the .EXE extension in the current directory and the subdirectory tree.

FLAGDIR

FLAGDIR is the equivalent of the FLAG command except that FLAGDIR operates only on directories.

FLAGDIR *path* [*options*]

- ■ *path*: Specifies the directory that FLAGDIR will display attributes for. If this is not specified, FLAGDIR will show information for the current directory. You can use the DOS wildcard character (*) to indicate all subdirectories within the current directory.

- ■ *options*: Specifies which attributes to change. You can include as many options as you like on the command line.

Viewing Directory Attributes

If you just want to see the attributes for the current directory, type **FLAGDIR**. If you want to see the attributes for all the subdirectories, type **FLAGDIR ***. Figure 8.2 shows an example of displaying the attributes of the subdirectories of SYS:TEST. Notice that SYS:TEST is a "fake root" directory for drive R:— it appears to be the root of drive R:.

```
R:\>flagdir *
ALC/SYS:TEST/*
      TEMP           DeleteInhibit Purge RenameInhibit
      DATA           DeleteInhibit RenameInhibit
      PROGRAM        DeleteInhibit RenameInhibit
      KEY            DeleteInhibit RenameInhibit
      UTILITY        Normal

R:\>
```

Figure 8.2   Attributes of SYS:TEST subdirectories.

Changing Directory Attributes

The following table lists the options that can be used.

 Note: There is no SUB option for this command, so there is no way to set attributes for an entire directory tree.

Table 8.3   Directory attribute options for FLAGDIR.

Option	Attribute
DI	Delete Inhibit
H	Hidden
N	Normal (the absence of all attributes)
P	Purge
RI	Rename Inhibit
SY	System

The following examples will give you a good idea how to use FLAGDIR to control directory attributes.

FLAGDIR DIRI   Sets the Delete Inhibit and Rename Inhibit attributes of the current directory.

8 — File and Directory Attributes

`FLAGDIR SYS:PUBLIC DIRI`	Sets the Delete Inhibit and Rename Inhibit attributes of the SYS:PUBLIC directory.
`FLAGDIR SYS:APPS N`	Removes all attributes from the SYS:APPS directory.
`FLAGDIR SYS:PUBLIC\* DI`	Sets the Delete Inhibit attribute of all SYS:PUBLIC subdirectories. This does not set attributes for directories below SYS:PUBLIC subdirectories.

Recommendations

Now that you've read about what attributes do and how you can change them, you may need some guidelines on how to apply this information.

Executable Files

Executable files are those which have .EXE or .COM extensions. These files are especially important because they are the most likely candidates for virus infection or replacement with a Trojan horse program. You should focus your attention on protecting these files first.

Shareable

Executable files should be set to Shareable. If you don't set executable files to Shareable, you may have contention problems when two or more users try to run the same program at the same time and the executable program file contains overlays. There is no significant security penalty for setting files to Shareable.

Read-Only

 Tip: Set executable files to Read-Only to prevent the files from being modified and deleted.

You should not set an executable file to Read-Only if the program is self-modifying. A good example of a self-modifying program is the DOS V5 SETVER program. If you set it to Read Only, it will not function correctly. You can solve the problem by removing the Read Only attribute. All the Novell-supplied programs are not self-modifying and can be set to Read Only.

Execute Only

If you set executable files to Execute Only, these files cannot be opened for either read or write access. This would make it difficult for viruses to infect these files.

However, you should not set a file to Execute Only if the file contains overlays or the program must read configuration information from its file. If you do, the program will not function correctly. Exactly what happens depends on the program.

Workstations running Windows open executable files for read access while the programs are being executed. DOS does not do this. So, you cannot set executable files to Execute Only if you plan on running them from within Windows. Does this mean that Windows is a less secure environment than DOS? In this case, yes.

Program-Related Files

There are probably many files on your file server that are not executable, but need to be present for programs to run properly. Examples are DOS overlay files and Windows INI files. DOS overlay files usually have an .OVL extension, but this is by convention only. An overlay file can have any extension.

Tip: Set overlay files to Read-Only and Shareable so they can't be modified by a virus or deleted by a user, but they can be shared by many users.

You may have noticed that NetWare utility programs use several DAT files such as ERRHELP.DAT, SYS$ERR.DAT, and SYS$MSG.DAT. These must be Shareable since many users may need access to these files concurrently.

 Tip: Set the NetWare DAT files to Read-Only in order to protect them from modification and deletion.

Data Files

How should user or application data files be set? Your goal is to protect these files as much as possible while still allowing legitimate users access to the information within the files.

For those applications where multiple users need access to the same data files, the files often need to be set to Shareable so that they can be opened by multiple users. An application that is not NetWare-aware is likely to create data files that default to Nonshareable.

If you deliberately want to restrict a data file's access to one user at a time, you can set the file to Nonshareable. This may occur when an application wants to be the sole user of a configuration file. An example of this is NetWare's Bindery files. These files are Nonshareable and are constantly held open by the NetWare operating system.

A data file may be set to Read-Only if the file will not normally be modified. Use this in a database application, for example, where a price list database should never be changed by users. If you want to update the price list, you'd first need to remove the Read-Only attribute.

You'd set the Transactional attribute for only those files that you want to be protected by the Transaction Tracking System (TTS). Another benefit of a Transactional file is that it cannot be deleted.

Temporary Files and Purge

You'd set files to Purge when you want them to automatically be purged when they are deleted. The usual reason for this is to purge temporary files when you delete them.

Practically speaking, this doesn't work because the program that creates the temporary files must set the Purge attribute itself. Few, if any, programs do this—including Novell's own programs.

 Tip: To set the Purge attribute for temporary files, tell an application to put its temporary files in a directory where you've set the directory Purge attribute. Now, anytime a file is deleted in that directory it is automatically purged.

Print jobs in the NetWare print queue directories provide a good example of temporary files. It's a good idea to set all your print queue directories to Purge. After a print server services a print job, the file is deleted from the print queue directory. Without the Purge attribute set, print jobs are recoverable and consume disk space. On a busy file server, disk space can be filled with deleted print jobs quickly.

Delete Inhibit

You can set a file to Delete Inhibit when you want users to have read and write access to the file. You can also do this when you don't want them to be able to delete the file even though they possess delete rights in the directory. This is nice for those cases where users need delete rights in a directory because the application creates and deletes temporary files. You're unable to tell the application to store its temporary files in another directory. You want users to be able to write to data files, but you don't want users to delete the data files.

 Tip: Set data files to Delete Inhibit when users don't need to delete the data files. This is a wonderful security feature of NetWare (version 3.x only), that most people don't know about.

Directories

There are some directories on your file server that should never be deleted or renamed:

- SYS:PUBLIC
- SYS:SYSTEM
- SYS:LOGIN
- SYS:MAIL

Even though users don't generally have the rights to affect these directories, it's best to protect them.

 Tip: Set these directories to Delete Inhibit and Rename Inhibit. You'll probably want to protect most other directories on your server in the same way.

If you set a directory to Delete Inhibit, you're unable to delete the directory, but that doesn't necessarily stop you from deleting files within the directory. Also, if you set a directory to Rename Inhibit, you're unable to rename the directory. But, that doesn't necessarily stop you from renaming files within the directory.

CHAPTER 9

NetWare Rights

To access files within directories on NetWare volumes, you must have rights to the directories the files are contained in. Rights are a powerful security mechanism in NetWare. You can use them to control who has access to program and data files. In this chapter you'll see that NetWare 2.x allows users to have rights to directories on a NetWare volume. NetWare 3.x allows users to have rights to individual files within directories, in addition to the directories themselves.

Take care to assign users rights only when they need them to do their jobs. This simple rule goes a long way toward securing your server from hostile users, as well as viruses and Trojan Horse programs.

- Types of Rights
- Trustee Rights
- Viewing Your Rights
- Controlling Rights
- Mailbox Directories
- NetWare 2.15 Rights
- Recommendations

Types of Rights

Table 9.1 summarizes the rights in NetWare 2.2 and 3.x. NetWare 2.15 rights are, in some cases, different and are presented later in this chapter.

 Note: NetWare 3.x allows you to have rights to files within a directory even though you do not have rights to the directory. This concept will be presented later in this chapter.

Table 9.1   NetWare 2.2 & 3.x directory and file rights.

Required Right	Action
Create	Create directories and files
Erase	Erase files and subdirectories
Read	Open files and read from them
Write	Open files and write to them
Modify	Modify file attributes
Modify	Modify filename, ownership and dates/times
File scan	Search for files in the directory
Supervisory	All rights for directory tree (3.x only)
Access control	Control the rights of others

 Note: There is no Close right in NetWare. Anyone is allowed to close a file they've opened.

The rights that you can possess in a directory are described in this section.

Create

The Create right allows you to create new files or subdirectories. When you create a new file, it is automatically opened and you can write to it as well as read from it. Of course, it doesn't make sense to read from a file that was just created and has a length of zero. However, you do have the right to position the file pointer. So, you can create the file, write to it, reposition the file pointer and read the data you just wrote.

 Caution: Once you close the file, you can no longer modify the file unless you have Read or Write rights. With NetWare version 3.x, the Create right is required to salvage a deleted file.

Erase

This right allows you to delete files in the current directory. Even though you may have Erase rights, you're not able to erase files whose attributes are set to Read Only, Transactional, or Delete Inhibit.

The Erase right also lets you delete subdirectories as long as the subdirectories are empty and are not in use by other users. Even though you may have Erase rights, you're not able to erase directories whose Delete Inhibit attribute is set.

Read

This right allows you to open files and read them. Even though you may have the Read right, you cannot open a file whose Execute Only attribute is set. Also, you may not be able to read from a file if another user has the file open and has denied you read access.

Write

This right allows you to open files and write to them. Even though you may have the Write right, you cannot open (and later write to) a file whose Read Only attribute is set. Also, you may not be able to write to a file if another user has the file open and has denied you write access.

Modify

This right enables you to change attributes, names and date/time stamps of files and directories.

 Caution: This is a powerful right and should not be given to users unless required for them to run their applications. Hostile users and programs (such as viruses) would have a great deal of control if they could control file attributes.

File Scan

The File Scan right makes the files within the directory visible to you when you scan for them.

Scanning for files means that programs can use the DOS function calls Find First and Find Next. One such program is the DOS resident command DIR. If you do not have File Scan rights, you will get a message saying that there are no files found when you run DIR. Similarly, any program that searches the current directory for file names, like WordPerfect, will not find any files without this right.

Supervisor

This right gives you all rights to the directory, files within the directory, and subdirectories.

 This right does not exist in NetWare 2.2.

Access Control

The Access Control right allows you to modify the rights of others as well as control your own rights. You can assign rights to others that you yourself do not possess (except the Supervisory right in NetWare 3.x). However, since you can control your own rights, for all practical purposes, you have all rights.

 Note: If you are not a Supervisor or workgroup manager, you must use the GRANT command to assign rights. SYSCON and FILER will not allow you to do so.

Trustee Rights

If you have rights to a directory or file, you are a "trustee" to that directory or file. The rights that you possess are called "trustee rights." A user acquires trustee rights in a directory in three ways. These are:

■ A user is assigned rights to a directory by a Supervisor or by a user with Access Control rights.

■ A user acquires rights to a directory as a result of being security-equivalent to another user who has rights to that directory.

■ A user is a member of a group that has rights to the directory. A group is assigned rights to a directory by a Supervisor or by a user with Access Control rights.

The combination of all of these rights is a user's *trustee rights*.

 NetWare 2.x only supported trustees who had rights to directories. They had those rights to all the files in that directory.

NetWare 3.x allows trustees to individual files within the directory as well as to the directory itself. This gives the Network Administrator much more flexibility in the assignment of rights. The administrator, for example, could assign a user rights to certain files within a directory without giving the user rights to all the files in the directory.

 Note: The Create right changes somewhat when assigned to a file. It doesn't make sense to expect that Create rights to a file will allow you to create a file within an existing file. So, the Create right only enables you to salvage the file if it's deleted.

Viewing Your Rights

If you want to see the trustee rights that you possess in a directory, there are two programs to use:

- The SYSCON program (menu-oriented)
- The RIGHTS program (command-line-oriented)

You cannot view trustee rights directly with the SYSCON program, since trustee rights are a combination of your user rights, your group rights, and your security-equivalence rights. It is far simpler to use the RIGHTS program, which displays the trustee rights directly.

`RIGHTS [directory|drive]`

This command shows you the rights that you possess in the current directory, or a specific drive or directory you include on the command line. Figure 9.1 shows an example—the rights a Supervisor has in the SYS:LOGIN directory.

 Note: The RIGHTS program actually displays a user's *effective rights*. This concept is explained later in this chapter.

205

```
I:\LOGIN>rights
ALC\SYS:LOGIN
Your Effective Rights for this directory are [SRWCEMFA]
     You have Supervisor Rights to Directory.   (S)
   * May Read from File.                         (R)
   * May Write to File.                          (W)
     May Create Subdirectories and Files.        (C)
     May Erase Directory.                        (E)
     May Modify Directory.                       (M)
     May Scan for Files.                         (F)
     May Change Access Control.                  (A)

 * Has no effect on directory.

     Entries in Directory May Inherit [SRWCEMFA] rights.
     You have ALL RIGHTS to Directory Entry.

I:\LOGIN>
```

Figure 9.1   RIGHTS program display.

Controlling Rights

You can assign and delete rights in several ways. You use the following Novell programs to control rights:

- SYSCON
- FILER
- GRANT
- REVOKE
- REMOVE

SYSCON and FILER

SYSCON and FILER are menu-oriented programs which can be used to view and assign trustee rights. You can use both programs to control the rights of users and user groups. Once you understand rights and how to assign and revoke them with the command line programs such as GRANT, REVOKE and RE-MOVE, the use of SYSCON and FILER become intuitive. In this chapter, we'll focus on the command line utilities. You may decide to use the menu-oriented programs instead.

GRANT

The GRANT command is used to give users or groups rights to a directory. The syntax for the GRANT command is as follows.

```
GRANT [ONLY|ALL EXCEPT] rights [FOR path] TO
[USER|GROUP] name [options]
```

- **ONLY** Assign only the rights which follow next on the command line.

- **ALL EXCEPT** Assign all rights except the ones which follow next on the command line.

- *rights* The rights you wish to assign to the user or group.

 Note: Some versions of GRANT require that rights abbreviations are separated from one another by spaces.

- **FOR** *path* If you specify a path with the FOR operator, you are granting the user or group rights to the directory specified in *path*. If you do not use FOR, the current directory is assumed.

- **TO USER** You are granting rights to a user whose name follows next on the command line. Since a user is assumed to follow, you can leave the TO USER parameter out of the command line. However, including it may help you to remember the correct syntax and prevent potential mistakes.

- **TO GROUP** You are granting rights to a user group whose name follows next on the command line. Remember that there may be a user and a user group by the same name. If you want to assign rights to a user group and forget to include the TO GROUP directive, you'll assign the rights to the user of the same name, instead of to the group.

- *name* This parameter can be a user's account name or a user group name.

- *options* The options allowed are /S for Subdirectories and /F for Files. Novell manuals do not describe the function of these options, and they appear to have no function in our testing. I assume that the nonfunctional /S option is a bug in the current version of GRANT.

Table 9.2 summarizes the different rights that can be assigned by the GRANT command.

Table 9.2   Rights options for the GRANT command.

Abbreviation	Right
ALL	All rights except Supervisory
N	No rights
R	Read
W	Write
C	Create
E	Erase
M	Modify
F	File Scan
A	Access Control
S	Supervisory

The following examples will give you an idea of how to use the GRANT command.

GRANT R W TO TERRY

This adds read and write rights to a user called TERRY. Any rights that TERRY had before remain.

GRANT ONLY R F C W TO JOHN

This grants Read, File Scan, Create, and Write rights to JOHN. Any other rights that JOHN previously had are removed.

GRANT ALL EXCEPT M TO BETTY

This assigns all rights except the Modify (and Supervisory) to BETTY.

Note: Consider this statement—GRANT ALL EXCEPT ALL.... Even though GRANT doesn't complain about it, this statement doesn't do what you expect. It is equivalent to GRANT ALL..., when it should be equivalent to GRANT N.... I experiment with things like this because it's my job. If you *like* to do things like this, you really need to get out more.

REVOKE

The GRANT program lets you easily remove all rights by specifying N rights. It also lets you remove rights by using the ONLY operator. However, Novell offers another program called REVOKE to accomplish the same thing.

 Tip: Some people prefer to use GRANT when they're adding rights and REVOKE when they're removing rights. Others prefer to not use REVOKE at all and simply use GRANT for everything. The choice is yours. There are reasons, however, why you may wish to use REVOKE rather than GRANT. The /S and /F options that don't work with GRANT do work with REVOKE.

The command line for the REVOKE command looks like this:

REVOKE *rights* [FOR *path*] FROM [USER|GROUP] *name* [*options*]

- *rights*   The rights you wish to remove from the user or group.

- FOR *path*   If you specify a path with the FOR operator, you are removing rights to that directory from the user or group. If you do not use FOR, you are removing rights to the current directory.

- **FROM USER**   You are removing rights from a user whose name appears next on the command line. Since a user is assumed to follow, you can leave the FROM USER parameter out of the command line. However, including it may help you to remember the correct syntax and prevent potential mistakes.

- **FROM GROUP**   You are removing rights from a user group whose name follows next on the command line. Remember that there may be a user and a user group by the same name. If you want to revoke rights from a user group and forget to include the FROM GROUP parameter, you'll revoke the rights from the user of the same *name*, instead of the group.

- *name*   This parameter can be a user's account name or a user group account name.

- *options*   The options allowed are /S for Subdirectories and /F for Files. The /S option causes REVOKE to work on all subdirectories beneath the current directory. The /F option causes REVOKE to remove rights from files. If you use both /S and /F, REVOKE will remove rights from all files within the current directory and all subdirectories beneath it.

The following examples show how to use the REVOKE command.

REVOKE ALL FROM BILL /F	This revokes BILL's file rights to the files in the current directory.
REVOKE M E FROM MARY /S	This revokes MARY's Modify and Erase directory rights in the current directory and all other subdirectories beneath it.

REMOVE

This command is used to remove a user or group from the list of trustees in a directory.

REMOVE [USER|GROUP] *name* [FROM *path*] [*options*]

- **USER**   Indicates that the name that follows is a user account name. It is assumed that a user account name follows, therefore the USER parameter is optional.

- **GROUP** Indicates that the name that follows is a user group name. If your intention is to remove a user group from a trustee list, you *must* use the GROUP parameter.

- *name* This parameter can be a user's account name or a user group name.

- **FROM** *path* If you specify a path with the FROM operator, you are removing the user or group from the trustee list for the specified directory. If you do not use FROM, you are removing the user or group from the trustee list for the current directory.

- *options* The options allowed are /S for Subdirectories and /F for Files. The /S option causes REVOKE to work on all subdirectories beneath the current directory. The /F option causes REVOKE to remove trustee rights from files. You cannot use both /S and /F in the same command.

Note: When a user is no longer a trustee of a directory, the user may still have trustee rights in the directory as a result of belonging to a group, being security-equivalent to another user, or simply inheriting rights which flow down from directories above the current one.

The following examples show how to use the REMOVE command.

REMOVE BOB	This removes BOB as a trustee of the current directory.
REMOVE JANE FROM SYS:WP /S	This removes JANE as a trustee of the SYS:WP directory tree.

TLIST

This command is used to view the users and groups who are trustees of the directory specified by *path* or the current directory.

TLIST [*path*] [USERS|GROUPS]

- *path* If you specify a path, TLIST will report on directory specified in that path. If you do not include a path, TLIST will report on the current directory.

- USERS If you want to view only the users who are trustees, include USERS on the command line.

- GROUPS If you want to view only the groups who are trustees, include GROUPS on the command line.

 Note: If you do not specify either USERS or GROUPS, both Users and Groups will be listed. If you do specify either one or the other, you must include a path (a period will do for the current directory), or TLIST will assume that USERS or GROUPS is the path.

Here are some examples of how TLIST might be used.

TLIST	Views all the trustees of the current directory.
TLIST . USERS	Views only the user trustees of the current directory.
TLIST M:	Views all trustees of the directory that M: points to.
TLIST FS1/SYS:PUBLIC GROUPS	Views only group trustees of the SYS:PUBLIC directory on file server FS1.

 Caution: If you specify a file server that you are not attached to, this command will fail. It will not log you in to that server like certain other NetWare programs (CAPTURE, MAP) will.

Inheritance

When you have trustee rights in a directory, those rights are inherited by (or flow down to) lower-level directories and the files within those directories. So, for example, if you have Read and File Scan rights to SYS:PUBLIC, you also have Read and File Scan rights to every directory and file below SYS:PUBLIC. This is called *inheritance*.

 Caution: If you assign rights to a user in the root of volume SYS, the user will inherit those rights in all subdirectories of the root—unless you protect the directories with a mask (described in the next section). It's best not to make anyone a trustee of the root of any volume—especially SYS.

Inherited Rights Mask

If you don't want lower-level directories to inherit the rights of the directories above, you can block some or all of these rights from being inherited. You do this with the *Inherited Rights Mask* (IRM). There is an Inherited Rights Mask for every directory on your file server.

There is also an Inherited Rights Mask for every file on your file server. A file's IRM can block some or all rights from being inherited from the directory it resides in.

 Note: Only NetWare 3.x has the Inherited Rights Mask concept. Inherited Rights Masks do not apply to the SUPERVISOR account, a Supervisor-equivalent account or a user account that has the Supervisory right in the directory.

Figure 9.2 illustrates how trustee rights can be blocked from flowing down to child directories by the IRM. In this example, a user has all rights in the directory SYS:ACCT.

The Network Administrator defined the IRM for directory SYS:ACCT\DATA as:

- Create
- File Scan
- Erase
- Read
- Write

The IRM allows these rights to flow down to the SYS:ACCT\DATA directory, but blocks the Access Control and Modify rights.

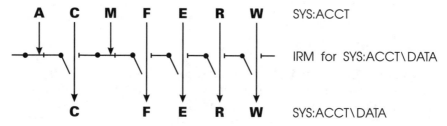

Figure 9.2   Example of the Inherited Rights Mask.

ALLOW

You can use the ALLOW program to view or set the Inherited Rights Mask of files or directories.

 Note: ALLOW is for NetWare version 3.x file servers only.

```
ALLOW path [TO INHERIT] rights
```

- ■ *path* If you want to view or change the IRM of a specific directory, path will point to that directory. If you want to view or change the IRM of a file or files, path will include a filespec.

- ■ `TO INHERIT` This parameter is not required but may help you remember the function of ALLOW. It cannot be abbreviated.

- ■ *rights* The rights that you want to assign to the IRM. Table 9.3 shows each right and the command abbreviation.

Table 9.3 Rights options for the ALLOW command.

Abbreviation	Rights
A	Access Control
ALL	All rights
C	Create
E	Erase
F	File Scan
M	Modify
N	No rights
R	Read
S	Supervisory
W	Write

Anybody can use ALLOW to view an IRM, but you must have Access Control rights (or be a Supervisor) to change the IRM. When you use ALLOW to set the IRM, the IRM will only have those inherited rights that you specify. Any rights that you do not specify are removed if they were present before.

ALLOW SYS:PUBLIC TO INHERIT F R

This sets the IRM of the SYS:PUBLIC directory to Read and File Scan. You'd do this to prevent SYS:PUBLIC from inheriting additional rights if those rights were present in the root of SYS:.

Controlling Rights

```
ALLOW SYS:PUBLIC\*.EXE R F
```
This sets the IRM of all files with the extension of EXE in the SYS:PUBLIC directory to Read and File Scan. This prevents the EXE files from inheriting any other rights from the SYS:PUBLIC directory.

Maximum Rights Mask

The *Maximum Rights Mask* (MRM) is similar to the Inherited Rights Mask in that they both have the words *Rights Mask* in them and they both affect user rights in some way. Beyond that, they are totally different concepts.

The MRM defines the maximum effective rights that any user account (except a Supervisor account) can have in a directory. Every directory on a NetWare version 2.x. file server has a MRM.

 Note: The Maximum Rights Mask does not apply to NetWare version 3.x.

The Maximum Rights Mask affects only the directory for which it is defined. A directory with a MRM will still inherit all the rights of its parent, but the MRM will not allow users to have rights not specified in the MRM. An MRM will *not* prevent rights from flowing down the tree to lower-level directories.

Effective Rights

Effective rights are the actual rights a user has in a directory (or to a file), when the following are all considered:

■ Trustee assignments
■ Inheritance

- Inherited Rights Mask (NetWare 3.x only)
- Maximum Rights Mask (NetWare 2.x only)

Effective rights on a NetWare version 3.x server are different from effective rights on a NetWare version 2.2 server.

Effective Rights (3.x)

Effective rights to a directory are determined in one of two ways:

- If you do not have a trustee assignment to the directory, your effective rights to the directory are equal to your effective rights to the parent directory, minus any rights blocked by the directory's Inherited Rights Mask.

- If you have a trustee assignment to the directory, your effective rights are equal to your trustee assignments, regardless of the parent directory or the Inherited Rights Mask.

Trustee Rights vs. Inherited Rights

There is a big difference between giving a user a trustee assignment of *no rights* and not giving a trustee assignment at all in a directory. By giving the user a trustee assignment of *no rights,* you prevent that user from inheriting any rights from the parent directory. By not giving a trustee assignment at all to a directory, you allow the user to inherit rights from the parent directory.

Effective rights to a file are very similar. If you do not have a trustee assignment to the file, your effective rights to the file are equal to your effective rights of the directory containing the file, minus any rights blocked by the file's Inherited Rights Mask. If you have a trustee assignment to the file, your effective rights to the file are equal to your trustee assignments.

Effective Rights (2.x)

Effective rights to a directory on a NetWare 2.x server are also determined one of two ways:

- If you have a trustee assignment to the directory, your effective rights are equal to your trustee assignment for the directory, minus the Maximum Rights Mask for the directory.

- If you do not have a trustee assignment to the directory, your effective rights are equal to your trustee rights in the parent directory, minus the Maximum Rights Mask of the directory. You can ignore the parent directory Maximum Rights Mask.

Mailbox Directories

When you install NetWare, a directory tree is created on volume SYS: which starts with the directory called MAIL in the root of the volume. The subdirectories of SYS:MAIL are *mailbox directories* for user accounts. They are called mailbox directories because they were once used by Novell's Electronic Mail System (EMS) to store e-mail messages. Novell no longer supplies EMS with NetWare, but the directory tree remains because it is used for other things.

Mailbox directories are used to store a user's login script and print job configuration file. Some electronic mail packages use the mailbox directories for storing mail messages. Postmaster and The Noteworks are examples of this.

In order to support electronic mail, NetWare's installation procedure assigns the user group EVERYONE Create and Write rights to the SYS:MAIL directory.

 Caution: Since all users are members of the EVERYONE group and since inheritance causes the Create and Write rights to flow down to all user mailbox directories, any user can create and write to a file in any other user's mailbox directory.

Login Scripts

A user's login script is kept in a file called LOGIN, located in the user's mailbox directory. You need to be very careful to ensure that you have a login script. If you don't, someone can give you one. If you're a Supervisor and you don't have a login script, someone can give you a hostile login script. Suppose the login script is as follows:

```
MAP R:=SYS:
DRIVE R:
#GRANT ALL TO EVERYONE
DRIVE F:
```

When you log in (using this script), you'll unknowingly give all rights to the root of SYS: to everyone. Since rights flow down to subdirectories, everyone will have rights everywhere—including SYS:SYSTEM.

Solutions

Novell has engineered a fix to this problem (first released with NetWare 3.11). It solves the problem by placing zero-length files called LOGIN and LOGIN.OS2 in the user mailbox directory whenever the user is created.

 Note: Earlier versions of NetWare do not have this feature and you must solve this problem in one of the ways discussed in the following sections.

Remove Group Rights

There are a few solutions to the security problem of mailbox directories. The first is to remove all rights for the group EVERYONE from the SYS:MAIL directory. Users will no longer have any rights in the mailbox directories of other users. They will continue to have rights in their own mailbox directories. They will need these rights for their login script and print job configurations. You cannot do this if you are using an electronic mail package that uses these directories.

Replace Missing Login Scripts

The second way to solve this problem is to make sure that all users have login scripts. The best way to ensure this is to always create users with the MAKEUSER or USERDEF utilities rather than manually with SYSCON. This solution is not bulletproof because a user may decide to eliminate his or her login script file in the mailbox directory. This also does not ensure that existing users have login scripts.

You can determine which user accounts on your server have no login scripts in a few ways. The most obvious is to use Novell's SECURITY program to check for user login scripts. Another program called SCANT will also report if a user does not have a login script. SCANT is a NetWare security scanning program which is meant to be used in conjunction with Novell's SECURITY program.

Disable User Login Scripts

A third solution is to prevent user login scripts from running. If you do this, you'll probably have to add a significant amount of functionality to the system login script to compensate for the lost functionality in the user login scripts. You disable user login scripts by placing an EXIT statement in the system login script.

 Caution: Users may resent having their login scripts taken away. If you do this, it's best to do it before your users discover the convenience of login scripts.

Even though you disable login scripts, users can still invoke DOS batch files automatically. This is done by creating home directories for all users. In the system login script, put the following statements at the end:

```
MAP H:=SYS:HOME\%LOGIN_NAME
DRIVE H:
EXIT "INIT"
```

Now create a DOS batch file called INIT.BAT and place it in each user home directory. This batch file will execute each time the user logs in. Unfortunately, DOS batch files don't have the rich set of NetWare identifier variables that a login script has.

NetWare 2.15 Rights

NetWare 2.15 has been replaced by NetWare 2.2 and is, therefore, obsolete. However, there are still a significant number of NetWare installations running 2.15, so this section deals just with NetWare 2.15 rights.

The names of rights in NetWare 2.2 are, in some cases, different than the names in 2.15. Table 9.4 shows the name differences. For some rights, the action that 2.15 takes is different from 2.2 or 3.x. These differences are discussed in more detail following the table.

Table 9.4   Rights in NetWare 2.15 vs. NetWare 2.2.

Actions	2.15 Rights	2.2 Rights
Control trustee rights	Parental	Access Control
Create directories and files	Create	Create
Erase files	Delete	Erase
Open files	Open	(not used)
Modify file attributes	Modify	Modify
Read from files	Read	Read
Search for files	Search	File Scan
Write to files	Write	Write

Parental

This right is similar to the Access Control right in NetWare 2.2 and 3.x. This allows you to control the rights of other trustees within the directory. NetWare versions below 2.15 require that you possess this right to create or delete subdirectories as well.

Open

This right is unique to NetWare 2.15 and earlier versions of NetWare. It does not exist in NetWare 2.2 or 3.x. You must possess this right to open a file before reading from it or to open an existing file before writing to it.

Read

This right lets you read from an open file. In NetWare 2.15 you also need to have the Open right to read from a file. In NetWare 2.2 and 3.x, the Open right is implied when you possess the Read right.

Write

This right allows you to write to open files. In NetWare 2.15, you could not write to an existing file if you did not also possess the Open right.

Recommendations

You may be overwhelmed with all the ways that you have to control user rights. Some recommendations are in order to start you on your way. You'll probably figure out other ways of controlling rights that work for you.

User Groups

Rather than assigning trustee rights to individual users, assign users to user groups. Then, assign trustee rights to the user group. This makes it easier to assign rights and to change those rights in the future.

Mask Rights

Even though users and groups have no trustee rights to SYS:SYSTEM, they could easily inherit rights if they are assigned trustee rights to the root of volume SYS. Even though you would never assign users rights to the root of SYS, it's best to protect the SYS:SYSTEM directory—just in case.

 For NetWare 3.x, set the Inherited Rights Mask for the SYS:SYSTEM directory to no rights.

 For NetWare 2.x, set the Maximum Rights Mask (using FILER) for the SYS:SYSTEM directory to *no rights.*

 Tip: You can use this technique to protect other directories as well. For SYS:PUBLIC, you can set the mask to Read and File Scan. Remember that the mask applies to all users except the Supervisor and equivalents.

Ensuring No Rights (3.x)

If you want to be sure that a user does not inherit rights to a directory, make that user a trustee of the directory, but assign the user no rights. Now the user does not have any rights regardless of the user's trustee rights in the parent directory.

Application Security

Many popular applications that run on personal computers today were developed in the days before local area networks were commonplace. As a result, these applications had little in the way of security. A common concern of users on a network is that the Network Administrator(s) have access to any information stored on the network file servers. Conventional wisdom says that you have no business being on a LAN if you can't trust your Administrators. After all, this is no different from mainframes. In a mainframe environment, there is always someone who has access to "your" data. However, Network Administrators do not necessarily need to have access to all data in an organization. In this chapter, I'll focus on the ways that user data can be kept private on a network.

There may be legitimate concern about keeping your data private on a network. The topics covered in this chapter will help you to do this. They are as follows:

■ Security Built into Applications
■ External Encryption

Security Built into Applications

Many application programs now have encryption features built in. This means that users can encrypt their data files when they store them to disk. If the "disk" is the NetWare file server, other users cannot see the contents of these data files without knowing the encryption "key" or "password." We'll now see how popular application programs handle this encryption.

WordPerfect

WordPerfect 5.x has a built in encryption mechanism that is user-controlled. The user can encrypt a document by assigning it a password.

The user does this by pressing **Ctrl-F5** and then selecting `Password`. Figure 10.1 shows the menu item that appears. You'd select item **1** to add a password to this document or change an existing password. If you no longer want the document encrypted, you'd select item **2**.

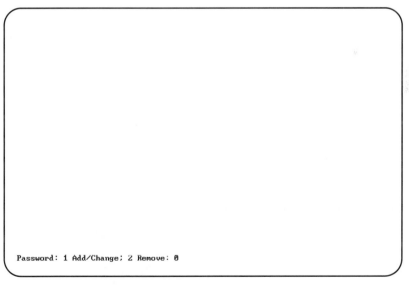

Password: 1 Add/Change: 2 Remove: 0

Figure 10.1   WordPerfect password prompt (Ctrl-F5, P).

Tip: If you use a mouse with WordPerfect, you can pull down the **File** menu and select `Password` as shown in Figure 10.2.

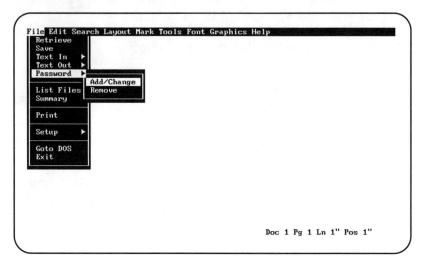

Figure 10.2   WordPerfect password menu.

In the future, when the user wishes to edit or print an encrypted file, he or she must first supply the password.

 Note: Many users and network administrators are not aware that WordPerfect can encrypt files. One reason for this is the WordPerfect manual refers to this feature as *locking.* To someone familiar with networks, *locking* is something an application does when only one user should be able to modify the document at a time.

Quattro Pro

Borland's Quattro Pro spreadsheet program lets you encrypt files by assigning them a password. The password you assign the file may be up to 15 characters.

Note: Quattro Pro passwords are case-sensitive.

 Encrypting Files in Quattro Pro

1. With the spreadsheet displayed on the screen, select /**File**, and then **Save As**.

2. Enter the file name, followed by a space and then the letter P. Press **Enter**. (See Figure 10.3.)

3. Enter a password (up to 15 characters), at the password prompt.

4. Enter the password a second time to verify.

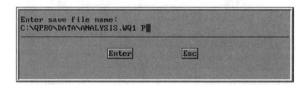

Figure 10.3   Saving a password-protected file in Quattro Pro.

Excel

Microsoft Excel encrypts files when you assign a password to the file. The password is case-sensitive and is limited to 16 characters.

Security Built into Applications

Encrypting Files in Excel

1. With the spreadsheet displayed on the screen, select **File**, and then **Save As**.

2. Click on the **Options** button.

3. Type a password in the Protection Password text box and choose OK. (See Figure 10.4.)

4. Retype your password and choose OK.

5. At the File Save As box, choose OK.

Figure 10.4   The Excel Save As Options dialog box.

When you open the file in the future, you'll be prompted for the password.

Lotus 1-2-3

Lotus *1-2-3* lets you encrypt files by assigning them a password. The password you assign the file may be up to 15 characters.

 Note: Lotus *1-2-3* passwords are case-sensitive.

Encrypting Files in Quattro Pro

1. With the spreadsheet dis-played on the screen, select /**File Save** command.

2. Enter the file name, followed by a space and then the letter **P**. Press **Enter**. (See Figure 10.5.)

 Note: If you are protecting a file that has already been saved, simply press the spacebar and then the letter P.

3. Enter a password (up to 15 characters), at the password prompt.

4. Enter the password a second time to verify.

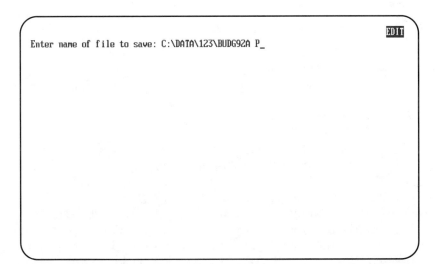

Figure 10.5   Saving a password-protected file in Lotus 1-2-3.

Forgotten Passwords

If the user forgets a file's password, the document cannot normally be recovered. Passwords also may not be available when the employer-employee relationship deteriorates to the point where the employee refuses to provide the passwords.

Most vendors of application software will not help you decrypt your file under these conditions. They worry about the legal ramifications. However, there are solutions to forgotten passwords.

Password Recovery Software

One solution to this concern is to have *password recovery software* available for those times. These software products allow you to break the password protection on many data files. One company that provides password recovery software is AccessData in Orem, Utah. They offer the following products:

Product	Decrypts files produced by:
WRPASS	WordPerfect
LTPASS	Lotus 1-2-3, Quattro Pro, Symphony
XLPASS	Microsoft Excel
PXPASS	Paradox

 Note: LTPASS recovers encryption passwords from most Lotus 1-2-3, Symphony, and Quattro Pro files. LTPASS successfully recovered encryption passwords from Symphony versions 1.2 (.WRK) and 2.0 (.WR1), Lotus 1-2-3 versions 2.01 and 2.2 (.WK1), Lotus Educational Version (.WKE), and Quattro Pro (.WQ1). LTPASS did not recognize Quattro Pro 1.x (.WKQ) and Quattro Pro's compressed formats (.WQ!, .WKZ, .WK$, .WK!) as being encrypted, even though they were.

Each program has its own unique features, but the steps for recovering a password are very similar for all of them. Here is an overview:

1. You're first prompted for the software access code. To prevent unauthorized use, an access code is coded into each program. This code is printed in the manual and is required to run the program.

2. After you've entered the access code, you're prompted for the encrypted file name. You can enter a file name with a full path, or press F5 to enter list files mode. You can then use the arrow keys to select a file to recover.

 Tip: If you want to recover multiple files, you can use wildcard characters in the file name, or select multiple files with the space bar while in list files mode.

3. You're now prompted for the type of file. This varies from one program to the next.

   - PXPASS prompts for a Paradox Table or Script file.

   - RPASS prompts for WordPerfect Version 4.2 or Versions 5.0–5.1.

   - LTPASS asks for Lotus 1-2-3 Versions 2.0–2.2 or 4.0–3.1.

   - XLPASS needs to know which of the three possible Excel passwords to recover.

   - Each program, except XLPASS, also has an Unknown option. You should select this option if you don't know the type of the file.

4. WRPASS, LTPASS, and XLPASS ask one additional question—the *level of analysis*. This determines how complex of a statistical model to use in determining the password. A more complex model takes longer, but has a better chance of success.

 Tip: Start with the *quick* recovery model. If this does not recover the password, move on to the *regular* and then to the *in-depth* models. You'll recover most passwords with the *quick* model.

233

5. If you selected multiple files to recover, the program will ask if you want to create an OUTPUT.DOC file. This is a text file that contains the name of each file recovered and the password for the file.

6. At this point, the program will start trying to recover a password. The WRPASS, LTPASS, and XLPASS programs run for a determined length of time and show a "thermometer" on the screen to show progress. When the meter reaches 100%, the program will display the recovered passwords.

 Note: The PXPASS program uses a different method to recover passwords. The decryption process is based on statistical patterns that exist in the encrypted file. This process could take from a few seconds to more than 30 minutes, depending on the file, and on the power of the computer running the program.

7. WRPASS, LTPASS, and XLPASS will display the actual password used to encrypt the file. PXPASS cannot recover the actual password used, but it will determine a password that will work to unlock the file.

There is a security feature to prevent WRPASS, LTPASS, and XLPASS from recovering a password. If the password contains an underscore (_) character, the program will refuse to display the recovered password. This gives users the ability to protect files against unauthorized access by someone with a copy of one of these programs. This feature does not exist in PXPASS.

External Encryption

When an application does not provide for encryption of data files, the encryption may still be done with external programs—but there are tradeoffs. On the negative side, encryption done outside

234

the application usually means another step for the user to perform if the external encryption process cannot be automated in some way.

On the positive side, external encryption products generally use more secure encryption techniques. It would be far more difficult to decrypt a WordPerfect file that was encrypted with Central Point's PC Secure program, for example, than if the file was encrypted by WordPerfect. There are numerous external encryption products on the market. The following is a partial list:

Company	Product
Central Point Software	PC Secure (part of PC Tools)
Fischer International	Watchdog
PKWare	PKZip
Richard Levey	Noah's File Encryption Utilities

These products use either standard encryption algorithms, like DES, or proprietary algorithms that the vendor has designed. Generally, DES encryption is more secure, but the proprietary algorithms are faster.

Performance Issues

One consideration with encryption is the time it takes to encrypt a file. I ran performance tests to determine how long it takes to encrypt and decrypt a standard test file. For the test file, I chose the !NETWARE.NFO file that usually resides in the SYS:PUBLIC directory.

This file is 1,114,112 bytes in size. All the following tests were done on a PC with a 80486-33 MHz processor, ISA (AT) bus running at 8 MHz, an Adaptec 1542 SCSI controller with a Seagate ST2209N SCSI drive. Both source and destination files were located on the local drive.

The first test encrypted the files using the full DES encryption. The results are shown in the following table:

Table 10.1   Encryption and decryption rates for !NETWARE.NFO—full DES encryption.

Program	DES encryption		DES decryption	
	Time to encrypt	Data rate	Time to decrypt	Data rate
Noah DES	17:39	1.00 KB/s	17:10	1.08 KB/s
Noah 386	7:52	2.36 KB/s	7:36	2.44 KB/s
PC Secure	1:36	11.60 KB/s	1:37	11.49 KB/s
Watchdog	0:40	27.85 KB/s	0:19	58.64 KB/s
Watchdog/ Armor	0:16	69.63 KB/s	0:09	123.80 KB/s

As you can see from the chart, the Noah DES programs are the poorest performers while the Watchdog products from Fischer International are the fastest of those tested. The Watchdog/Armor product uses a circuit card which included DES hardware.

Table 10.2 lists those programs that use encryption techniques other than DES. The table includes a column (%) which tells you the percentage of file compression. Central Point Software's PC Secure can also compress files as it encrypts. Note that, once again, Watchdog turns in the best performance numbers.

Table 10.2   Encryption and decryption rates for !NETWARE.NFO—non-DES encryption techniques.

Encryption technique	Encrypt the test file			Decrypt the test file	
	(%)	Time (min:sec)	data rate (KB/s)	Time (min:sec)	data rate (KB/s)
PC Secure					
DES/compress	17	0:56.9	19.58	1:02.7	17.77
Quick/compress	17	0:25.7	43.35	0:32.1	34.71
Quick/no compress	0	0:18.4	60.55	0:18.8	59.26
PKZip					
-s option	37	0:27.5	40.56	0:09	123.79
Watchdog					
Proprietary	0	0:05	222.80	0:04	278.5

10 — Application Security

Noah's File Encryption Utilities

These programs are notable because they're available for download on CompuServe. They are called DES.ZIP and DES386.ZIP. You can find them in the NOVLIB forum. These are shareware programs written by Richard Levey. They both implement the DES encryption algorithm, but DES386 is meant to run on a 80386-based workstation.

PC Secure

This program is included with Central Point's PC Tools package. It uses DES encryption as well as the vendor's own proprietary encryption algorithm. Since it is bundled with PC Tools, there are probably more copies of PC Secure in the hands of LAN users than any other DES encryption product.

 Caution: Our tests show that PC Secure has difficulty encrypting an entire directory tree. Certain directories get skipped in both the encryption and decryption process. They are not always the same directories—*ouch!* To be safe, encrypt one directory at a time.

PKZip

PKZip is a well-known file compression program, offered by PKWare, that can also encrypt your files as it compresses them. The encryption is proprietary. Given its encryption performance and compression, it makes a very usable general-purpose encryption tool.

CryptDir

You're likely to have files on your file server that have been encrypted by various programs. In the same directory, you may have files encrypted by WordPerfect, Lotus 1-2-3, and PC Secure. How do you tell them apart?

External Encryption

CryptDir is a program offered by the Accelerated Learning Center that scans your directory and lists encrypted files and the program that was used to encrypt them. Figure 10.6 shows a sample CryptDir display.

```
H:\>cdir
CryptDIR V1.0  by The Network LockSmith
ED.TMP        is encrypted by WordPerfect
LAU.XLS       is encrypted by Microsoft Excel
NUMBER1.WQ1   is encrypted by Quattro Pro
NUMBER2.WQ1   is encrypted by Quattro Pro
TEST.DOC      is encrypted by WordPerfect
TEST.SEC      is encrypted by WordPerfect
TEST.TXT      is encrypted by WordPerfect
WP.SEC        is encrypted by WordPerfect

H:\>
```

Figure 10.6   *Displaying encrypted files with CryptDir.*

 Note: CryptDir is able to detect only those encrypted files where the vendor places information in the file that identifies the encrypting program.

Noah's programs, for example, do not place such information in the files, so CryptDir is unable to detect these encrypted files. PC Secure also includes version information, so CryptDir will tell you which version of PC Secure encrypted your files.

CHAPTER 11

Menus

One of most Network Administrators' concerns is to protect users from the intricate details of "being on a network." It's best to hide as much of this detail as possible. One way to do this is to provide each user with a menu. The user simply selects the application they want to run from the menu. Everything else happens automatically.

Some Network Administrators view menus not only as a user convenience, but as a security mechanism as well. The thinking is, "If a user can get to the DOS prompt, there's opportunity for trouble." This chapter focuses on the security aspects of providing users with menus.

- NetWare Menus
- Batch File Menus
- Applications Which Call DOS
- NetMenu

NetWare Menus

Novell's menuing system (supplied with NetWare), is used by many network administrators to insulate users from the underlying details of the network. At times, these Network Administrators also find it desirable to restrict certain (or all) users to the menu so they never get out of the menu to the operating system.

This is difficult to ensure with the Novell menu system, because you can escape from the menu by using the Escape key. Also, Novell's MENU program was created with a C language library package called C-Worthy. The C-Worthy package provides a back door to all of these menus via the Alt-F10 key sequence. Figure 11.1 shows what happens when you press the Alt-F10 key sequence. If you answer Yes, you find yourself back at the operating system prompt.

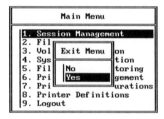

Figure 11.1   Example of a NetWare Menu.

Batch File Menus

Many Network Administrators build their own menuing systems out of DOS batch files. The advantage to this is the absence of a back door to DOS. You can build a menuing system that is very difficult to escape from, as long as you include the BREAK OFF statement within your batch file.

Note: It's not impossible to break out of a DOS batch file program—just difficult.

Within your batch file you can use DOS programs to put up menu items on the screen and prompt for menu choices. Usually one choice is to log out of the network. You may elect to put in the capability to exit to DOS if you choose, or you can write the batch file program to prevent it.

The Accelerated Learning Center has developed programs that can be used within DOS batch files to create professional-looking menus.

There are other commercially available menuing systems that are very secure. One very popular package is the Saber Menuing System. Saber is popular because it was one of the first menuing systems for NetWare. Menus that you design with Saber can be very secure. The Saber Menuing System now includes features such as software metering and auditing. It can prevent a user from escaping out of the menu to DOS. Recent versions of Saber support Windows.

Note: Saber is not a product that works "right out of the box." Expect to spend several days working with Saber before you're an "expert" menu designer.

Applications Which Call DOS

Prohibiting a user from exiting the menuing system does little good if the user can run an application which supports an Exit to DOS function. These functions work by loading in another copy of the DOS command processor, usually the COMMAND.COM program supplied with PC DOS and MS-DOS. When you're finished running your applications from the secondary command processor's DOS prompt, you type **EXIT** to return to your original application.

Most programs provide no way to disable this Exit to DOS feature. One way to disable it is to set the user's COMSPEC variable (in the child environment), to a directory that does not contain a copy of COMMAND.COM. To do this, just set the COMSPEC variable before calling the application, as in the example below.

```
SET COMSPEC=C:\TEMP\COMMAND.COM
```

In this example, there is no COMMAND.COM in the C:\TEMP directory.

 Caution: The downside of this is that the workstation will lock up with no way to get back to the parent program. The user must reboot DOS, reload the NetWare shell, and so forth—an awful solution.

Dummy Command Processors

There is a much more clever approach to disabling an application's Exit to DOS function. You can set the COMSPEC variable to point to a directory which contains your own special program called COMMAND.COM. Instead of providing the normal Command processor, your program tells the user that escape is impossible and to press any key to go back to the menu system, then exit. Control will return to the calling program. You'll find this easy to do if you're a programmer. If you're not a programmer—find one.

Alternatively, your program can produce screen output which appears as if the real COMMAND.COM is loading. You can even print a DOS prompt and wait for keyboard input, returning interesting error messages when users try to run applications. When they type **EXIT**, you can return them to the menu. Make sure that they don't call IBM or Microsoft to complain about the strange operation of their programs.

Custom Command Processors

Probably the ultimate solution is to build your own command processor, which *includes* the menuing system. This has many benefits:

- You totally control the user environment.
- There is no PATH variable (unless you implement it).
- There is no APPEND command.
- It restricts programs that the user can run.
- It can prompt for passwords when appropriate.
- It can implement an inactivity keyboard-locking feature.

With a custom command processor that is written to be a menuing system, an application that tries to Exit to DOS is calling the menuing system. So, escape from the menuing system is nearly impossible.

While building a custom command processor is beyond the scope of this book, there are books which do show you how. One such book is *Advanced MSDOS*, written by Ray Duncan and published by Microsoft Press. This book gives examples of a simple command processor in both C and 808X assembler. You can then add your own functionality.

NetMenu

NetMenu is a NetWare-aware menu program from Network Enhancement Tools, Inc. that solves many of the security problems mentioned previously in this chapter. My associates and I selected NetMenu as an example of a commercial product because we were attracted to its security features and its flexibility in menu design. People who feel the need to "roll their own" menu system will probably like NetMenu. Those who expect a menu system to work "right out of the box" will likely hate NetMenu.

With NetMenu, a network administrator can design menus that automatically adapt to changes in the users, equipment, or user access. Figure 11.2 shows an example of a menu created with NetMenu.

```
┌─ NETinc NetMenu(tm) User Interface ─┐
│ C - Check Today's BBS Messages      ↑│
│ 1 - NetMenu(tm) Demo Instructions    │
│ 2 - Create "NetWare-Aware" Executables│
│ 3 - Software Metering Example        │
│ 4 - Show Multiple Menu Windows       │
│ 5 - Display A NetMenu(tm) Audit Trail│
│ 6 - Sort A NetMenu(tm) Audit Trail   │
│ 7 - The Electronic Registration Form │
│ 8 - New Features of NetMenu(tm)      │
│ 9 - Change To Another Menu          ↓│
└──────────────────────────────────────┘
```

Figure 11.2   Example Menu built with NetMenu.

A NetMenu menu is a simple text file, called a *Menu Definition File* (*MDF*), that contains lines that define the menu title, titles of pop-up windows, and descriptions of individual menu items. Each menu selection contains the commands to execute the selection. When a selection is made from a menu, a batch file is created containing the commands. NetMenu then places the name of the batch file in the keyboard buffer and exits.

The MDF is a plain ASCII text file that contains a command character in the first column of each line. Any text following the command character on the line is the parameter(s) for the command.

Note: Network Enhancement Tools refers to these command characters as "control characters."

Tables 11.1 through 11.3 give details on NetMenu control characters.

Table 11.1   NetMenu window command characters.

Character	Description
%	Determines titles, placement, and colors of a menu window. The format is:
	%*Window Title Text, Row, Column, Color Palette.*
	If a −1 is given for the row coordinate, the window will be centered vertically on the screen. If a −1 is given for the column coordinate, the window will be centered horizontally on the screen. If the coordinates place the window off-screen, the window will be relocated.
*	Defines selection descriptions. Text following the * appears as the menu selection. Every * command character entry defines a selection that will appear in the window defined by the previous % command character. Only 10 selections will appear in a window, with scroll bars indicating more selections. There can be a maximum of 20 selections in a window.
. or space	This line is considered a remark and will be ignored.

The following command characters control attributes of each menu selection. Because a command character must always be in the first column, each command character and its related parameters will be on their own line. Each of these command characters affect attributes of the menu selection defined by the nearest preceding * command character.

Table 11.2   NetMenu selection attributes control characters.

Character	Description
+	Indicates a batch file command line. Batch file command lines follow the selections they are associated with. Each line beginning with a + is used to build a batch file. The batch file is built with each successive + line until a % or * is encountered. At that point, the name of the created batch file is placed in the keyboard buffer and NetMenu is exited.
^	Specifies a password for a selection. This line would follow the selection it's associated with. The characters following the ^ become the password. The maximum password length is 20 characters.

Character	Description
~	Specifies an encrypted password. Passwords are decrypted by shifting each character of the password to the next lower letter. For example, if the text following the ~ was OFU, the required password would be NET.
>>	Tells NetMenu to branch to another window defined in the current MDF file. Each window defined in an MDF file is numbered sequentially. The main window, window #1, is displayed when NetMenu is first run. Subsequent windows must be defined with the % character.
(	Defines additional help text for each menu selection. The text after the (sign is displayed at the bottom of the screen when the cursor is highlighting the associated selection.
'	This command character defines the maximum number of users allowed to execute this option simultaneously. The NetRun TSR must be loaded for this option to work. When a user attempts to access a selection that has reached its maximum count, a dialogue box explains the maximum has been reached. Console operators see an additional list of the actual users, their login times and connections.
}	Defines a timed option. If a user selects a menu option that contains the } character, the menu will clear the screen, lock the keyboard, and wait for the amount of time specified after the }. At that point, it will execute the commands.

The following command characters define attributes of the entire menu, such as titles and file locations.

Table 11.3 NetMenu MDF file attributes command characters.

Character	Description
!	Defines the menu master title. Text following the ! is displayed centered in the top area of the menu screen. Replaceable parameters in this text are updated every 30 seconds. See the section "Nouns" for information on replaceable parameters.
=	Determines the path where the exit batch file will be created. If no path is specified, the exit batch file is created in the current directory.

continues

247

Table 11.3 Continued.

Character	Description
.	Defines the parent menu. The text following this character is the name of an MDF file to execute when the ESC key is pressed to exit this menu. This allows a submenu to return to its calling menu.
[	Defines the menu status line. This line appears just below the master menu line.
{	Defines the bulletin board file name. A bulletin board is a text file that users can post entries to and read.
]	Defines the menu help file name. The menu help file is a text file that the users can read by pressing F1.
|	If this command character appears in an MDF file, the menu will not run unless the TSR NetRun is loaded. This TSR prevents a user from using Ctrl-Break or Ctrl-C to break out of a program or menu. This command character prevents a user from accessing a menu without NetRun loaded.
#	Denotes the end of the MDF file. Any text after this character will be ignored.

Nouns

Nouns are NetMenu replaceable parameters, similar to NetWare login script replaceable parameters. Nouns can replace any text following any control character in an MDF file. The noun will be replaced with its value before the text is used.

Nouns may also be used to determine if a menu selection is available. Consider this example:

```
*FoxBase, 4, %MEMBER_OF"FOXBASE"
```

This selection would only appear in the menu if the user is a member of the NetWare group FOXBASE.

Tables 11.4 through 11.7 list the nouns which are used by NetMenu and give examples of their output.

248

Table 11.4 NetMenu date/time nouns.

Noun	What it returns
AM_PM	am or pm
BETWEEN"hh:mm,hh:mm"	Yes
DAY	Numeric day of the month (1–31)
DAY_OF_WEEK	Name of the day of the week (Monday through Sunday)
GREETING_TIME	morning, afternoon, or evening
HOUR	Numeric hour of the day (1–12)
HOUR24	Numeric hour of the day (1–24)
MINUTE	Numeric minute of the hour (1–59)
MONTH	Numeric month of the year (01–12)
MONTH_NAME	January through December
NDAY_OF_WEEK	Numeric day of the week (1–7)
SECOND	Numeric second (0–59)
SHORT_YEAR	Numeric year (92–??)
YEAR	Full year (19??)

Table 11.5 NetMenu miscellaneous nouns.

Noun	What it returns
AT_LEAST"???k"	Yes or No—Is there at least the specified amount of conventional memory?
AT_LEAST_CPU"processor #"	Yes or No—Does this machine have at least the specified processor?
CPU_TYPE	The three-digit Intel CPU type. Example: 286.
CURRENT_DIR	The current directory. Example: \NETMENU.
CURRENT_DRIVE	The current drive letter without the colon. Example: H.
DISPLAY	MGA, CGA, EGA, VGA, MONO.
EOF	Puts a DOS end-of-file character into the batch file.
TOTAL_MEM	Total conventional memory. Example: 640K.
FREE_MEM	Available conventional memory. Example: 431K.
FREE_EMS	Available expanded memory. Example: 248K.

continues

Table 11.5 Continued.

Noun	What it returns
FREE_XMS	Available XMS (extended) memory Example: 000K.
FREE_SPACE"drive"	Available space on the disk drive specified. Example: 208644K.
ITEM_NUMBER	Menu item number. This is not easily described (see the manual).
MOUSE	Yes or No—Is a mouse driver loaded?
RCOUNT	An iteration counter (see the manual).
FIRST_MDF	The top level menu definition file— used to return to a parent menu. Example: MAIN.MDF.
THIS_MDF	The name of the current menu definition file. Example: UTILITY.MDF.
PREVIOUS_MDF	The MDF that called the current MDF—used to back up through menus. Example: PARENT.MDF.
XBATCH_DIR	The directory that the exit batch file will be created in. Example: H:\NETMENU.
XBATCH_NAME	The name of the exit batch file that will be created in the XBATCH_DIR directory. Example: N006.BAT.

Table 11.6 NetMenu identifier variables.

Noun	What it returns
BROADCAST	On or Off—Can your workstation receive SEND broadcasts?
CURRENT_VOL	Name of current volume. Example: SYS.
FIRST_NAME	First word of the Full Name in the Bindery. Example: David.
FULL_NAME	Full Name from the Bindery. Example: David Chamberlain.
LOGIN_NAME	User account name. Example: DAVE.

Noun	What it returns
MACHINE	Name of the workstation. Derived from the LONG MACHINE TYPE statement in the SHELL.CFG file when NETX is loaded. Example: IBM_PC.
MEMBER_OF"group"	Yes or No—Is this user a member of the group "group?"
NETWORK	Network address. Example: 00000001.
NICK_NAME	Taken from the user's Full Name in the Bindery. The nickname is defined as a word in the Full Name that is enclosed by single quotation marks. Example: If John 'David' Perot is the Full Name, David is the Nick Name.
NOS_VERSION	Version of the NetWare operating system running on the server. Example: 3.11.
OS	Name of the workstation operating system. Example: MSDOS.
OS_VERSION	Version of the workstation DOS. Example: V5.0.
P_STATION	Node address of the workstation. Example: 0000000000A2.
PRINT_Q"port number"	Name of current print queue capturing the LPT: port number. Example: POSTSCRIPT. Returns Local if port is not currently captured.
QUEUE_EXISTS"queue name"	Yes or No. Tests for the existence of a print queue and your right to place jobs in the queue.
SERVER	Name of current server. Example: ALC.
SERVER_EXISTS"server name"	Yes or No. Checks for the file server name in the Bindery.
SERVER_ATTACHED"server name"	Yes or No. Checks to see if the workstation has a connection to the file server.

continues

Table 11.6   Continued.

Noun	What it returns
SERVER_MAPPED"*drive*"	The name of the file server that the specified drive letter is mapped to. Example: FS1.
S_FULL_NAME	The user account's full name from the Bindery minus any nickname. Example: If the Full Name is Betty 'Bubbles' Smyth, the S_FULL_NAME is Betty Smyth.
SMACHINE	The short machine name from the NetWare shell. Example: IBM.
STATION	The logical connection to the current file server. Example: 006.
SUPERVISOR	Yes or No. Is the current user account equivalent to Supervisor?
USER_EXISTS"*user name*"	Yes or No. Does the user account name exist in the current file server's Bindery?
USER_ID	The object ID from the Bindery. Example: 10030001.
GROUP_MGR	Yes or No. Is the user a workgroup manager?
SECURITY_EQUAL"*group/user name*"	Yes or No. Is the current user equivalent to the specified user or group account name?

Table 11.7   NetMenu shell identifiers.

Noun	What it returns
IPX_LOADED	Yes or No. Is the IPX loaded?
NETX_LOADED	Yes or No. Is the NetWare shell loaded?
NETBIOS_LOADED	Yes or No. Is NETBIOS loaded?

Security Features

NetMenu can provide a good measure of system security. The NetMenu nouns offer a number of security features, which are detailed in the previous section. A variety of security features that can be realized with NetMenu follow:

Restrict User Access NetMenu can read from the NetWare Bindery. A menu can be designed to allow users access to menu areas depending on their group membership or other aspects of the network, such as their cable segment or node address. Menu selections can also be password-protected so that a user cannot access a selection unless he or she knows the password.

Prevent Rebooting or Access to DOS The system administrator can design menus that the user cannot escape from, preventing a user from accessing the DOS prompt. A small TSR called NetRun can disable the Ctrl-Break and Ctrl-C keys to prevent a user from breaking from a menu or a program. NetRun can also capture a Ctrl-Alt-Del and ask for a password. You can design a menu so that an application cannot exit to DOS. NetMenu handles this by supplying its own dummy command processor.

Control Access to Applications NetMenu allows an administrator to restrict simultaneous access to a menu selection. This would prevent more than a set number of users from executing a program. This is achieved through semaphore calls to the NetWare server.

Log Menu Activity NETLOG is a program that will record the date, time, station, node address, login name, and up to 70 characters of text into a log file. NETLOG could be called from within a NetMenu MDF, and it would record the activity of menu selections on the network. This gives you an audit trail of menu selections.

Timed Execution of Programs You can define the time that a selection will execute. For example, if an administrator with supervisor access executed a selection to back up the file server, the selection would lock the keyboard, preventing access from the keyboard, until the time specified. The administrator then could leave the workstation unattended without the possibility of someone accessing the workstation.

253

Auto Logout of User   NetMenu has the capability to log a user out of the server if a workstation remains idle past a certain length of time. It is important to note that this feature only works if the workstation is left at a menu. NetMenu is not a TSR and cannot control the workstation after an application is loaded.

CHAPTER 12

Time and Date

Time is a security mechanism in NetWare. You can restrict access to the file server based on time-of-day and day-of-week. You can also charge users based on time with NetWare accounting. You wouldn't want users to bypass security or accounting by controlling the server time. You also wouldn't want incorrect server time to impact security and accounting. This chapter shows you ways of securing your server's time as well as keeping it correct.

- Handling Time and Date
- DOS/NetWare Time
- File and Directory Time Stamps
- Securing the Server Console
- Time and Date Synchronization

Handling Time and Date

In Chapter 1, you saw how a network administrator could restrict user access to a file server based on time-of-day and day-of-week. NetWare accounting also uses date and time to determine what rates to charge when measuring a user's consumption of server resources. Since date and time are important, this chapter examines how NetWare handles date and time.

DOS/NetWare Time

Two of the most difficult problems for a manager of a network based on NetWare are time zones and multiple server environments. Time zones are a problem because NetWare does not have automatic ways of dealing with time zones—so you must. Multiple file servers can be a problem when they are not time synchronized to one another.

Time Zones

Since DOS is a single-user operating system, there is no need for time-zone support with stand-alone PCs. This is because a user is always in the same time zone as the PC. However, this lack of time-zone support can be a problem if your DOS PCs are workstations on networks that span time zones.

NetWare, like DOS, does not handle time zones. Consider the following dilemmas.

- If a workstation in a certain time zone attaches to a file server in another time zone and creates a file, is the time stamp on the file set to the server's time or the workstation time?

- If your workstation is attached to multiple file servers and each of those servers is in a different time zone, what time should your workstation time be set to if you run the SYSTIME command?

■ If you set account time restrictions for a user, but the user is located in another time zone, are the restrictions based on file server time or the user's local time?

NetWare's lack of time zone support is interesting considering Novell's claim that NetWare 3.x is an "enterprise-wide networking solution." While NetWare does not support time zones, Novell is beginning to address the issue; NetWare 3.1 does have a SET TIMEZONE server command. However, only NLMs that make calls to CLIB can make use of time-zone information. The NetWare operating system and utilities do not make use of time-zone information presently.

 Tip: A solution to the problem of time zones can be neatly solved if you're willing to adopt a "universal" time for all of your file servers regardless of location. The most obvious choice for a universal time is Greenwich Mean Time (GMT). An alternative is to adopt the time at the corporate office location. While this may work well for the network managers, users will likely have problems with this concept.

12- and 24-Hour Time

Most NetWare utility programs can handle time in both 12- and 24-hour formats, based on your workstation's DOS environment. You can control whether your workstation uses 12- or 24-hour time by setting the DOS country code. If you reside in the United Kingdom, for example, place the following statement in the workstation's CONFIG.SYS file to set the appropriate country code (044):

```
COUNTRY=044,,C:\DOS\COUNTRY.SYS
```

Consult your DOS documentation for additional information on country codes.

SYSCON is an example of a program that considers country code when displaying screens. Figure 12.1 shows how SYSCON displays the Default Time Restrictions screen (in the Supervisor

Options menu), when the workstation environment is set to the United Kingdom country code.

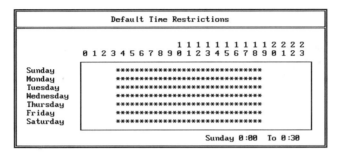

Figure 12.1   How SYSCON displays 24-hour time.

If there is no country statement in the CONFIG.SYS file, DOS assumes time and date settings for the United States and the same screen will now look like the one shown in Figure 12.2.

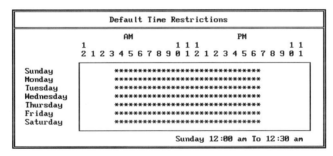

Figure 12.2   How SYSCON displays 12-hour time.

Whose Time Is It Anyway?

NetWare utilities do not always make it clear what time and date they are displaying. Consider the FCONSOLE utility program. When you run FCONSOLE, a banner appears at the top of the screen which includes the date and time. Whose time is this? It's the workstation time. Figure 12.3 shows an example where the workstation time (in the upper right hand corner), is different from the server time displayed in the File Server Status box.

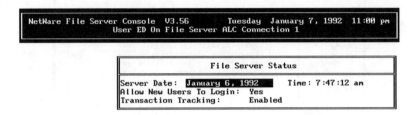

Figure 12.3   Differences between workstation time and server time.

Considering that the principal use of FCONSOLE is to function as a remote console for the file servers on your network, the time should be the time of the current server—but it's not.

If the server you're logged in to and your workstation are in different time zones or even different countries, there is nothing you can do to reconcile the different times you'll see in FCONSOLE. Don't worry about it—just be aware the difference can exist.

Time Synchronization

A workstation's DOS time and date is automatically synchronized with a file server's time and date in the following cases:

- When the Netware shell is loaded
- When a user logs in to a file server

When the NetWare shell is loaded in a workstation and the shell establishes a connection with a file server, the shell reads the server's time and date and updates the workstation's DOS time and date.

Tip: If you find it undesirable to synchronize your workstation's DOS time and date to the server when the shell loads (because you're in a different time zone), you can include the following statement in your SHELL.CFG file to disable the synchronization:

```
SET STATION TIME=OFF
```

When a user logs in to a NetWare file server by using Novell's LOGIN program, the workstation's DOS time and date is also synchronized with the server's time and date. Beginning with version 3.63 of the LOGIN program, you can now suppress this synchronization by placing the following statement in the login script:

```
SET_TIME OFF
```

If you want to control when time synchronization occurs, you can use the SYSTIME program. This program is used to display a file server's date and time, but it also synchronizes your workstation's DOS date and time to the file server.

```
SYSTIME servername
```

- If you do not specify a server name, you will get the date and time from the current server.

- If you specify a server name, your workstation's date and time will be synchronized to the specified server.

You cannot change a server's date and time with this command. Even though time synchronization may have occurred when you loaded the shell and when you logged in to a server, the clock in your workstation can drift and, over time, the server's date and time will be different from your workstation. The SYSTIME command is a way to resynchronize these clocks.

File and Directory Time Stamps

NetWare's file system is very different from DOS in its handling of file and directory time and date stamps. In DOS, directories and files have a date and a time associated with them. A directory's time and date are set when it is created. A file's time and date are set when it is created and, from then on, when the file is updated.

In this chapter, I'll use the term *updated* to represent the following actions taken against a file.

- The file is opened for write access
- The file is written to
- The file is closed

I'll use the term *accessed* when the following actions occur:

- The file is opened for read access
- The file is closed

File Date and Time

The NetWare file system has four dates associated with each file. These dates are:

- Creation date
- Last Accessed date
- Last Updated (Modified) date
- Last Archived date

Additionally, files have three time stamps. These are:

- Creation time
- Last Updated (Modified) time
- Last Archived time

You can view all of these dates and times for files by using this command:

```
NDIR /DATES
```

Figure 12.4 shows an example of what you will see.

```
H:\CD>ndir /dates
ALC/SYS:HOME\ED\CD

Files:              Last Updated    Last Archived  * Accessed  Created/Copied
---------------     -------------   -------------  - --------  -------------
CHKCD       EXE     4-16-89  6:08p  0-00-00  0:00  - 1-02-92  12-03-91  1:07a
EJECTCD     EXE     2-02-91  1:50p  0-00-00  0:00  - 1-02-92  12-03-91  1:07a
INSTALL     EXE     4-10-91  1:38p  0-00-00  0:00  - 1-02-92  12-03-91  1:07a
LOCKCD      EXE     2-02-91  1:50p  0-00-00  0:00  - 1-02-92  12-03-91  1:07a
MBOXRES     EXE     4-09-91  9:38p  0-00-00  0:00  - 1-02-92  12-03-91  1:07a
MBOXRES     OVL     4-09-91  9:01p  0-00-00  0:00  - 1-02-92  12-03-91  1:07a
MSCDEX      EXE    10-15-90 12:00a  0-00-00  0:00  - 1-02-92  12-03-91  1:07a
MUSICBOX    DOC     4-10-91  1:09p  0-00-00  0:00  - 1-02-92  12-03-91  1:07a
MUSICBOX    EXE     4-09-91  9:38p  0-00-00  0:00  - 1-02-92  12-03-91  1:07a
NECCDR      SYS     6-13-91 12:31p  0-00-00  0:00  - 1-02-92  12-03-91  1:07a
READ        ME      4-10-91  1:15p  0-00-00  0:00  - 1-02-92  12-03-91  1:07a
SCSITEST    EXE     6-11-91  8:28p  0-00-00  0:00  - 1-02-92  12-03-91  1:07a
UNLOCKCD    EXE     2-02-91  1:50p  0-00-00  0:00  - 1-02-92  12-03-91  1:07a

* Files marked A are flagged for subsequent archiving.
     357,180 bytes in   13 files
     380,928 bytes in   93 blocks

H:\CD>
```

Figure 12.4   How NDIR displays dates.

Creation Date and Time

When you create a file in a NetWare directory, the file's Creation Date and Time are set to the file server's current date and time. If you subsequently access or modify the file, the Creation Date and Time are not affected.

Last Accessed Date

A file's Accessed Date is set to the file server's current date when the file is accessed. When a file is created, the Accessed Date is set to the file server's current date.

 Note: When you use the DOS COPY, XCOPY, or Novell's NCOPY command to copy a file, the Accessed Date of the old (source) file is changed to the file server's current date. The new (target) file's Accessed Date is the same as it's Creation Date since it is created during the copy operation.

Updated Date and Time

Note: Novell documentation and other sources refer to both "Modified Date and Time" and "Updated Date and Time." These both refer to the same thing and the terms are used interchangeably.

When you create a file in a NetWare directory, the Modified Date and Time are set to the file server's current date and time. A file's Modified Date and Time are set to the file server's current date and time when it is modified.

Note: Accessing a file does not change it's Modified Date and Time.

If you open a file for read/write access, but don't write to it, the Modified Date and Time are not changed when you close the file. When you use the DOS COPY, XCOPY, or Novell's NCOPY command to copy a file, the Modified Date and Time of the new (target) file is the same as the original (source) file.

Archived Date and Time

A file's Archived Date and Time are not set automatically as a result of accessing or modifying the file. It must be set by a NetWare function call. The intention of this date and time is to allow backup software to date/time stamp files it has backed up.

Note: Novell's NBACKUP program does not set the Archived Date and Time. Third-party (NetWare-aware) backup or archive software may set the Archived Date and Time.

Directory Date and Time

A NetWare directory has only one date and time associated with it. This is the Creation Date and Time. A directory's Creation Date and Time are set to the file server's current date and time when the directory is created. Renaming the directory has no effect on the Creation Date and Time.

Securing the Server Console

A file server's time and date are used to enforce some of NetWare's security features. These features could be bypassed if the file server's time and date could be changed by someone who wanted to bypass security.

A file server's time and date can be changed from the file server's console. You would normally prevent access to the console by providing physical security for the server, but this may not be possible in your environment.

NetWare 3.x provides a mechanism to prevent the file server date and time from being changed from the console. When you type the command SECURE CONSOLE at the file server console, you will no longer be allowed to set the server's time or date from the console. Figure 12.5 illustrates this.

```
:set time 8:30:00
Time set to Tuesday  January 7, 1992  8:30:00 am
:secure console
DOS removed and its memory given to the disk cache
The console is secure
:set time 12:00:00
The console has been secured, the time can no longer be changed
:
```

Figure 12.5   Securing the server console.

 Note: You also cannot change the file server date and time by accessing the server remotely with RCONSOLE.

Once you secure the console with the SECURE CONSOLE command, it cannot be undone. You'll need to take down the server and bring it up again to enable date and time changes. However, you can still change the file server date and time by running FCONSOLE at a workstation even after you secure the console. You must be a Supervisor, Supervisor-equivalent user or a console operator to change a file server's date and time with FCONSOLE.

 Tip: If you can't prevent people from being near the file server, then use SECURE CONSOLE to prevent tampering with date and time.

When you secure the server console, other security-oriented things happen in addition to disabling date and time changes. These are:

- NLMs can only be loaded from the SYS:SYSTEM directory.
- DOS is removed from file server memory.
- You cannot enter the NetWare 3.x debugger.

Time and Date Synchronization

Time and date may be an important security consideration in a NetWare environment. Some of NetWare's security mechanisms rely on the server's time and date being set correctly. One of these mechanisms is login restrictions based on time-of-day and day-of-week. These restrictions can be easily bypassed if an intruder could change the time and date of the server.

In a multiserver environment, it may also be important that each server is running with the same time and date of other servers.

There are a few ways to keep server time accurate. Some of these techniques are performed manually by the network administrator or console operator. Some of these techniques can be automated so they can run periodically.

266

Time Broadcasts via Phone Lines

A NetWare administrator can use direct-dial telephone services to listen to time broadcasts. In the United States, the National Institute of Standards and Technology (NIST), in Colorado and the US Naval Observatory in Washington DC offer these services. In Canada, the National Research Council (NRC), in Ottawa provides this service (in both French and English). These are sources of extremely accurate time—far more accuracy than needed by a typical network. The telephone numbers are listed in Table 12.1.

 Note: A dial-up telephone line connection represents an unknown delay. So, while these time sources broadcast extremely accurate time, you have little idea how accurate it is by the time it reaches you.

Table 12.1   Organizations offering time broadcasts via phone lines.

Organization	Telephone number
US Naval Observatory	1-202-653-1800
US Naval Observatory	1-900-410-8463
NIST	1-303-499-7111
NRC	1-613-745-1576 (English)
NRC	1-613-745-9426 (French)

 Tip: Most telephone companies have a time service that you can dial, but the time resolution is usually limited to the minute. This resolution may be adequate for your network.

A way to automate the setting of a server's time is by running a program periodically which dials up a service that broadcasts time messages in data form. In the United States, the US

Naval Observatory runs a dial-up service at telephone number 1-202-653-0351 that sends Universal Coordinated Time (UTC) every second. An example of the message follows:

```
48131 240 154236 UTC
```

This is a message that was sent at 15 hours, 42 minutes and 36 seconds UTC (or 1542 hours and 36 seconds, as expressed in the UK), on the 240th day since January 1.

 Note: Universal Coordinated Time is an internationally agreed upon time standard based on an atomic definition of time rather than an astronomical definition of time (like GMT). For those of us who don't need very precise time-keeping, GMT and UTC are equivalent measures of time. Organizations like NIST would prefer that we use UTC.

There is a program available on NetWire called NAVALTI.ZIP that dials in to the Naval Observatory and sets your workstation time and, optionally, your current server time.

Time Broadcasts via Radio

There are also radio stations which broadcast time signals.

In the United States, there is radio station WWV located in Fort Collins, Colorado and WWVH located in Hawaii (both run by NIST). In Canada, there is radio station CHU located in Ottawa (run by the National Research Council). For other countries, consult the chart below.

Table 12.2 Internationally broadcast time signals.

Radio station	Location	Country	Frequency (kHz)		
BPV	Shanghai	China	5000	10000	15000
CHU	Ontario	Canada	3330	7335	14670

Radio station	Location	Country	Frequency (kHz)			
DCF77		Germany	77.5			
France Inter		France	162			
HBG		Switzerland	75			
IAM	Rome	Italy	5000			
JJY	Tokyo	Japan	2500	5000	8000	10000
				15000	20000	
LOL		Argentina	5000	10000	15000	
MSF	Rugby	England	60			
RID	Irkutsk	Russia	5004	10004	15004	
RWM	Novosibirsk	Russia	4996	9996	14996	
VNG	Lyndhurst	Australia	7500			
WWVB	Ft. Collins	Colorado	60			
WWV	Ft. Collins	Colorado	2500	5000	10000	15000
						20000
WWVH	Kauai	Hawaii	2500	5000	10000	15000
WWV	(Geosynchronous satellite)		468 MHz			
ZUO	Pretoria	S. Africa	2500	5000		

A Network Administrator could simply listen to these broadcasts and manually set a server's time once a day. It may be necessary to set a server's time more than once each day if the machine's time-of-day clock drifts too much.

Note: Radio station WWVB does not transmit voice messages. It transmits data-encoded time messages, as does the WWV satellite transmitter. Other stations transmit voice, but also include tones that make it possible for these broadcasts to be machine-readable.

Automating Received Broadcasts

There are receivers available that decode time broadcasts into data messages. One such device is the Model 8170 Receiver/Clock available from Spectracom Corporation in East Rochester, New York. It converts broadcasts from WWVB into ASCII-coded messages. It is available with RS-232, RS-422, and parallel BCD interfaces. To use this device to keep your NetWare file server(s) in sync, you would need to write the software. In the future, expect a commercial implementation.

Time Servers

It is possible to establish one server on the network as the master timekeeper for other file servers. This server could broadcast time signals over the network. All other servers on the network could receive the time broadcasts and update their time.

A Shareware implementation of a time server is offered by Jovandi International, Inc. The following programs are implemented as NLMs:

■ Time Master (TM.NLM)

■ Time Slave (TS.NLM)

These programs can be downloaded from CompuServe or obtained directly from Jovandi.

An interesting challenge for a time server is to broadcast its time message over the internetwork so propagation delays and other forms of delays are considered when updating the time on the slave servers. CSMA collisions on an EtherNet, for example, may introduce time-costly error recovery that will cause these time broadcasts to deliver old time information to the slaves.

 Note: Most applications do not require such accurate time and these delays can be ignored.

13

Audit Trail

So you've tightened up security on your network as much as you can without affecting user productivity, and now you feel fairly safe. You can't completely secure your server without affecting user productivity, so you know that there's a possibility that a security breach could occur, or users could still innocently destroy data.

There's always the possibility that you've overlooked something, and there's a security hole in your system. Perhaps someone will discover a previously undocumented feature of NetWare and exploit it to your disadvantage. What do you do now?

This chapter focuses on how you would add audit trail capability to your NetWare file server. We begin by looking at audit trail concepts and finish with an example of LT Auditor.

- Audit Trail Programs
- LT Auditor

Audit Trail Programs

An audit trail program collects information about user activity over time and stores that information in an audit database. Reports can be produced from information in the database. The reports list historical activity on the network. Typical audit trail programs record the following activities:

- Running programs
- Reading from files
- Writing to files
- Creating new files or directories
- Deleting files and directories
- Renaming files
- Logging in to a file server
- Logging out of a file server

Audit trail programs do not prevent hostile actions from occurring and are not a substitute for other security and backup procedures. They simply tell you what's been going on. By having a window into the past, you can better protect your network in the future.

 Note: Don't confuse audit trail programs with those popular programs which take inventory of the hardware that exists on your network, such as Intel's LANSight. Even though some of these products talk about "auditing," and one product has "auditing" in its name, they do not serve the same function as an audit trail program.

Collecting Data

The information about user activity is typically collected at the point closest to where the services are being performed. On a mainframe, audit trail data collection is done within the mainframe. In a LAN environment, audit trail data collection should be done within the server.

Unfortunately, Novell did not include an adequate audit trail capability within the NetWare operating system. Until they do, you need to rely on third-party products for audit trails that collect data at the workstation.

Figure 13.1 shows how data collection occurs at the workstation. This data collection is done by a RAM-resident (TSR) program in the PC called an *audit shell*. The audit shell intercepts DOS function calls from the application program.

If these functions represent activity that must be audited, an audit trail record is then sent to the audit database (here called a *history file*) in the server. The function call is then allowed to flow down to the NetWare shell (here called *shell*), where the request is processed normally.

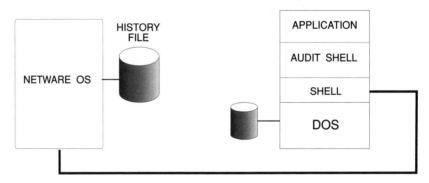

Figure 13.1   Audit trail data collection.

> **Note:** When the network is alive with users running applications and making DOS function calls, there is a significant amount of user activity occurring that must be audited. The audit shells send their audit information to the audit trail database on the file server. This can represent a significant amount of network traffic and adds an additional burden to your file servers. The storage requirements for the audit trail database can be massive.

13 — Audit Trail

There is one good thing about client-based audit trail data collection. You can easily audit activity on a workstation's local disk drives—right down to the floppy drive, if you want. You can discover who's been copying software from the network and taking it home. You can find out who installed the virus-infected program on your file server.

Filtering

An audit trail program can implement a technique called filtering to dramatically reduce the amount of network traffic and server storage. Filtering allows you to define the type of user activity that you want to collect and exclude all other user activity from the audit trail database. The audit trail database is smaller and there is less network traffic.

The dark side of filtering is not collecting user activity that you want to see. If, in the future, you decide that you want to see user activity that you filtered out, you can't go back in time and collect it. You need to spend time in advance planning on which user activity is (and will be) important to know about.

There is currently only one audit trail product for NetWare that uses filtering when collecting audit trail data—LT Auditor. This chapter will focus on this product.

LT Auditor

LT Auditor is sold by a company called Blue Lance. It was called LANTight in the past, but now LANTight refers to a family of products of which LT Auditor is a member. It is a NetWare-only audit trail package that is licensed per file server. There is no limit to the number of audited users per copy of LT Auditor.

 Note: Currently, LT Auditor will audit only DOS clients. Those DOS clients may be running Windows.

LT Auditor implements a comprehensive filtering facility, which is one of its strengths. You can define a *filter script* for each user. Your script can include any combination of these options to audit:

- Drive
- Directory or directory tree
- Filespec
- Filespec to exclude
- File and directory operations

You can be very selective in your filter scripts and keep audit trail database growth to a minimum. You can also declare that everyone and every file and directory operation should be audited in case you want a complete audit trail (and you have disk space and network bandwidth to spare).

At any time, you can look at the contents of the audit trail database and/or print reports. You can be as selective as you like in defining the contents of the reports. For example, you can produce a report when your concern is: "What files did John delete on January 23, 1991 from the SYS:APPS\DBASE directory between the hours of 8:00 and 15:00?"

Audit Shell

LT Auditor includes two audit shells—one for DOS users and one for Windows users. There are tradeoffs to consider when deciding which to use.

DOS Audit Shell

The RAM411 audit shell is a DOS TSR program. The 411 in the name of the file represents the version number of the program. This program requires about 27 KB of conventional memory.

Even though it's a DOS TSR, it can be loaded from a NetWare login script without trapping the memory used by LOGIN.EXE. It avoids trapping memory by loading itself into the highest conventional memory addresses possible and then telling DOS that top-of-memory is now 27 KB less than what it was before. On a 640 KB workstation there is about 613 KB of conventional memory left after RAM411 loads. The program overlays the transient portion of the DOS command processor (COMMAND.COM), but DOS reloads the command processor when it regains control.

By changing DOS top-of-memory, RAM411 is stealthy. You cannot see it by looking at the contents of memory with a program like MAPMEM or Manifest. This means that users may not know that they're being audited.

 Note: The savvy user may notice that top-of-memory is 27 KB less than what it should be, and they may get suspicious or spend a lot of time troubleshooting this "problem."

 Caution: As this book goes to press, RAM411 does not work with DR DOS. It does work with all versions of MS-DOS and PC DOS, including version 5.0.

Windows Audit Shell

Enhanced-mode Windows will not run with the RAM411 audit shell because Windows sees fragmented conventional memory from the top-of-memory adjustment. You would use the HIRAM411 audit shell instead. It is designed to load into high memory on a machine running QEMM. Unfortunately, it does not load in high memory if you use the MS DOS version 5 LOADHI command.

 Note: This audit shell HIRAM411 will work for DOS users (who have available high memory), as well as Windows running in any mode.

The disadvantage of HIRAM411 is it isn't stealthy. Users will see it if they run a program like QEMM's LOADHI that looks at the memory contents. Figure 13.2 shows an example of LOADHI output showing the HIRAM411 TSR.

```
H:\>loadhi

Region    Area      Size     Status
  1     B000 - B37E   13K    Used (QEMM386)
  1     B37F - B385  0.1K    Used (NDE)
  1     B386 - B38F  0.1K    Used (HIRAM411)
  1     B390 - B7FE   17K    Available
  2     D000 - D7FE   31K    Available
  3     DA00 - DF22   20K    Used (SMARTDRV)
  3     DF23 - E0CB  6.6K    Used (NECCDR)
  3     E0CC - E141  1.8K    Used (FILES)
  3     E142 - E461   12K    Used (MOUSE)
  3     E462 - E512  2.7K    Used (NDE)
  3     E513 - E967   17K    Used (IPX)
  3     E968 - F3D1   41K    Used (NETX)
  3     F3D2 - FA8F   26K    Used (HIRAM411)
  3     FA90 - FFFC   21K    Available

H:\>
```

Figure 13.2   QEMM LOADHI showing HIRAM411 loaded.

 Tip: There is a way to achieve a degree of stealth with HIRAM411 if you feel this is important. The HIRAM411 program does not care what it is called when it runs. You can rename it so when you load it, LOADHI will show the new name of the program.

Figure 13.3 shows an example of LOADHI output where HIRAM411 was renamed *NETBIOS*. Most users would probably not be concerned that NETBIOS is loaded on their workstation and not have a clue that it is really an audit trail program masquerading as NETBIOS.

LAN Access Reports

LT Auditor produces a *LAN Access Report* that tells you who has been connected to your server and for how long. Figure 13.4 shows a small segment of a LAN Access report.

13 — Audit Trail

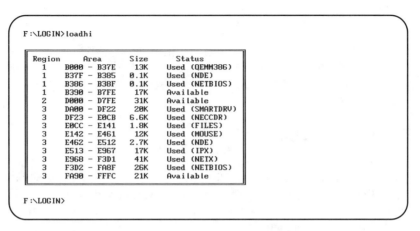

```
F:\LOGIN>loadhi

  Region      Area       Size       Status
    1      B000 - B37E    13K     Used (QEMM386)
    1      B37F - B385    0.1K    Used (NDE)
    1      B386 - B38F    0.1K    Used (NETBIOS)
    1      B390 - B7FE    17K     Available
    2      D000 - D7FE    31K     Available
    3      DA00 - DF22    20K     Used (SMARTDRV)
    3      DF23 - E0CB    6.6K    Used (NECCDR)
    3      E0CC - E141    1.8K    Used (FILES)
    3      E142 - E461    12K     Used (MOUSE)
    3      E462 - E512    2.7K    Used (NDE)
    3      E513 - E967    17K     Used (IPX)
    3      E968 - F3D1    41K     Used (NETX)
    3      F3D2 - FA8F    26K     Used (NETBIOS)
    3      FA90 - FFFC    21K     Available

F:\LOGIN>
```

Figure 13.3   HIRAM411 masquerading as NETBIOS.

```
STN: 2608C488026
        ****   **:**    ?????     12/28/91  09:26   Logout
     12/28/91  09:26   Login        ****   **:**    ?????
```

Figure 13.4   A segment of a LAN Access report.

The first line in the report shows an example of a user who has logged out, but LT Auditor doesn't have information about when that user logged in. You see a series of question marks where the word Login would normally be. This can occur if a user logs out sometime after the administrator purges the LAN Access database. The information about the user's login time is no longer in the database.

The second line shows the user logging in, but there is no logout time. That's because the user was still logged in when the LAN Access report was produced.

The next report segment (Figure 13.5), shows what happens if a user logs out abnormally. This could occur if the user reboots the workstation without first logging out. Notice that the second line in the report has substituted Improper Logout for the question marks. Another line was added to indicate the new login.

```
: 2608C488026
     ****   **:**    ?????     12/28/91  09:26   Logout
  12/28/91  09:26   Login        ****   **:**    Improper Logout
  12/28/91  09:47   Login        ****   **:**    ?????
```

Figure 13.5   LAN Access report segment showing improper logout.

File Access Report

The *File Access Report* is used to see the file and directory activity that has occurred. Figure 13.6 shows a small portion of a report where a user started Windows from a network directory.

Bindery Access Report

The *Bindery Access Report* records any user activity that modifies the contents of the Bindery. There is no filtering for Bindery access. Typical Bindery activities are creating and deleting users, changing passwords, creating print queues, and so on. Figure 13.7 shows a report that monitored three users being deleted from the Bindery.

```
10:09   [O        ] [   ]   win.com        SYS:WINDOWS\
10:09   [O        ] [   ]   emmxxxx0       SYS:WINDOWS\
10:09   [ C       ] [   ]   emmxxxx0       SYS:WINDOWS\
10:09   [O        ] [   ]   emmxxxx0       SYS:WINDOWS\
10:09   [ C       ] [   ]   emmxxxx0       SYS:WINDOWS\
10:09   [O        ] [   ]   win386.exe     SYS:WINDOWS\
10:09   [ C       ] [   ]   win386.exe     SYS:WINDOWS\
10:09   [O        ] [   ]   win386.exe     SYS:WINDOWS\
10:09   [O        ] [   ]   smartaar       SYS:WINDOWS\
10:09   [ C       ] [   ]   smartaar       SYS:WINDOWS\
10:09   [O        ] [   ]   system.ini     SYS:WINDOWS\
10:09   [ C       ] [   ]   system.ini     SYS:WINDOWS\
10:09   [O        ] [   ]   win386.exe     SYS:WINDOWS\
10:09   [O        ] [   ]   vpicda.386     SYS:WINDOWS\
10:09   [ C       ] [   ]   vpicda.386     SYS:WINDOWS\
10:09   [O        ] [   ]   vnetware.386   SYS:WINDOWS\
10:09   [ C       ] [   ]   vnetware.386   SYS:WINDOWS\
10:09   [O        ] [   ]   emmxxxx0       SYS:WINDOWS\
```

Figure 13.6   Sample File Access report.

```
12:34   DELETED BINDERY OBJECT
            Object Name  : Aaaa
            Type         : User  (1)

12:34   DELETED BINDERY OBJECT
            Object Name  : Test
            Type         : User  (1)

12:34   DELETED BINDERY OBJECT
            Object Name  : Test1
            Type         : User  (1)
```

Figure 13.7   Sample Bindery Access report segment.

Security Problems

LT Auditor is not bulletproof. Unfortunately, it is possible for users to bypass or destroy the audit trail.

Disabling the Audit Shell

A problem with using an audit shell on the workstation to audit user activity is the possibility that a user can disable the audit shell and not be audited. This is undesirable because the decision to audit a workstation should be the Network Administrator's—not the user's. This highlights a fundamental weakness with LT Auditor—auditing is done at the workstation. Blue Lance supplies an uninstall program for the RAM411 audit shell. They recommend that you install it in a directory where normal users don't have access.

It would be better for auditing to occur on the server, but Blue Lance claims the NetWare operating system doesn't allow server-based, third-party programs to easily tie in to the file system. If auditing is ever done on the server, it will likely be Novell that provides this facility.

Corrupting the Audit Trail Database

Since auditing is done at the workstation and the workstation is connected to the file server with a user account, the user has write rights to the audit trail database. This would allow the user to corrupt the database and, perhaps, render it unusable.

Suggestions

There is a way to make workstation-based auditing a bit more secure. If the server could occasionally poll the audit shell to see if it is still running in the workstation, you could be notified if the workstation audit shell is ever unloaded. This technique is already used by Brightwork Development in their SiteLock product for ensuring that SWATCHER is loaded. Although SiteLock is not an audit trail program, there is no reason why the same technique cannot be used in auditing products like LT Auditor. Unfortunately, there's nothing you can do to implement this—the solution must come from Blue Lance.

Some additional security can be realized by implementing LT Auditor in a client/server fashion. The audit shell would not write to the audit trail database directly. Rather, a server-based application (NLM) would receive audit trail records from the workstations and would then update the audit trail database. Workstation users would not have rights to the directory in which the audit trail database is kept.

 Note: Client/Server audit trail is a feature of the not-yet-released LT Auditor version 4.0.

FCBs

LT Auditor causes a great deal of network activity when a program running on a workstation does file I/O using older DOS function calls. These function calls use *File Control Blocks* (FCBs), rather than the newer file handle approach used in more modern versions of DOS. The disadvantage of FCB I/O is the audit trail program sends an audit trail record to the audit database anytime an FCB function is called.

When LT Auditor is auditing a DOS application that uses "handle" function calls, it applies some intelligence to the auditing process to lessen the amount of network traffic and to keep the history file to a minimum.

Suppose that an application opens a database file and reads a thousand records from the file. Each record is read with a separate DOS function call. LT Auditor will compress these thousand reads into one audit trail record. If, using the same example, the application uses FCB function calls, there would be one thousand audit records generated. Fortunately, modern DOS applications do not use FCB function calls. However, you may be running an application that was designed several years ago that uses FCB function calls. If you are, you may notice a significant performance problem when LT Auditor is used.

LT Auditor Version 4.0

Blue Lance is scheduled to release a new version of LT Auditor. Version 4.0 may be generally available by the time you read this. Previous information in this chapter was written before Blue Lance revealed details of the new product.

LT Auditor 4.0 is dramatically different from previous versions of the product. Version 4.0 is a client-server audit trail product. Instead of an audit trail shell that writes to the audit trail database directly, there is now an NLM that does this. This means that the audit trail database cannot be corrupted by a user writing to it directly, because users do not have rights to that file.

Filtering is no longer the responsibility of the audit trail shell; it is now done by the NLM. This provides a significant benefit—the shell size is reduced to about 8 KB. (The version 3.0 shell is about 27 KB.)

You may be wondering about increased LAN traffic as a result of filtering at the file server. Yes, the audit trail shells will now have to report any auditable activity to the NLM. This means sending that information in an IPX packet. Does this mean there will be a lot more IPX packets flowing on your network cables? Blue Lance thinks not.

With version 3.0 of LT Auditor, there is a significant amount of overhead involved in having the audit trail shell write directly to the audit trail database. Since the audit shell no longer writes to the file directly, there is a significant amount of LAN traffic eliminated. On balance, the new technique may actually lessen network traffic, but the testing has not been done to confirm this.

 Note: Since the audit trail shell communicates with the NLM via an IPX socket, this means a user can be audited without even being logged in to the file server. The practical application for this is to audit local drive activity.

Software metering is included with version 4.0; it can generate reports that list unsuccessful attempts to load metered programs. You can use the reports to justify additional licenses for your popular application programs.

Version 4.0 supports both active software metering and passive software metering. Active software metering is where users cannot run an application if all licensed copies are in use. Blue Lance uses the term *passive software metering* to mean that you can allow users to load copies of an application beyond the license limit, but a message will be sent to users of your choice notifying them of the "violation."

LT Auditor version 4.0 will now sport a Windows front end. Even if you're not a Windows enthusiast, you'll probably admit that the new user interface is more intuitive. Figure 13.8 shows the Filter Editor screen.

 Note: Even though the LT Auditor management program is Windows-based, users do not have to run Windows to be audited.

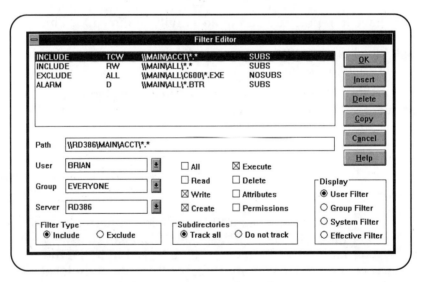

Figure 13.8   LT Auditor version 4.0 Filter Editor screen.

Figure 13.9 shows the Configure Meters screen. This is used to define software metering.

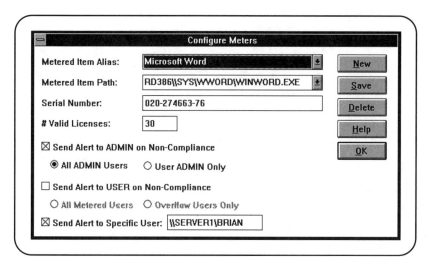

Figure 13.9   LT Auditor version 4.0 Configure Meters screen.

LT Auditor version 4.0 will do a lot to make an audit trail more secure by preventing users from accessing the audit trail database directly. The reduction in size of the TSR is a most welcome change. Finally, the Windows-based management program certainly seems like it should be easier to use than the current character-based program.

Backups and Archives

Computer viruses have changed both the reasons you perform backup and the way that you perform backup. In the past, you were concerned that a hard disk crash would destroy your data files. You backed up your data files regularly so that when the hard disk crash occurred, you could make repairs and restore your hard disk to the way it was at the last backup. You'd only lose the new data that was placed on the hard disk after the most recent backup. You'd backup often to minimize this loss.

Today, you back up your data so you can restore it in the event of a computer virus attack—in addition to your concern about hardware failures. With a hardware failure, you'd know that your data files were all right prior to the failure. The hardware failure itself was an easily identifiable event.

A computer virus attack, however, may not be easily recognizable. You may notice the effects of a computer virus attack sometime after the attack begins. It could be days or months before you know that you've fallen victim to a virus.

 Note: Another reason to back up is to aid network administrators in recovering data that a user has accidentally deleted.

Backup Strategies

For hardware failures, it was all right to buy a box of five tapes and label them Monday through Friday. On Monday, you'd backup to the Monday tape. On Tuesday, you'd backup to the Tuesday tape and so on. On the following Monday, you'd reuse the Monday tape—destroying last Monday's backup. If you experienced a hardware failure on Wednesday, you'd restore from the Tuesday tape. If the Tuesday tape happened to be bad, you could restore from the Monday tape.

 Note: Throughout this appendix, the term "tape" is used to describe the backup medium. Even though tape is most often used today to do server backups and archives, optical disk technology is increasingly being used.

With this technique, you had a backup cycle of five days. Certainly this was enough redundancy to protect you from hardware failures. Now that you have to protect your data from computer viruses, this simplistic approach no longer works, because you can't be certain when the virus attack starts.

Suppose you were infected by a virus that looks for files with the file extension .DBF. Rather than destroy these files, the virus modifies the contents of these files a little bit at a time. A user who notices that the file is changed slightly may attribute the change to a data-entry error by a fellow office worker. It may be weeks or months before somebody realizes the errors were caused by a virus. By this time, there is no copy of the file on tape which is not corrupted.

Archives

To protect yourself from a computer virus, you need to increase your backup cycle from five days to a much longer period of time. Suppose you want to protect your data from this sort of corruption for one year. Would you have to buy 260 tapes—one tape for every weekday of the year? You could, but there are less expensive ways of achieving the same goal.

A simple technique is to periodically save one of your tapes in the vault and replace it with a new tape. This is called *archiving*, and your archived tapes would be stored for a few years before (if ever) being reused.

With archiving, you can restore data files to the way they were anytime in the past. How often should you archive? That's up to you. The more often you archive, the more money you spend on media (tapes, optical disks, and so forth).

Grandfather-Father-Son Backups

A backup technique that you can use to increase the backup cycle (without significantly increasing the number of tapes or disks), is called a "Grandfather-Father-Son" backup. This name is used because it establishes a hierarchy of tapes. There are daily tapes, weekly tapes and monthly tapes—analogous to Sons, Fathers and Grandfathers.

This method of backup requires fewer tapes than the simplistic backup strategy above. The following example assumes that all of your data files will fit on one tape, but the same principle applies if your backups require more than one tape. The example shows you how you can back up four weeks of data on only eight tapes.

Begin by labeling your eight tapes as follows:

- Monday
- Tuesday
- Wednesday
- Thursday
- Friday 1
- Friday 2
- Friday 3
- Month

Here is how you would implement this backup strategy:

1. On Monday, Tuesday, Wednesday and Thursday back up to the appropriately labeled tapes. These backups may be *incremental* if you choose. This means that you can back up only those files that have been modified since the last full backup.

2. On the first Friday of the month, perform a full backup to the Friday 1 tape.

 Caution: This *must* be a full backup. Do not perform an incremental backup, or the backup set will be incomplete.

3. On the second Friday of the month, perform a full backup to the Friday 2 tape.

4. On the third Friday of the month, perform a full backup to the Friday 3 tape.

5. On the fourth Friday of the month, perform a full backup to the Month tape.

You've now protected your data for one month using only eight tapes.

For a one year cycle, you'd modify the procedure to archive your monthly backup tapes. Instead of having one tape labeled *Month*, you'd have 12 tapes labeled *January* through *December*. At the end of each month, you'd take the month tape and put it in the vault. At the end of the year, you now have 12 months of history on tape at monthly intervals. You should be able to recover from nearly any virus-attack scenario.

Incremental Backups

Backup strategies usually involve some combination of full and incremental backups. In the Grandfather-Father-Son procedure described above, the Monday through Thursday backups were incremental. This saves time, because the entire disk does not need to be backed up—only the files which have been modified since the last backup.

A — Backups and Archives

When a file is modified, the file's Archive Needed attribute is set. When the file is backed up, the backup software resets the Archive Needed attribute. With this technique, each incremental backup is relative to the previous backup. If the file server should fail and you need to restore your data, you'll first need to restore from the last full backup and then restore from all the following incremental backups in the proper order.

Your backup software may allow you to modify the way you perform incremental backups to make each incremental backup relative to the last full backup. You do this by having your backup software *not* reset the Archive Needed attribute when it does an incremental backup. The Archive Needed attribute is reset only when you do a full backup. Now, if you need to restore, you restore from the most recent full backup and then from the last incremental backup.

Keeping Backups Secure

Another backup issue is keeping the backed up data secure. All too often, backup media are left lying on desktops or put into a desk drawer or cabinet that is not secure. Anyone who can steal a tape may have access to all your data.

Treat backup media like you treat money. When you store it, it must be protected from theft. You would store money in different places depending upon the amount. Similarly, you would use more secure techniques for storing your backup media as the value of your data increased. You may keep the backup of office correspondence word processing files in a locked drawer, while your customer database might be locked in the vault.

You should provide a suitable place for the storage of backup media and implement procedures that ensure that your backup media is always there when not in use.

 Caution: The place where you store your backup media should not be the same place your file server is located. A fire or flood that destroys your server will also destroy your backups.

You might decide to implement a system where the person responsible for backup must "sign out" the backup media. If you did, this would not necessarily mean you are paranoid. It's best to have one person responsible for the secure storage of your backup media and another person responsible for performing the backup. This dual responsibility provides a system of checks and balances to ensure that the procedures are being followed.

Backup Encryption

If you're unable to provide a physically secure place for your backup media or you can't ensure that procedures are being followed to keep the backup media secure, there is an alternative. You can keep your backed up data secure even though the backup media is not—by storing your data on the backup media in encrypted form.

Few vendors of backup products provide you with the ability to encrypt your data as you store it on the backup media. The Accelerated Learning Center conducted a survey of fifteen manufacturers of backup products that would be used to backup NetWare file servers. Only one responded that they had an encryption feature. This was Contemporary Cybernetics Group.

Their CY-S Security Encryption option is available for their 8mm tape backup units. This option uses a *card key*, which is about the size of a credit card. You must insert the card key into the front of the unit when backing up your data. You must use the same card key when restoring from tape. You cannot recover your data if you use a different card key.

Other companies responded that they supported encryption when their product simply implemented password-protected backups. This means that you must supply a password to run the backup (or restore) software, but your data files are stored on tape in unencrypted form.

A — Backups and Archives

Tip: If the idea of encrypted backups is attractive, but your backup product doesn't support encryption, there's still a way to do this. In Chapter 10, "Application Security," you saw how you could use PKZIP to encrypt compressed files. You can modify your backup procedures to first compress and encrypt your important data files before backing them up with your backup software.

Unattended Backups

Many backup products let you schedule a backup session so that backup occurs late in the evening when nobody is using the server. This increases your chances of backing up all of your data files. If you back up during the day, nonshareable files that users have open will not be backed up.

 Note: If your backup software backs up your NetWare Bindery and Trustee rights, the backup software needs to run as a Supervisor account.

If you schedule your backups so the workstation is unattended, be sure that the workstation is physically secure—in a locked room. Leaving an unattended workstation logged in as Supervisor is risky. It's possible that someone can acquire Supervisor access from that workstation.

Novell's NBACKUP program, for example, tries to prevent this by not allowing you to exit the NBACKUP program without knowing the Supervisor password if it is set for a scheduled backup. Other backup products do not offer this protection.

Testing Backups

You should test your ability to restore from your backup and archive media. You'd be disappointed to learn that you couldn't restore from your backup tapes if your file server hard disk crashed.

> **Note:** When you install a new backup product, you should test your ability to restore as part of the installation and checkout procedure. You should also test your ability to restore when you purchase new backup media.

Testing your backup media does not only mean running a *verify operation* on the media. You should also test to see that you can actually restore to a real hard disk. When you do this, it's best to restore to something other than your production file server, in case the restore operation destroys data on the server.

Another benefit of this testing is that it allows you to practice performing a restore. Many network administrators perform a restore for the first time after the file server has crashed. They must then restore data under time pressures—and mistakes are likely.

Backup Media Lifetime

There are two classic problems with tape media of which you should be aware. Magnetic tapes degrade with use and the data stored on tapes degrades as the tape sits on the shelf.

You cannot use a tape forever. At some point, you should take the tape out of service and destroy it. When should you do this? The answer is elusive. Let experience or advice from the tape manufacturer guide you. You may decide to take a tape out of service after one year even though it still appears to work.

When you archive a tape, the data (stored in magnetic form), tends to degrade as time passes. Eventually, you'll be unable to restore from that tape reliably.

Tip: To reduce the risk of using degraded tape, you should use new tapes for your archives. Do not use a tape that has been in use for your daily backups for several months.

When you store your tapes, they should be stored in an environmentally friendly place. When you purchase tapes, the manufacturer usually supplies operating and storage recommendations for the tapes, which include temperature and humidity specifications. In addition, your tape storage place should be fireproof.

The problems of backup media lifetime can be reduced dramatically by using optical media instead of magnetic tape. Optical media do not degrade with use because the read/write head does not touch the medium. Your data does not degrade as the medium is sitting on the shelf, because the data can only change when a laser writes to the medium.

Vendors of Security Products

■ **Accelerated Learning Center**

V^2Scan, CryptDir, SCANT, Security-oriented training

311 B Avenue, Suite A
Lake Oswego, OR 97034
Phone: (503) 635-6370
FAX: (503) 636-9501

■ **Access Data**

WRPASS, XLPASS, LTPASS, PXPASS

87 East 600 South
Orem, UT 84058
Phone: (800) 658-5199
FAX: (801) 224-6009

■ Baseline Software

Password Coach

P.O. Box 1219
Sausalito, CA 94966
Phone: (415) 332-7763
FAX: (415) 332-8032

■ Blue Lance

LT Auditor

1700 W Loop South, Suite 1100
Houston, TX 77027
Phone: (713) 680-1187
FAX: (713) 622-1370

■ Brightwork Development

SiteLock

766 Shrewsbury Avenue
Jerral Center West
Tinton Falls, NJ 07724
Phone: (201) 530-0440, (800) 552-9876
FAX: (201) 530-0622

■ Centel Federal Systems, Inc.

NetAssure

11400 Commerce Park Drive
Reston, VA 22091
Phone: (703) 758-7000
FAX: (703) 758-7320

■ Central Point Software Inc.

Central Point Anti-Virus, PC Secure

15220 NW Greenbrier Parkway, Suite 200
Beaverton, OR 97006
Phone: (503) 690-8090
FAX: (503) 690-8083

■ **Certus International**

Certus LAN

13110 Shaker Square
Cleveland, OH 44120
Phone: (216) 752-8181, (800) 722-8737
FAX: (216) 752-8188

■ **Citadel Systems**

NETOFF

P.O. Box 7219
The Woodlands, TX 77387-7219
Phone: (713) 363-2384, (800) 962-0701
FAX: (713) 292-0617

■ **Contemporary Cybernetics Group**

Tape backup products with encryption option

Rock Landing Corporate Center
11846 Rock Landing
Newport News, VA 23606
Phone: (804) 873-9000
FAX: (804) 873-8836

■ **Datamedia Corp.**

SECUREcard

20 Trafalgar Square
Nashua, NH 03063
Phone: (603) 886-1570
FAX: (603) 886-1782

■ **Fischer International Systems Corp.**

Watchdog, Watchdog Armor

4175 Merchantile Avenue
P.O. Box 9107
Naples, FL 33942
Phone: (813) 643-1500, (800) 237-4510

■ **Hersey Micro Consulting Inc.**

FANSI-Console

P.O. Box 8276
Ann Arbor, MI 48107
Phone: (313) 994-3259

■ **Intel Corp.**

LANSight Support, NetPort II, LANProtect

3311 N University Avenue, Suite 200
Provo, UT 84604
Phone: (801) 379-2220
FAX: (801) 379-1599

■ **Jovandi International**

Time Master, Time Slave

233 Peachtree Street NE, Suite 404
Atlanta, GA 30303
Phone: (404) 523-1772
FAX: (404) 522-7116

■ **LAN Support Group Inc.**

Bindview Plus, BVDEBUG

2425 Fountain View, Suite 390
Houston, TX 77057
Phone: (713) 789-0882, (800) 749-8439
FAX: (713) 977-9111

■ **LANWORKS Technologies Inc.**

BootWare, Bootware MSD

3218 Wharton Way
Mississauga, ON L4X 2C1
Phone: (416) 238-5528
FAX: (416) 238-9407

■ McAfee Associates

VIRUSCAN, NETSCAN

4423 Cheeney Street
Santa Clara, CA 95054
Phone: (408) 988-3832
FAX: (408) 970-9727

■ Metz Software

MetzLock

4018 148th Avenue NE
Redmond, WA 98052-5165
Phone: (206) 641-4525

■ MTEK International

Risk Management Specialists

311 B Avenue, Suite 200
Lake Oswego, OR 97034
Phone: (503) 636-3000
FAX: (503) 636-8439

■ NetWave, Inc.

LANTrail

145 6th Avenue, Suite 207
New York, NY 10013
Phone: (212) 242-3200
FAX: (212) 242-3222

■ Network Enhancement Tools

NetMenu

20218 Bridgedale
Humble, TX 77338
Phone: (713) 974-1810, (800) 365-6384
FAX: (713) 781-0257

- ■ **Nu-Mega**

  NET-Check, NLM Profile

  102 Perimeter Road
  Nashua, NH 03063
  Phone: (603) 889-2386
  FAX: (603) 889-1135

- ■ **OnTrack Computer Systems Inc.**

  NetUtils, Dr. Solomon

  6321 Bury Drive
  Eden Prairie, MN 55346
  Phone: (612) 937-1107, (800) 752-1333
  FAX: (612) 937-5815

- ■ **PKWare, Inc.**

  PKZIP

  7545 N Port Washington Road, Suite 205
  Glendale, WI 53217
  Phone: (414) 352-3670
  FAX: (414) 352-3815

- ■ **Procomp USA, Inc.**

  Serv+

  6801 Engle Road
  Cleveland, OH 44130
  Phone: (216) 234-6387
  FAX: (216) 234-2233

- ■ **RSA Data Security Inc.**

  RSA development tools

  10 Twin Dolphin Drive
  Redwood City, CA 94085
  Phone: (415) 595-8782
  FAX: (415) 595-1878

■ Spectracom

Time receivers

101 Despatch Drive
East Rochester, NY 14445
Phone: (716) 381-4827

■ STX Information Security Group

STXPRESS Stealth

1577 Spring Hill Road
Vienna, VA 22182
Phone: (703) 827-6600, (800) 423-6807
FAX: (703) 827-6724

■ Saber Software

Saber Menuing System

P.O. Box 9088
Dallas, TX 75209
Phone: (214) 361-8086, (800) 338-8754
FAX: (214) 361-1882

■ Software Publishers Association

Anti-Piracy Hotline

Phone: (800) 388-7478

■ Symantec

Norton Anti-Virus

10201 Torre Avenue
Cupertino, CA 95014
Phone: (408) 253-9600

NetWare Security Commands

This appendix provides a list of those NetWare commands which affect security. In presenting the syntax for these commands, the following conventions are used:

User-supplied parameters are presented in *lowercase italic computer font*.

Optional parts of a command are enclosed in **[ ]** brackets.

A vertical bar **[|]** indicates a choice; for example, USER | GROUP indicates that you can specify either USER or GROUP, but not both.

Switches are sometimes listed by their full names; uppercase letters in a switch indicate the minimum information required to specify the switch. For example, to specify /No Tabs, you can type /**NT**.

ALLOW

This lets you set the Inherited Rights Mask from the command line.

Syntax

ALLOW *path* [TO INHERIT] [*rightslist*]

path is any valid path name. The path must be present. You can refer to the current directory by simply using the period character.

rightslist is the list of rights you want the path to inherit. Enter one or more of the following:

ALL	All rights
N	No rights
S	Supervisory
R	Read
W	Write
C	Create
E	Erase
M	Modify
F	File Scan
A	Access Control

CAPTURE

This lets you tell the NetWare shell to redirect LPT ports to a
NetWare print queue.

Syntax

CAPTURE [*options*]

options include one or more of the following:

/AUtoendcap	Use this option if you want the shell to end a print job and send the job to the printer every time you exit an application.
/Banner=*bannername*	This option specifies the text that appears on the lower part of the banner page. Replace *bannername* with a string of characters, 12 maximum.
/Copies=*n*	Include this option to indicate how many copies of the print job to print. The default is 1.
/CReate=*path*	Use this option to capture printed output to a file instead of a print queue. Replace *path* with any valid network path and/or filename.

/Form=*form*	This option specifies what form to use when printing the job. Replace *form* with a form name or number. The default is form 0.
/FormFeed	This option will cause a form feed to be sent to the printer after every job.
/Job=*jobconfiguration*	Use this option to specify which print job configuration to use. Replace *jobconfiguration* with the name of a print job configuration created with PRINTCON.
/Keep	This option causes the file server to keep all data it has received if your workstation hangs or loses power while you are capturing. If this option is not used, the file server will discard the data.
/Local=*n*	This option determines which of the local LPT ports to capture. Replace *n* with 1, 2, or 3.
/NAMe=*name*	Use this option to specify the text that appears in the upper part of the banner page.

`/No Tabs`	Use this option to ensure that tab characters in your print job are not expanded into spaces.
`/No FormFeed`	Use this option to prevent form feeds from automatically being sent to the printer at the end of every print job.
`/No Banner`	Use the option to prevent a banner page from being printed with each print job.
`/No Autoendcap`	Use this option to prevent the shell from ending a print job and sending it to the printer every time you enter and exit a program.
`/NOTIfy`	Use this option to be notified when your data has been printed.
`/No NOTIfy`	Use this option to skip notification when your data has been printed.
`/Queue=`*queuename*	Replace *queuename* with the name of the print queue to receive your print jobs.
`/Server=`*fileserver*	Replace *fileserver* with the name of the file server to receive your print jobs.

/SHow	Use this option to display the current capture status of all three LPT ports. You cannot use this option with any other CAPTURE option.
/Tabs=*n*	Use this option if you want tab characters to be expanded into spaces. Replace *n* with the number of characters between tab stops.
/TImeout=*n*	This option tells the shell to end a print job and send the data to the printer if no characters are received after *n* seconds.

C — NetWare Security Commands

DOSGEN

This is used to create a boot file for use by diskless workstations.

Syntax

```
DOSGEN [drive] [output_file]
```

drive is the drive identifier of a local floppy drive used to create a boot image. If you do not specify a drive letter, drive A: is assumed.

output_file is the name of the boot image file to create. If you do not specify a file name, NET$DOS.SYS is assumed.

FLAG

This is used to view and set file attributes.

Syntax

FLAG [*path*] [+|-] *attributes* [*options*]

path is any valid path and/or filename; wildcards are allowed. If no path is specified, all files in the default directory are assumed.

attributes is the list of attributes to modify. A + or – may be used to add or subtract all attributes except All and Normal. If + or – is not used, + is assumed. All + attributes and – attributes must be grouped together. The attributes and their values are as follows:

A	Archive Needed
X	Execute only (cannot be removed once set)
RO	Read Only
S	Shareable
H	Hidden
SY	System
T	Transactional
P	Purge
RA	Read Audit
WA	Write Audit
CI	Copy Inhibit
RI	Rename Inhibit
ALL	Adds all attributes
N	Normal (Clears all attributes)

options are:

SUB   Causes FLAG to operate on the indicated files in the current directory, as well as all subdirectories which are below the current directory.

/C   Causes continuous scrolling when filenames are displayed.

FLAGDIR

This is used to view and set directory attributes.

Syntax

`FLAGDIR [path] attributes [/C]`

path is any valid path name. If path is not used, the default directory is assumed.

attributes is the list of attributes to apply to a directory.

The attributes are:

N	Normal (Clears all attributes)
H	Hidden
SY	System
P	Purge
DI	Delete Inhibit
RI	Rename Inhibit

`/C` causes continuous scrolling when filenames are displayed.

GRANT

This is used to give Trustee rights to users and groups.

Syntax

GRANT *rightslist* [FOR *path*] TO [USER|GROUP] *name* [*options*]

rightslist is the list of rights to assign. Each right must be separated by a space. Rights are listed below.

ALL	All rights
N	No rights
S	Supervisory
R	Read
W	Write
C	Create
E	Erase
M	Modify
F	File Scan
A	Access Control

path is any valid path leading to the directory or file to modify. Wildcards are allowed. If path is not used, the default directory is assumed.

USER or GROUP must be included if a user and a group with the same name exist.

name is the name of the user or group to which rights are assigned.

options are:

/F	Modify files
/S	Modify subdirectories

MAP

This is used to view, create, and delete DOS drive letters which point to directories on NetWare volumes. MAP commands are normally placed in login scripts.

Syntax

```
MAP [options] [ROOT] [drive:] [= [drive:|path]]
```

options may be replaced with one of the following:

INS	To insert a search drive mapping in the search path ahead of other drives.
DEL or REM	To delete a drive mapping.
N	To map the next available drive to a specified path. Do not use an equal sign when using the N option.

ROOT can be included to map a fake root.

drive: indicates the drive letter to be mapped. You can also indicate *Sn:* to indicate a search drive. Replace *n* with a number indicating placement in the PATH variable. If *drive:* is not included, the default drive will be assumed.

drive:|path indicates the drive letter or path of the directory to map to. If *drive:|path* is not used, the default directory is assumed.

Use no option, or MAP *drive:*, to view all drive mappings or the drive mapping for any drive.

NPRINT

This is used to place a file in a NetWare print queue.

Syntax

`NPRINT path [options]`

`path` refers to the path and name of the file to print. Several files can be printed by including the names of files separated by commas, or by using wildcards.

`options` are as follows:

/AUtoendcap	Use this option if you want the shell to end a print job and send the job to the printer every time you enter or exit an application.
/Banner=bannername	This option specifies the text that appears on the lower part of the banner page. Replace bannername with a string of characters, 12 maximum.
/Copies=n	Include this option to indicate how many copies to print. The default is 1.
/CReate=path	Use this option to capture printed output to a file instead of a print queue. Replace path with any valid network path and/or filename.

`/Delete`	Use this option to automatically erase the file after it is printed.
`/Form=`*`form`*	This option specifies what form to use when printing the job. Replace *form* with a form name or number. The default is 0.
`/FormFeed`	This option will cause a form feed to be sent to the printer after every job.
`/Job=`*`jobconfiguration`*	Use this option to specify which print job configuration to use. Replace *jobconfiguration* with the name of a print job configuration created with PRINTCON.
`/Keep`	This option causes the file server to keep all data it has received if your workstation hangs or loses power while you are capturing. If this option is not used, the file server will discard the data.
`/Local=`*`n`*	This option determines which of the local LPT ports to capture. Replace *n* with 1, 2, or 3.

/NAMe=*name*	Use this option to specify text that appears in the upper part of the banner field.
/No Tabs	Use this option to ensure that tab characters in your print job are not expanded into spaces.
/No FormFeed	Use this option to prevent automatic form feeds from being sent to the printer at the end of every print job.
/No Banner	Use this option to prevent a banner page from being printed with each print job.
/No Autoendcap	Use this option to prevent the shell from ending a print job and sending it to the printer every time you enter and exit a program.
/NOTIfy	Use this option to be notified when your data has been printed.
/No NOTIfy	Use this option to skip notification when your data has been printed.
/Queue=*queuename*	Replace *queuename* with the name of the print queue to receive your print jobs.

/Server=*fileserver*	Replace *fileserver* with the name of the file server to receive your print jobs.
/SHow	Use this option to display the current capture status of all three LPT ports. You cannot use this option with any other CAPTURE option.
/Tabs=*n*	Use this option if you want tab characters to be expanded into spaces. Replace *n* with the number of characters between tab stops.
/TImeout=*n*	This option tells the shell to end a print job and send the data to the printer if no characters are received after *n* seconds.

C — NetWare Security Commands

PURGE

This is used to permanently delete previously erased files.

Syntax

PURGE [*path*] [/ALL]

path can be to any valid path and file name. If path is not used, all deleted files in the current directory will be purged.

/ALL is a switch which tells PURGE to recurse through subdirectories.

REMOVE

This is used to remove a user or group as a trustee of a file or directory.

Syntax

REMOVE [USER|GROUP] *name* [FROM *path*] [*options*]

USER or GROUP must be included if a user and a group with the same name exist.

name refers to the user or group name from which you wish to remove rights.

path is the path and name of the directory or files to be modified. Wildcards are allowed for multiple file operations.

options can be any of the following:

/SUB	Causes REMOVE to recurse subdirectories.
/F	Causes REMOVE to remove trustees from all files in path.

REVOKE

This is used to take away rights from a trustee.

Syntax

REVOKE *rightslist* [FOR *path*] FROM [USER|GROUP] *name*

rightslist is the list of rights to revoke. Each right must be separated by a space. Rights are listed below.

ALL	All rights
N	No rights
S	Supervisory
R	Read
W	Write
C	Create
E	Erase
M	Modify
F	File Scan
A	Access Control

path is any valid path leading to the directory or file to modify. Wildcards are allowed. If a path is not used, the default directory is assumed.

USER or GROUP must be included if a user and a group with the same name exist.

name is the name of the user or group from which to revoke rights.

RIGHTS

This is used to view your effective rights in a directory.

Syntax

```
RIGHTS [path]
```

path can be any valid path name. If no path is specified, the current directory is assumed.

C — NetWare Security Commands

SECURITY

This produces a report on possible security problems with your file server.

Syntax

```
SECURITY [/C]
```

/C is for continuous scrolling.

TLIST

This produces a list of trustees for a directory.

Syntax

```
TLIST [path] [USERS|GROUPS]
```

path is the path leading to the directory or file to be viewed. If you don't specify a path, the default directory will be assumed.

USERS or GROUPS is added if you only wish to display User or Group trustees. If neither USERS or GROUPS is specified, both will be displayed.

D

Sample Policy Statement

The Computer Policy Statement that follows is for the mythical XYZ company. This is a very simple statement, which you will likely want to add to. Once you formulate your own version, you will want to distribute it to all employees who have access to the network.

To make this more than just a "statement," you could add language that defines the consequences for violating this policy. If you wish to do this, you will need your employees to sign the statement—and you should probably consult legal counsel first. The policy addresses five areas of concern:

- Electronic Mail
- Privacy of Your Screen
- Security
- Viruses
- Software Piracy

Computer Policy Statement

This is the official computer policy of *Company XYZ*. Please read this thoroughly and ask questions if there is anything you do not understand.

1. Electronic Mail

XYZ's computer system includes an electronic mail facility for which you have a mailbox. Messages that you send and receive are normally private, but *XYZ* management reserves the right to inspect mail messages and search for messages that are relevant to *XYZ* business. Do not use the electronic mail facility for messages that you expect to remain private since we cannot guarantee your privacy.

The electronic mail system has the ability to store (archive) messages that you've sent and received. This is so that we can look at messages that have been sent in the past. Do not remove messages from your archives without the knowledge of *XYZ* management.

2. Privacy of Your Screen

XYZ has computer programs which allow a Network Administrator to look at your computer screen from other computers connected to the network. These programs are normally used for diagnostic or network-management purposes. We don't anticipate the need to do this often. However, understand that others in the office may be able to see your screen from time to time. We would normally advise you that this is being done unless we are investigating possible security problems and would deliberately not notify you. If you use your computer exclusively for *XYZ* business purposes, you should not have privacy concerns.

3. Security

XYZ places emphasis on computer security in order to protect its programs and data files from damage or from people getting access to data that they shouldn't have access to. Do not let others know your password. Even *XYZ* management cannot see your password.

Do not attempt to bypass system security or to use *XYZ* computers to subvert or break into other computer systems.

4. Viruses

Computer viruses can do great damage to computer systems. *XYZ* has taken precautions to protect its computer system from viruses, but it is impossible to provide complete protection. Do not install software onto the network without first checking with *XYZ* management. Even if you install a program in your own home directory, you are placing the entire system at risk.

5. Software Piracy

It is illegal to steal software. Do not remove software from *XYZ*'s computer system or software library and take it home to use. Do not load a copy of a software product on *XYZ*'s computers which you've borrowed from someone else without the knowledge of *XYZ* management, even if it is a "legal" copy.

XYZ wishes to honor the licensing agreements for any software products we've acquired. If you know of a situation where *XYZ* or an *XYZ* employee or representative is not complying with a licensing agreement, please bring it to the attention of *XYZ* management so we can take steps to comply.

Glossary

account   A name (and all information associated with that name), that identifies a user or other entity allowed access to a network.

Account Manager   A user account that is able to control the directory and file rights of other users within a workgroup. User accounts are assigned Account Manager status by the Workgroup Manager.

Archiving   The process of saving your data to a medium which can be stored away for an indefinite period of time.

audit shell   A TSR program run on a workstation for the purpose of collecting audit trail data.

audit trail   A database of user activity collected over time by an audit shell program.

backdoor account   A Supervisor-equivalent user account created for the purpose of accessing the server should the Supervisor account become locked by intruder detection or if the Supervisor password is forgotten.

Bindery   The database that NetWare uses to identify users, groups, file servers, and other network entities.

boot image file   A file that contains an image of a boot diskette. It resides in the file server's SYS:LOGIN directory. This file is used by a workstation's boot PROM to emulate a local disk for booting the workstation.

boot index file   A file (usually called BOOTCONF.SYS) that contains the internetwork addresses of diskless workstations and the name of the boot image file that they should boot from.

checksum   A computed number used to determine if a file has been modified. A file's checksum is calculated by summing all of the byte values in the file. This number can be calculated for a file, stored, and checked against the file later to see if the file has changed. Some people use the term *checksum* as a generic term which describes any technique to validate a file's contents, including a Cyclical Redundancy Check (CRC).

Collision Detection (CD)   A technique used by LAN cards to determine if two or more machines on the network cable are sending at the same time. When machines send data at the same time, this results in a collision; other procedures must recover from this error condition.

Coordinated Universal Time (UTC)   UTC is roughly equivalent to Greenwich Mean Time (GMT). UTC is a term used mostly by the scientific community, while GMT is used by military organizations and the general public. GMT is based on astronomical observation, while UTC is based on atomic clocks.

CRC   Cyclical Redundancy Check. A more accurate form of a checksum. It is possible for a file to be changed without changing the checksum. It is unlikely (though possible), that a file's contents can change without changing its CRC. While a detailed explanation of the CRC algorithm is beyond the scope of this book, it can be simply described as a mathematical division process. The result of any division process is a quotient and a remainder. The "CRC" is the remainder.

CSMA   Carrier Sense Multiple Access. A method of transmitting data over a shared communications medium, where the transmitting station listens for activity on the medium before transmitting. CSMA is usually used with Collision Detection (CD), where the transmitting station listens as it transmits to ensure it is not transmitting while another station is also attempting to transmit. If the transmitting station detects a collision, it negotiates with the other colliding stations to determine who should transmit next.

decryption   The action of converting an encrypted file back to its original form.

DES encryption   Data Encryption Standard. A standard encryption algorithm.

device driver   A software module which provides support for a specific hardware device.

diskless workstation   A workstation that has no local storage and must be booted from the file server. Some people consider a workstation to be diskless if it has no local hard disk drives but does have floppy disk drives. This book assumes that a workstation is diskless if there are no local drives at all.

dynamic   In the NetWare Bindery, objects may be either dynamic or static. A dynamic object is one which is purged from the Bindery when a file server boots NetWare.

effective rights   The actual rights a user has to a directory or file when the Trustee assignments, Inheritance, and Masks are all considered.

encryption   Modifying data using a mathematical algorithm so the file cannot be read without an encryption key.

EtherNet   A local area network topology developed by Xerox in the 1970s. The term *EtherNet* is used to describe any physical network topology adhering to the IEEE 802.3 standard.

file attributes   Those characteristics of a file which specify actions that are allowed or prohibited on a file (for example, Read Only or Shareable).

filter script   In audit trail products, a list of statements which determines which file and directory activity should be audited.

filtering   Third-party audit trail products may post only information about certain events to the audit history file. If so, this is called filtering because other events are filtered out.

Full Name   The identity of the person who owns a user account. The Full Name normally includes the user's first and last name (given and family name). The Full Name can be accessed in the system login script, or by other software which can read the NetWare Bindery.

Grandfather-Father-Son backup   A technique for backing up your file server that increases your backup cycle without requiring a significant increase in the number of tapes or disks.

Greenwich Mean Time (GMT)   The current time in Greenwich, England. It is used as an international time standard when it is desirable to refer to a standard or universal time.

hostile server process   A process (program) running on your file server whose main purpose is to steal processor time from other processes, destroy other processes, or otherwise try to prevent the server from running normally.

hot key   A keystroke sequence entered at the keyboard for the purpose of invoking a sequence of events or transferring control to a TSR. For example, Ctrl-Alt-Del is a hot key to reboot a workstation.

identifier variables   Variables that can be accessed in a login script.

incremental backup   A technique for backing up only the data files which have changed since your last backup.

infected disk   A disk containing a virus or Trojan Horse program. An infected diskette is usually altered by a computer virus so that its boot sector, File Allocation Table, directory structure, or files are changed—usually for the purpose of accomplishing a hostile task.

internetwork address   A combination of the network address and the node address. The internetwork address uniquely identifies each machine in the network. See *network address* and *node address*.

Interrupt Service Routine   A program segment invoked by a processor interrupt. The program's purpose is to deal with whatever event caused the interrupt.

intruder   A user or other entity attempting to gain illegal access to the file server.

Intruder Detection   A feature of NetWare that detects an intruder by a certain number of failed attempts at logging in within a window of time. NetWare will optionally lock the account under attack for a specified period of time, so subsequent login attempts will fail.

kernel   An Operating System process which is responsible for scheduling and running other processes.

key file   A file that must be present before a program will run. A key file is usually used for copy protection purposes.

Menu Definition File (MDF)   A file that defines a menu for the NetMenu program.

NetWare Shell   A TSR program loaded at the workstation that traps requests for file and print services and routes them to a file server whenever appropriate.

network address   A number associated with each physical cabling system (network) in an internetwork.

NLM   NetWare Loadable Module. A special program designed to run on a NetWare 3.x file server.

node address   A number associated with each node (workstation or server), on a physical network. The node address is determined by the LAN card.

noun   A variable similar in nature to login script identifier variables, but used in a NetMenu Menu Definition File.

object   A record in the Bindery database. There is an object associated with every user, print server, file server, or other entity on a network.

passive software metering   A term used by Blue Lance to describe what happens when users are allowed to load more copies of an application than the license allows. These events are recorded so you can determine that additional licenses may be purchased.

polling   **1.** The process of regularly checking devices in a computer to see if they require attention. For example, a program may poll the serial port to see if a character has been received. **2.** The process of regularly checking nodes on a network to see if they are still active. For example, the NetWare file server polls workstations regularly to see if they are still attached.

335

preemption This occurs when a process is halted by the operating system scheduler (kernel) so another process can run. NetWare is a *nonpreemptive* operating system, which means that the NetWare kernel does not preempt a server process.

process An executing program.

PROM Programmable Read Only Memory. In a workstation, this memory is usually used to boot the computer and contains low level programs.

properties Field names in the Bindery database for information related to a Bindery object.

rights Actions a user is allowed or disallowed to perform on files and directories on a file server.

ring A level of privilege on an Intel 80286, 80386, or 80486 processor.

SAP Service Advertiser Protocol. A Novell-designed protocol which allows a device or process to advertise its existence and services to other machines on the internetwork.

scanning **1.** The act of checking a program or file for the presence of a virus. **2.** The act of reading a file for the purpose of calculating a checksum, or performing some other action based on the contents of the file.

security-equivalent A user account that is given all the security attributes of another user account or user group.

semaphore A variable stored in file server memory. Semaphores are similar to DOS environment variables. They are often used for software metering, but can be used generally for the purpose of coordinating processes.

signatures Information stored about a file, usually including a CRC, that can be periodically checked to determine if the file has been tampered with.

static In the NetWare Bindery, objects may be either dynamic or static. A static object is one which remains in the Bindery even when the file server is taken down and later boots NetWare.

Supervisor's Working Account   An account used by the Network Manager or Administrator for doing routine work which does not require Supervisor-equivalence. You would use the working account rather than the SUPERVISOR account to reduce the damage in the event of a virus or Trojan Horse attack.

token   The Watchdog product from Fischer International uses a four-character "token" when you use their dual-password feature. The token is to tell the user that he or she is entering the password into the real system and not responding to a Trojan Horse LOGIN program.

Transaction Tracking System   A NetWare feature that protects data files from corruption in the event of a workstation or file server failure. It can restore data files to the condition they were in before the failure.

Trojan Horse   A program with hostile intent that masquerades as a normal program. A Trojan Horse program is usually given a misleading name in an attempt to lure a user into running it. It is different than a computer virus in that it does not normally propagate and does not infect other program files.

Trustee Rights   Rights to a directory or file directly or indirectly assigned to a user or user group. They are a combination of your user rights, your group rights, and your security-equivalence rights. In NetWare 2.x, these are the rights that a user possesses before the Maximum Rights Mask is applied.

unique password   A password that is different from any password used before.

user group   An account that represents a collection of user accounts who are members of the group. The members of this group can then be treated as a single identity.

UTC   See *Coordinated Universal Time*.

VAP   Value-Added Process. A special program written specifically to run on a NetWare 2.x file server.

virus A program which reproduces itself when it is run. It can corrupt and infect other programs, and spread from one computer to another. A virus usually has hostile intent and corrupts data files or causes other damage.

warm booting The process of reloading a computer's operating system via software means without turning off or shutting down the computer.

work group A group of users that is administered by a Workgroup Manager.

Workgroup Manager A user that is given Supervisory rights over a group of users and a certain directory structure.

Working Account See *Supervisor's Working Account.*

Index

339

LAN Desktop Guide to Security NetWare Edition

encrypting
  Lotus 1-2-3, 230-231
  Microsoft Excel, 229-230
  Quattro Pro, 228-229
  with external programs,
    234-238
  WordPerfect, 227-228
erasing, preventing, 181
hidden, 185-186
hiding, 180
history, 274
key, 166-167, 335
Menu Definition File (MDF),
  335
opening, Read right, 202
overlay, 184, 194-195
purging, 182, 196
read-only, 180, 194
reading, Read right, 202
renaming, preventing, 183
rights, accessing, 203
scanning for, 203, 336
sharing, 183, 193
time and date, 262-263
  Accessed Date, 263
  Archived Date and Time,
    264
  Creation Date and Time, 263
  Updated Date and Time, 264
trustee rights, 204-205
writing to, 203
filter scripts, 333
filtering, 275, 333
Find First, DOS function call, 203
Find Next, DOS function call, 203
Fischer International Systems
  Corp., 299
FLAG command, 312-313
  changing file attributes, 189-191
  viewing file attributes, 187-189
FLAGDIR command, 314
  changing directory attributes,
    192–193
  viewing directory attributes,
    191
Force Periodic Password Changes
  account restriction, 28-29

formats
  password, 21
  time, 258-259
formatting virus infected diskettes,
  116

G

GDIR DOS command, 87
GP1 virus, 99
Grandfather-Father-Son backup
  strategy, 289-290, 334
GRANT command, 204-209, 315
Greenwich Mean Time (GMT), 258,
  334
group accounts
  adding users, 162
  creating with SYSCON, 162-164
  deleting users, 163
groups, viewing, 211-212
GUEST user account, 4-5

H

hardware
  failures, 94
    NetWare 2.x drives, 95
    NetWare 3.x drives, 95
HELP DOS command, 87
Hersey Micro Consulting Inc., 300
Hidden file attribute, 180
hidden files, 185-186
hiding
  directories, 180
  files, 180
HIRAM411 audit shell, 277-278
history files, 274
hostile server process, 334
hot keys, 334

I

identifier variables, 334
  NetMenu, 250-252
incremental backups, 290-291, 334
Index file attribute, 182

infected disks, 334
INFO DOS command, 87
inheritance
    Inherited Rights Mask, 213-216
    Maximum Rights Mask, 216
trustee rights, vs. inherited rights,
    217
Inherited Rights Mask, 213-216,
    223
installing
    diskless workstations, 68-78
    SiteLock program, 129-130
Intel Corp., 300
internetwork addresses, 334
Interrupt Service Routine, 334
intruder detection, 39, 334
    account lockout, 41-42
    address of intruder, 42-43
    node address problems, 43-45
intruders, 334
item property, 159

J-K

Jovandi International, 300

kernel, 141-142, 335
key files, 166-167, 335
keyboards, locking, 91-92

L

labeling diskettes, 106-107
LAN access reports, 278-279
LAN Support Group Inc., 300
LANWORKS Technologies Inc.,
    300
Limit Concurrent Connections
    account restriction, 27
LIST DOS command, 87
locking keyboards, 91-92
Logged, Bindery security level, 160
LOGIN program
    login scripts, bypassing, 48
    password entry, automating,
        48-49

login scripts
    bypassing, 48
    disabling, 220-221
    replacing missing, 220
    storing in mailbox directories,
        219
Lotus 1-2-3, encrypting files,
    230-231
LT Auditor, audit trail program,
    275
    Bindery Access Report, 280
    corrupting database, 281
    disabling audit shells, 281
    DOS audit shell, 276-277
    File Access Report, 280
    File Control Blocks (FCB), 282
    LAN Access Report, 278-279
    suggestions, 281-282
    version 4.0, 283-285
    Windows audit shell, 277-278
LTPASS password recovery
    software, 232-234

M

mailbox directories, 218
    disabling login scripts, 220-221
    group rights, removing, 219
    login scripts, 219
MAKEUSER command, 6-7
MAP command, 316
Maximum Rights Mask, 216, 223
McAfee Associates, 301
MDF (Menu Definition File), 245
Menu Definition File (MDF), 245,
    335
menus
    batch files, 241-242
    NetWare, 241
METZ Lock (auto-logout)
    program, 52-54
Metz Software, 301
Microsoft Excel, encrypting files,
    229-230
Modify right, 203
MONITOR (NLM) command,
    91-92, 143-146
MTEK International, 301

N

names, account
  length, 9-10
  misleading, 11-12
  valid characters, 10-11
naming
  Bindery objects, 156
  Bindery properties, 158
  users, 163
National Institute of Standards and
  Technology (NIST), 267
National Research Council (NRC),
  267
NET-Check program, 150-151
NETLOG command, 253
NetMenu (Network Enhancement
  Tools), 244
  MDF (Menu Definition
    File), 245
    file attributes command
      characters, 247-248
    nouns, 248
      date/time, 249
      identifier variables, 250-252
      miscellaneous, 249-250
      shell identifiers, 252
  security features, 253-254
  selection attributes control
    characters, 246-247
  window command characters,
    246
NetOFF (auto-logout) program,
  50-51
NETSCAN command, 102, 116-119
NetUtils, 85
  breaking into file servers, 89
NetWare
  file attributes, 180-183
  menus, 241
  preemption, protection
    mechanism, 141-142
  rings, protection mechanism,
    142-143
NetWare 2.15, rights, 221-222
NetWare 2.x
  drive failures, 95
  file server
    locking keyboards, 91
    breaking into, 88-89

NetWare 3.x
  drive failures, 95
  file server, locking keyboards,
    91-92
NetWare, Bindery security level,
  159-160
NetWare Shell, 335
NetWave, Inc., 301
network address, 335
Network Enhancement Tools,
  244-248, 301
network loadable module (NLM)
  programs, 335
  MONITOR, 91-92, 143-146
  NET-Check, 150-151
  NLM-Profile, 146-149
  testing, 143
  virus-infected, 101
NLM-Profile program, 146-149
Noah's File Encryption
  utilities, 235
node address, 335
nondedicated file servers,
  viruses, 99-100
Norton Anti-Virus, 102
nouns, NetMenu, 248, 335
  date/time, 249
  identifier variables, 250-252
  miscellaneous, 249-250
  shell identifiers, 252
NPRINT command, 4, 317-320
Nu-Mega, 302
NWSETUP command, 8

O

Object, Bindery security level, 160
objects, 335
  Bindery, 156
    counterfeit, 170
    dynamic, 158
    naming, 156
    security levels, 159-161
    static, 158
    types, 156-157
  dynamic, 333
  static, 336
OnTrack Computer Systems Inc.,
  302
Open right, 222

P

347

Index

Purge file attribute, 182, 196
purging files, 182, 196
PXPASS password recovery
    software, 232-234

Q-R

Quattro Pro, encrypting files,
    228-229
radios
    decoding time broadcasts, 270
    synchronizing time, 268-269
RAM411 audit shell, 276-277
Read Audit file attribute, 182
Read right, 202-222
Read-Only file attribute, 180, 194
rebooting, preventing with
    NetMenu, 253
REMOVE command, 210-211, 322
Rename Inhibit file attribute, 183,
    197
Require Password account
    restriction, 28
Require Unique Passwords account
    restriction, 29-30
REVOKE command, 209-210, 323
rights, 199-201, 336
    Access Control, 204
    controlling, 206-212
    Create, 202-205
    effective, 216-218, 333
    Erase, 202
    File Scan, 203
    inheritance, 213-216
    maximum, defining, 216
    Modify, 203
    modifying, 204
    NetWare 2.15, 221-222
    Open, 222
    Parental, 221
    Read, 202, 222
    recommendations, 222-223
    Supervisor, 203
    trustee, 204-205, 337
        vs. inherited rights, 217
    viewing, 205
    Write, 203, 222

RIGHTS command, 205, 324
rings, 142-143, 336
RPLFIX.COM patch program, 79
RSA Data Security Inc., 302

S

Saber Menuing System, 242
Saber Software, 303
SACS (Sergeant Access Control
    System), 92
    defeating, 93-94
    memory requirements, 93
SAP (Service Advertiser Protocol),
    336
SBACKUP DOS command, 87
scanning for files, 203, 336
SCANT command, 220
scripts
    filter, 333
    login
        bypassing, 48
        disabling, 220-221
        replacing missing, 220
        storing in mailbox
            directories, 219
SECURE CONSOLE command, 142,
    265-266
SECURITY command, 173-175, 325
    login scripts, checking for, 220
security equivalent user
    accounts, 17
    backdoor accounts, 18-19
    rules for equivalence, 18
    Supervisor working
        accounts, 19
semaphores, 166, 336
Sergeant Access Control System,
    see SACS
SERV+ program, 86-87
SERVER.EXE program, 100-101
servers
    file
        dedicated, viruses, 100-101
        nondedicated, viruses,
            99-100
        physical security, 85-95
        preventing viruses, 102-103

software protection
programs, 127-140
time and date, 260-261
print, creating, 165
time, 270
set property, 159
Shareable file attribute, 183, 193
shell identifiers, NetMenu, 252
shells
DOS audit, 276-277
Windows audit, 277-278
signatures, 336
SiteLock (virus-protection)
program, 65, 127-129
execute-only program files,
134-135
home directory, defining, 138
installing, 129-130
local drives, disabling, 137
maintaining, 137-139
non-virus checked files, 132
overlay files, 135-136
scanning intervals, 136
setting up, 130-132
software
passive metering, 335
password recovery, 232-234
protection programs, 127-139
see also programs
Software Publishers Association,
303
Spectracom, 303
static objects, Bindery, 158, 336
STX Information Security
Group, 303
subdirectories
creating, Create right, 202
rights, accessing, 203
Supervisor, Bindery security
level, 160
Supervisor right, 203
SUPERVISOR user account, 3-4
Supervisor's Working Account, 336
Symantec, 303
synchronizing time and date
decoding broadcasts, 270
time broadcasts via phone
lines, 267-268
time broadcasts via radio,
268-269
time servers, 270

SYSCON program, 6
Bindery functions
groups, creating, 162-164
users, adding, 161-162
security equivalent user
accounts, creating, 17-19
trustee rights, viewing, 205
user accounts, creating, 8-12
System file attribute, 180
SYSTIME command, 261

T

temporary files, purging, 196
time and date, 257
12-and 24-hour formats,
258-259
directories, 265
files, 262
Accessed Date, 263
Archived Date and Time,
264
Creation Date and Time, 263
Updated Date and Time, 264
securing file server, 265-266
synchronizing, 260-261
decoding time broadcasts,
270
time broadcasts via phone
lines, 267-268
time broadcasts via radio,
268-269
time servers, 270
time zones, 257-258
workstation time vs. server
time, 259-260
Time Master program, 270
Time Slave program, 270
time zones, 257-258
TLIST command, 211-212, 326
token, 337
topologies, EtherNet, 333
Transaction Tracking System, 183,
337
Transactional file attribute, 183
Trojan Horse programs, 120, 337
ANSI.SYS driver, 121-122
dual password protection, 56-57
LOGOUT programs, 122

349

Index

protecting against, 123-124
Supervisor equivalence,
  accessing, 123
troubleshooting
  diskless workstations, 78-81
  LOGIN program, 48-49
trustee rights, 204, 337
  viewing, 205
  vs. inherited rights, 217
TYPE DOS command, 87

U

/UNATTEND (NETSCAN) option,
  118-119
user accounts, 3
  account restrictions, 25-33
  adding to Bindery, 161-162
  creating, 5-8
    with SYSCON, 8-12
  GUEST, 4-5
  passwords, 20-25
  security-equivalence, 17-19
  SUPERVISOR, 3-4
user group accounts, creating,
  12-13
USERDEF command, 7-8
users
  adding to group accounts, 162
  auto logout (NetMenu), 254
  deleting from group
    accounts, 163
  naming, 163
  restricting access with
    NetMenu, 253
  viewing, 211-212

V

V^2 Scan program, 143
VALIDATE command, 106,
  119-120
Value-Added Process (VAP), 337
  keyboard lock, 91
  testing, 143
  virus-infected, 101
VER DOS command, 87

viewing
  directory attibutes, 191
  file attributes, 187-189
  groups, 211-212
  rights, 205
  users, 211-212
VIRUSCAN program, 111-116
  automating, 115-116
  command line options, 112-114
  formatting infected floppy
    disks, 116
  removing viruses, 116
viruses, 99, 337
  dedicated file servers, 100-101
  diskettes
    labeling, 106-107
    receiving procedures,
      107-108
    scanning, 105-106
    write-protected, 103-105
  nondedicated file servers,
    99-100
  protecting against, 101-103
  scanning for, 108-110
    NETSCAN, 116-119
    VALIDATE, 119-120
    VIRUSCAN program,
      111-116
  software protection
    programs, 127
    LANProtect, 139-140
    SiteLock, 127-139

W

warm booting, 337
Watchdog, 54, 235
  access control, 55-57
  Armor card, 57
  bootup protection, 57
WordPerfect, encrypting files,
  227-228
work groups, 337
Workgroup Manager, 338
  creating, 15
Working Account, 338
workstations
  diskless, 333
    advantages, 61-62
    AUTOEXEC.BAT file,
      editing, 79-80

X

Sams—Covering The Latest In Computer And Technical Topics!

Audio

Advanced Digital Audio $39.95
Audio Systems Design and Installation . .$59.95
Compact Disc Troubleshooting and Repair . .$24.95
Handbook for Sound Engineers:
   The New Audio Cyclopedia, 2nd Ed. . .$99.95
How to Design & Build Loudspeaker
   & Listening Enclosures $39.95
Introduction to Professional
   Recording Techniques $29.95
The MIDI Manual $24.95
Modern Recording Techniques, 3rd Ed. . .$29.95
OP-AMP Circuits and Principles $19.95
Principles of Digital Audio, 2nd Ed. $29.95
Sound Recording Handbook $49.95
Sound System Engineering, 2nd Ed. $49.95

Electricity/Electronics

Active-Filter Cookbook $24.95
Basic Electricity and DC Circuits $29.95
CMOS Cookbook, 2nd Ed. $24.95
Electrical Wiring $19.95
Electricity 1-7, Revised 2nd Ed. $49.95
Electronics 1-7, Revised 2nd Ed. $49.95
How to Read Schematics, 4th Ed. $19.95
IC Op-Amp Cookbook, 3rd Ed. $24.95
IC Timer Cookbook, 2nd Ed. $24.95
RF Circuit Design $24.95
Transformers and Motors $29.95
TTL Cookbook $24.95
Understanding Digital Troubleshooting, 3rd Ed.$24.95
Understanding Solid State Electronics, 5th Ed. $24.95

Games

Master SimCity/SimEarth $19.95
Master Ultima $16.95

Hardware/Technical

First Book of Modem Communications $16.95
First Book of PS/1 . . . .$16.95
Hard Disk Power with the Jamsa Disk Utilities $39.95
IBM PC Advanced Troubleshooting & Repair $24.95
IBM Personal Computer Troubleshooting
   & Repair $24.95
Microcomputer Troubleshooting & Repair . .$24.95
Understanding Fiber Optics $24.95

IBM: Business

10 Minute Guide to PC Tools 7 . . . . . .$ 9.95
10 Minute Guide to Q&A 4 . . . .$ 9.95
First Book of Microsoft Works for the PC . . .$16.95
First Book of Norton Utilities 6 . . . .$16.95
First Book of PC Tools 7 . . . .$16.95
First Book of Personal Computing, 2nd Ed. . .$16.95

IBM: Database

10 Minute Guide to Harvard Graphics 2.3 . . . $9.95
Best Book of AutoCAD $34.95
dBASE III Plus Programmer's
   Reference Guide $24.95
dBASE IV Version 1.1 for the First-Time User $24.95
Everyman's Database Primer Featuring dBASE IV
   Version 1.1 . . . .$24.95
First Book of Paradox 3.5 . . . .$16.95
First Book of PowerPoint for Windows $16.95
Harvard Graphics 2.3 In Business $29.95

IBM: Graphics/Desktop Publishing

10 Minute Guide to Lotus 1-2-3 . . . . . .$ 9.95
Best Book of Harvard Graphics $24.95
First Book of Harvard Graphics 2.3 . . . . .$16.95
First Book of PC Paintbrush $16.95
First Book of PFS: First Publisher $16.95

IBM: Spreadsheets/Financial

Best Book of Lotus 1-2-3 Release 3.1 . . . . $27.95
First Book of Excel 3 for Windows $16.95
First Book of Lotus 1-2-3 Release 2.3 . . . . $16.95
First Book of Quattro Pro 3 . . . . $16.95
First Book of Quicken In Business $16.95
Lotus 1-2-3 Release 2.3 In Business $29.95
Lotus 1-2-3: Step-by-Step $24.95
Quattro Pro In Business $29.95

IBM: Word Processing

Best Book of Microsoft Word 5 . . . . $24.95
Best Book of Microsoft Word for Windows . $24.95
Best Book of WordPerfect 5.1 . . . . $26.95
First Book of Microsoft Word 5.5 . . . . . . $16.95
First Book of WordPerfect 5.1 . . . . $16.95
WordPerfect 5.1: Step-by-Step $24.95

Macintosh/Apple

First Book of Excel 3 for the Mac $16.95
First Book of the Mac $16.95

Operating Systems/Networking

10 Minute Guide to Windows 3 . . . . $ 9.95
Best Book of DESQview $24.95
Best Book of Microsoft Windows 3 . . . . . . $24.95
Best Book of MS-DOS 5 . . . . $24.95
Business Guide to Local Area Networks . . . $24.95
DOS Batch File Power
   with the Jamsa Disk Utilities $39.95
Exploring the UNIX System, 2nd Ed. $29.95
First Book of DeskMate $16.95
First Book of Microsoft Windows 3 . . . . . . $16.95
First Book of MS-DOS 5 . . . . $16.95
First Book of UNIX $16.95
Interfacing to the IBM Personal Computer,
   2nd Ed. $24.95
The Waite Group's Discovering MS-DOS,
   2nd Edition $19.95
The Waite Group's MS-DOS Bible, 4th Ed. . $29.95
The Waite Group's MS-DOS Developer's Guide,
   2nd Ed. $29.95
The Waite Group's Tricks of the UNIX Masters$29.95
The Waite Group's Understanding MS-DOS,
   2nd Ed. $19.95
The Waite Group's UNIX Primer Plus, 2nd Ed.$29.95
The Waite Group's UNIX System V Bible . . $29.95
Understanding Local Area Networks, 2nd Ed. $24.95
UNIX Applications Programming:
   Mastering the Shell $29.95
UNIX Networking $29.95
UNIX Shell Programming, Revised Ed. . . . $29.95
UNIX: Step-by-Step $29.95
UNIX System Administration $29.95
UNIX System Security $34.95
UNIX Text Processing $29.95

Professional/Reference

Data Communications, Networks, and Systems $39.95
Handbook of Electronics Tables and Formulas,
   6th Ed. $24.95
ISDN, DECnet, and SNA Communications . $49.95
Modern Dictionary of Electronics, 6th Ed. . $39.95
Reference Data for Engineers: Radio, Electronics,
   Computer, and Communications, 7th Ed. $99.95

Programming

Advanced C: Tips and Techniques $29.95
C Programmer's Guide to NetBIOS $29.95
C Programmer's Guide
   to Serial Communications $29.95
Commodore 64 Programmer's
   Reference Guide $24.95

Developing Windows Applications
   with Microsoft SDK $29.95
DOS Batch File Power $39.95
Graphical User Interfaces with Turbo C++ . .$29.95
Learning C++ $39.95
Mastering Turbo Assembler $29.95
Mastering Turbo Pascal, 4th Ed. $29.95
Microsoft Macro Assembly Language
Programming $29.95
Microsoft QuickBASIC
   Programmer's Reference $29.95
Programming in ANSI C $29.95
Programming in C, Revised Ed. $29.95
The Waite Group's BASIC Programming
   Primer, 2nd Ed. $24.95
The Waite Group's C Programming
   Using Turbo C++ $29.95
The Waite Group's C: Step-by-Step $29.95
The Waite Group's GW-BASIC Primer Plus .$24.95
The Waite Group's Microsoft C Bible, 2nd Ed. $29.95
The Waite Group's Microsoft C Programming
   for the PC, 2nd Ed. $29.95
The Waite Group's New C Primer Plus $29.95
The Waite Group's Turbo Assembler Bible . .$29.95
The Waite Group's Turbo C Bible $29.95
The Waite Group's Turbo C Programming
   for the PC, Revised Ed. $29.95
The Waite Group's Turbo C++Bible $29.95
X Window System Programming $29.95

Radio/Video

Camcorder Survival Guide . . . . $ 14.95
Radio Handbook, 23rd Ed. $39.95
Radio Operator's License Q&A Manual,
   11th Ed. $24.95
Understanding Fiber Optics $24.95
Understanding Telephone Electronics, 3rd Ed. $24.95
VCR Troubleshooting & Repair Guide $19.95
Video Scrambling & Descrambling
   for Satellite & Cable TV $24.95

For More Information,
See Your Local Retailer
Or Call Toll Free

1-800-428-5331

All prices are subject to change without notice.
Non-U.S. prices may be higher. Printed in the U.S.A.